BORN OF WAR IN COLOMBIA

Genocide, Political Violence, Human Rights Series
Edited by Alexander Laban Hinton, Nela Navarro, and Natasha Zaretsky

For a list of titles in the series, see the last page of the book.

BORN OF WAR IN COLOMBIA

Reproductive Violence and Memories of Absence

TATIANA SANCHEZ PARRA

RUTGERS UNIVERSITY PRESS
New Brunswick, Camden, and Newark, New Jersey
London and Oxford

Rutgers University Press is a department of Rutgers, The State University of New Jersey, one of the leading public research universities in the nation. By publishing worldwide, it furthers the University's mission of dedication to excellence in teaching, scholarship, research, and clinical care.

Library of Congress Cataloging-in-Publication Data

Names: Sanchez Parra, Tatiana, author.
Title: Born of war in Colombia : reproductive violence and memories of absence / Tatiana Sanchez Parra.
Description: New Brunswick : Rutgers University Press, [2023] | Includes bibliographical references and index.
Identifiers: LCCN 2023041259 | ISBN 9781978832466 (paperback) | ISBN 9781978832473 (hardback) | ISBN 9781978832480 (epub) | ISBN 9781978832503 (pdf)
Subjects: LCSH: Rape as a weapon of war—Colombia. | Children of rape victims—Colombia. | Restorative justice—Colombia.
Classification: LCC HV6569.C7 S263 2023 | DDC 362.8839209596—dc23/eng/20240117
LC record available at https://lccn.loc.gov/2023041259

A British Cataloging-in-Publication record for this book is available from the British Library.

Copyright © 2024 by Tatiana Sanchez Parra
All rights reserved
No part of this book may be reproduced or utilized in any form or by any means, electronic or mechanical, or by any information storage and retrieval system, without written permission from the publisher. Please contact Rutgers University Press, 106 Somerset Street, New Brunswick, NJ 08901. The only exception to this prohibition is "fair use" as defined by U.S. copyright law.

References to internet websites (URLs) were accurate at the time of writing. Neither the author nor Rutgers University Press is responsible for URLs that may have expired or changed since the manuscript was prepared.

♾ The paper used in this publication meets the requirements of the American National Standard for Information Sciences—Permanence of Paper for Printed Library Materials, ANSI Z39.48-1992.

rutgersuniversitypress.org

A las mujeres del norte del Cauca, quienes me enseñaron
que "viejo es Cauca, y más sin embargo corre"

CONTENTS

	List of Illustrations	ix
	Introduction: Gendered Victimhood, Reproductive Violence, and Layers of Unintelligibility	1
1	Between Political Struggles: Gendered Victimhood and Unwanted Lives	26
2	The Bureaucracies of Victimhood in the Making: A Record of the Unintelligible and the Uncertain	55
3	Contested Identities: Reproductive Violence, Reproductive Labor, and War	85
4	Memories of Absence: Collective Reparations and Impossible Witnesses	110
	Conclusion: Toward Futures of Reproductive Justice	141
	Acknowledgments	157
	Notes	161
	Bibliography	169
	Index	181

ILLUSTRATIONS

Figure 1.	San Miguel (Cauca, Colombia), 2016	3
Figure 2.	Main entrance to the community, San Miguel, 2022	15
Figure 3.	A woman on her way to run errands, San Miguel, 2017	87
Figure 4.	Path by the creek, San Miguel, 2022	111
Figure 5.	Detail from men's social cartography, San Miguel, 2016	127
Figure 6.	Poultry farm viewed from the community cemetery, San Miguel, 2022	143

BORN OF WAR IN COLOMBIA

INTRODUCTION
Gendered Victimhood, Reproductive Violence, and Layers of Unintelligibility

I traveled to the Colombian municipality of Buenos Aires following whispers about children born of sexual violence perpetrated by paramilitaries. I had seen traces of them in a 2010 magazine article and in a footnote in an ombudsman's report.[1] I had heard stories about them in conversations with human rights lawyers who worked in national nongovernmental organizations (NGOs) based in Bogotá, Colombia's capital city, and who, at some point when it was considered safer to travel to the area after the paramilitary demobilization in December 2004, had participated in projects that involved working with women who had endured conflict-related sexual violence in that part of the country. Although these whispers never grew into fully fledged stories, they all spoke of children who were born of paramilitary sexual violence and how people in their communities were referring to them as *paraquitos* (little paramilitaries). I followed those whispers through the red-soil mountains in the north of the department of Cauca, where Buenos Aires is located, across the narrow, winding roads that meander up the mountains and away from the valley and its landscapes of endless expanses of sugar cane that reward travelers with breathtaking views of the Cauca River that always offer a sense of relief to someone prone to car sickness, like me. Following those whispers led me to San Miguel, a small, rural, Afro-Colombian community that endured a paramilitary occupation lasting more than four years in the early 2000s and that is now going through the process of implementing collective reparations under the country's domestic reparations program.

However, when I first arrived in San Miguel, I lost track of the whispers. I traveled the dirt roads, paths, and community-built bamboo bridges that convey people across the fields, over the creeks, and up and down the hills. I got lost walking from one place to another, not understanding the directions people gave me, which were expressed in terms of crops and coffee and casava plants or mango, oak, *encenillo*, and *mochilon* trees. I gradually became familiar with the names of the hills, curves, wells, and rock formations. I learned to respect the pace of the day, to seek out the shade of trees in the hot midday sun, and to find shelter when the torrential rain came. I learned to be patient, to enjoy the wait and become aware of the changing sounds throughout the day. I started learning people's names, and they reciprocated, and over time, they began sharing parts of their lives with me. I was always listening closely, all my senses primed and eagerly awaiting evidence of the whispers that had brought me there. I was looking for those children labeled after their biological fathers' violence, but despite my preconceptions about what I imagined to be their uncomfortable presence in the community, I was unable to find them. I met their neighbors, teachers, grandmothers, siblings, aunts, and uncles. I met their mothers, and I also met them, and yet I could not *see* them, as the very label that I assumed would make them visible was long gone.

This book addresses why people born of conflict-related sexual violence in Colombia remain unseen within human rights and transitional justice agendas despite their physical presence and multiple forms of sociolegal visibility. Throughout six decades of ongoing armed conflict in Colombia, but particularly in the latter decades, left-wing guerrillas, right-wing paramilitaries, government forces, and international troops have perpetrated different forms of sexual violence against the population. Official figures refer to more than thirty-seven thousand victims of conflict-related sexual violence across the country, most of them women and girls from Afro-Colombian, Indigenous, and peasant communities.[2] As a result, there are generations of people born of these abuses in Colombia. Mentions of them appear in the testimonies of their mothers, who became pregnant as a result of sexual violence committed by members of armed groups and, for different reasons—among them, a lack of access to safe and free abortion—gave birth to their sons and daughters. Human rights practitioners, for their part, have drawn attention to stories about how, in some communities, people have used naming practices to single these children out, labeling them as *paraquitos*. In addition to these forms of visibility and their physical presence in their communities and in their mothers' lives, in Colombia, they also exist within one of the country's transitional justice legal frameworks: in 2011, they were recognized as victims of the armed conflict by the law that created the domestic reparations program.

These forms of visibility, however, have yet to translate into concrete strategies for working with them and their mothers, understanding their experiences and situations, and guaranteeing their rights and well-being. I argue that the ways in which we in Colombia, as a society, have *seen-them-without-really-seeing-them*

FIGURE 1. San Miguel (Cauca, Colombia), 2016

are the result not of a social or political intention to deny and conceal their existence, as is the case in other contexts where they have been understood as threats to nationalistic projects, but of an inability to see them as independent subjects within the geographies of war, victimhood, and peace building.[3] The lenses through which we have approached them have configured different layers of their *unintelligibility*. Throughout the book, I reveal how a past-oriented and harm-centered model of transitional justice has converged with a notion of gendered victimhood that primarily focuses on conflict-related sexual violence and the patriarchal politics of social reproduction and care to render the bodies and experiences of people born of conflict-related sexual violence unintelligible to the eyes of those who are seeking to understand, think and write about, and address the consequences of war in Colombia.

TRANSITIONAL JUSTICE, GENDERED VICTIMHOOD, AND POLITICS OF REPRODUCTION

The contemporary model of transitional justice that is founded on the search for truth, justice, and redress emerged in the late 1980s and early 1990s as part of the human rights regimen and within the legal framework of international human rights law. This model adopted the goal of achieving the stability of nation-states that had experienced oppressive regimes or periods of mass violence through the consolidation of democratic systems. Its emergence marked a political shift from struggles for social justice that questioned structural systems of oppression to those that prioritized individual human rights and understood them as universal.

This meant that instead of seeking to transform the socioeconomic conditions that were central to the class and anticolonial struggles, which lay at the heart of many armed and political conflicts across the world, this model took as its coordinates the propagation of liberal human rights, practices, and institutions. To this end, the model viewed events through the lens of human rights violations, adhered to a linear notion of time that was clearly defined and restricted to the recent past, and proposed truth-seeking bodies, tribunals, and eventually, programs of reparations as the privileged mechanisms of operation.[4]

An essential part of transitional justice was the ability to draw a distinction between the periods "before and after" the human rights violations took place, for the model was not about addressing the human experience of suffering and injustice but about translating those experiences into concrete, legally defined violations of human rights; seeking to hold the perpetrators accountable; and eventually, offering the victims forms of reparations for the harms that the violations had caused.[5] Criticisms of transitional justice have highlighted the tension embedded in the model's main goals of simultaneously pursuing the stability of the nation-state and seeking justice for victims, as the notion of stability on which the model is grounded focuses on redressing human rights violations while overlooking the historical root causes of the abuses.[6] Under the guise of stabilizing the nation-state, political transition can act as a platform not only to maintain but also to legitimize the power relations and hierarchical structures of the dominant system, which has historically thrived by exploiting feminized and racialized bodies, who are often the very ones who have suffered the human rights violations. "Stabilizing the nation-state," argues Pascha Bueno-Hansen, "leads to dependence on established social hierarchies, while changing deep-rooted conditions of injustice requires questioning and further destabilizing the same hierarchies."[7]

Although in its initial stages, the model followed a more retributive approach to justice that shone the spotlight on the perpetrators, in the case of the contemporary transitional justice model that has assumed a victim-centered approach and has been interpellated by feminist, decolonial, and queer studies, it is unquestionable that there will be no justice without redress.[8] Nevertheless, the notion of redress—with its measures of rehabilitation, restitution, compensation, satisfaction, and guarantees of non-repetition—continues to reference the past in order to reimagine the future: the past of the victim before the specific human rights violations occurred, the historical past of the context that allowed the violations to be perpetrated, and the future that the victim was deprived of due to the violations.

In this book, I argue that people born of conflict-related sexual violence will remain illegible as independent subjects within transitional justice systems for as long as they continue to be viewed according to a notion of justice defined by legal harms that are firmly rooted in the past. They are their mothers' children, the result of the sexual and reproductive violence perpetrated by members of armed groups and by other actors such as the state, which did not guarantee access to safe abortion services in those cases where women wanted such access. Integral reparations for victims of conflict-related sexual violence need to be streamlined, including providing sustained psychosocial, emotional, and spiritual support for women who gave birth to children resulting from sexual abuse, while strategies need to be put in place to guarantee that there is no repetition.[9] But the experiences of people born of conflict-related sexual violence are not the same as those of their mothers. Attaining justice for them involves challenging harm-centered logics and demanding that we think creatively and strategically about how to achieve a present and a future free from reproductive violence.

The last few years have witnessed growing interdisciplinary efforts to gain recognition for reproductive violence as an independent category of concern and action on international peace and security agendas.[10] Thanks to the work of the women's and feminist movements, gender-based violence and gendered victimhood now have much better-defined places in international human rights, including transitional justice and peace-building endeavors.[11] As a result of this, sexual violence in contexts of armed and political violence is no longer understood as a regrettable but unavoidable collateral damage of war, and it is widely acknowledged that redressing and preventing sexual violence must constitute essential facets of peace building.[12] While the significance of such developments in the mission to combat sexual violence perpetrated against women and girls in war contexts should not be overlooked, there is also a need for criticisms of and revisions to the frameworks through which gender and gendered victimhood have predominantly been understood.[13]

It has been pointed out that the prevailing notion of gender that has been adopted is binary and understands sex as the main way men exercise oppression over women.[14] One of the consequences of this is that a gendered approach to transitional justice has become equated with focusing on cisgender women as victims of sexual violence.[15] Not only has this notion tended to render invisible the experiences of cisgender men and people with diverse gender identities, expressions, and sexual orientations, but it has also reproduced patriarchal power relations in institutional or community-oriented projects of political transitions and peace building.[16] Men are understood as either perpetrators of sexual violence or protectors of "their" women, while women are understood as passive victims of sexual violence.[17] Similarly, this approach has obstructed the achievement of a better understanding of the role of masculinities and nonheteronormative identities and sexualities in those same contexts.[18] Meanwhile, attention has also been drawn to the conceptual and policy risks of applying reductive explanatory logics to conflict-related sexual violence and concluding that it is either strategic or opportunistic.[19] The opportunism-strategy dichotomy, which sees conflict-related sexual violence as either sex driven or gender oriented, overlooks the complex entanglements of power relations—for example, of class, age, ethnicity/race, gender, and sexuality—that shape not only people's experiences of sexual violence but also the strategies they employ to cope with its consequences and navigate transitional justice mechanisms.[20]

Understanding gendered victimhood through these lenses has restricted the transformative potential of transitional justice, as there are other layers of people's experiences of war that are also gendered but fall outside the dominant perspective.[21] In this regard, people's experiences of reproductive violence in contexts of armed and political violence have tended to be overlooked within human rights and transitional justice agendas.[22] On the rare occasions when they are considered, this tends to happen within the conceptual and policy-making scope of conflict-related sexual violence, even in instances where there is no sexual component—such as in cases of forced sterilization or forced contraception[23]—and not in relation to women's reproductive autonomy but in relation to harms caused to the group to which women belong. An example of this can be found in the Rome Statute, where the definitions of the crimes of forced pregnancy and forced sterilization underscore the connection between sexual violence and ethnic cleansing rather than making the connection with women's reproductive autonomy.[24]

Increasingly, interdisciplinary efforts within the feminist and women's movements across the globe are advocating for the recognition of conflict-related reproductive violence as an independent category within human rights and transitional justice frameworks. The disentanglement of the sexual from the reproductive will contribute to broadening understandings of gendered victimhood while advancing concrete knowledge about the ways in which people's reproductive lives, capacities, and futures have been harmed, claimed, and destroyed in contexts of armed and political violence. Producing this knowledge constitutes an urgent step toward advancing issues of gendered justice, not only in terms of accountability and reparations for the harms specific practices like forced contraception have caused to victims and their life paths, but also to reveal the entrenched systems of oppression that lay behind, for instance, colonial eugenic rationales for population control deployed in relation to forced sterilization or patriarchal notions of identity transmission associated with forced pregnancies.[25]

In this book, I contribute to these interdisciplinary efforts by shining the spotlight on the unintelligibility of people born of conflict-related sexual violence. The case of Colombia illustrates how, despite the existence of the sociolegal category of children born of conflict-related sexual violence, these people remain unseen by actors seeking to understand and address the consequences of war, as their scope of vision is limited to the sexual components of the violence perpetrated against women. The aspects that involve the reproductive dimensions of that violence—such as pregnancy, giving birth, and parenting—are often understood as collateral damage resulting from sexual violence and as women's "natural" labor. By questioning the ways in which we have not seen people born of conflict-related sexual violence, I also unmask the patriarchal politics of social reproduction and care that have functioned to render women's experiences of conflict-related reproductive violence invisible.

Marxist feminists have exposed capitalism's coercion of women's reproductive functions and the way that it feeds on the reproductive work of women and other racialized and feminized bodies.[26] Both procreation and care were harnessed to serve capitalist accumulation, and motherhood became women's expected, "natural" duty.[27] In some contexts, such as the wars in Bosnia and Herzegovina and Uganda, following patriarchal notions of identity transmission, sexual violence has been perpetrated with the intention to impregnate women and force them to give birth to children based on the rationale that it would destroy the women's social group or enlarge the perpetrator's group.[28] In those contexts, the children have been discriminated against, marginalized, and physically harmed, as they are understood as a manifestation of "otherness" and hence a risk to the women's social group. This is not the case in Colombia, as children's identities, no matter how they were conceived, are also linked to those of their mothers. However, while women are not understood merely as vessels who are unable to transmit identity to their children, they are still expected to perform their role as nurturers, regardless of their own experiences of violence.[29]

I show that patriarchal expectations of women's gender role as nurturers through the labor of motherhood have contributed to the unintelligibility of the children born of conflict-related sexual violence. The stories that tell of the situations, experiences, needs, and dreams of those people born of this type of violence are yet to be heard. For now, those stories remain subsumed under the accounts of the sexual violence perpetrated against their mothers, within which they are enunciated as part of its consequences. At the same time, women—regardless of what stage they are at in their healing process, the economic hardships they may be enduring, or how they are coping with the various ways in which the lives they had dreamed of for themselves have been thwarted—are expected not only to raise and love their children but to navigate the convoluted victimhood system to seek justice for themselves and their sons and daughters.

At the international level, we are witnessing a period of unprecedented attention to the situation of children born of conflict-related sexual violence across the world, as the need for urgent action to guarantee their rights, wellbeing, and futures becomes increasingly recognized. Examples of this include the United Kingdom's 2021 Call to Action to Ensure the Rights and Wellbeing of Children Born of Sexual Violence in Conflict, which is endorsed by several countries, United Nations entities, and global civil society organizations. This call was followed in 2022 by the Platform for Action, a collaborative, multiactor effort to work with and for children born of conflict-related sexual violence, who face various challenges that endanger the social, physical, mental, and emotional well-being of themselves and their mothers; exacerbate their marginalization; and may even threaten their lives. Prior to this, the 2019 U.N. Security Council Resolution 2467, an instrument designed to strengthen the prevention of and response to conflict-related sexual violence through a survivor-centered approach, includes concerns about the situation of women who become pregnant as a consequence of sexual violence in conflict and their children born of these abuses. The ensuing 2022 secretary-general's report entitled *Women and Girls Who Become Pregnant as a Result of Sexual Violence in Conflict and Children Born of Sexual Violence in Conflict* highlights some of the challenges and risks they face and underscores the knowledge gap that still exists concerning these children as well as the need to fill it in order to move forward.

Such unprecedented attention draws on the work that human rights advocates and scholars from various disciplines have undertaken since the 1990s to make visible the plight of children born of sexual violence in war contexts in different periods of time and across the globe.[30] As part of their individual and collective work, three broad and interconnected aspects have been emphasized. First, children born of conflict-related sexual violence experience several forms of discrimination based on the circumstances of their conception, their biological fathers' identities, and their biological fathers' roles not just as individual perpetrators of violence but also as members of specific armed groups.[31] Discrimination against these children takes different forms as they grow older, ranging from stigmatizing naming practices intended to signal connections between the children and their biological fathers or their mothers' experiences of suffering, to obstructing their access to land, education, citizenship, or the opportunity to grow up as part of a loving family.[32] The marginalization and ostracism that many of them endure, together with the fact that many of them live in conditions of severe economic hardship and ongoing conflict, make them vulnerable to other forms of violence such as recruitment, trafficking, and sexual exploitation.[33]

Second, despite the widespread awareness of the hardships these children might endure, there has been a lack of concrete initiatives from private entities or the public sector, policies, and normative frameworks to guarantee their rights and development in safe and caring environments.[34] Third, and closely connected with the second element, is the acknowledgment that there remains a knowledge gap that, time and again, has been presented as an explanation for both the lack of tangible action taken and the urgent need to move forward in terms of finding ways of working with and for these children.[35] Questions about what filling the knowledge gap entails, who should take a leadership role in these matters, and most importantly, how to fill it in ways that do not represent further risks for either the children or their mothers have been central to these debates for several decades.[36]

I contribute to interdisciplinary efforts to advance these matters by posing questions and seeking ways forward by adopting a reproductive justice and feminist approach to issues of transitional justice and peace building. The reproductive justice framework adheres to three main principles: "(1) the right *not* to have a child; (2) the right to *have* a child; and (3) the right to *parent* children in safe and healthy environments."[37] With a commitment to sexual autonomy and gender freedom, and drawing on strategic alliances between scholarship and political action, reproductive justice exposes the connections among capitalist exploitation; the conditions of social groups defined by intertwined power relations such as class, gender, sexuality, age, and ethnicity; and the enjoinments and constraints on people's sexual and reproductive lives.[38] For women and communities who live in contexts of armed and political violence, their reproductive lives are also influenced by the policies, economies, logics, and practices of war. Feminist approaches to war and peace have underscored that peace-building endeavors must go beyond the scope of confrontations between armed groups to address the coconstitutive systems of war: patriarchy, capitalism, colonialism, and militarization.[39] Learning from Latin American feminisms, this book offers an invitation to move forward along the path to obtaining justice for people born of conflict-related sexual violence by broadening and interconnecting the political struggles through which we seek to find them.[40]

No one should have to endure sexual violence, just as no one should have to go through a pregnancy resulting from any of its forms. Safe, legal, and free abortion must be a right that all bodies who can conceive should have access to. However, there is more to consider in regard to the stories of women who become pregnant as a consequence of sexual violence perpetrated by members of armed groups and their children born of those abuses. In cases where women give birth, their children should be able to grow up in nonmilitarized contexts where their presents and futures are not defined by colonial, patriarchal, and economic violence. For those women who continue their pregnancies and want to raise their children, their well-being and that of their children should be a priority. This means providing access to integral health services, including emotional, psychosocial, and spiritual support for the person who gave birth after experiencing conflict-related sexual violence and their child, but it also means having access to resources to parent the child in safe and healthy contexts. No one should be coerced into giving away their children because they cannot afford to nurture them, for legal or social reasons, or because war itself takes them away.

This book also contributes to the knowledge gap by shining a spotlight on the specific case of Colombia. Colombia has established a series of judicial and nonjudicial remedies designed to deliver reparations to victims of conflict-related sexual and reproductive violence, including children born as a result of it. Although gaining access to integral reparations has not been straightforward, and the process is often described by victims as revictimizing due to the fragmented nature of its delivery and the highly bureaucratized system that they have to navigate, Colombia is one of the few countries in the world that has a robust infrastructure through which to advance issues of redress for victims of conflict-related sexual and reproductive violence.[41] Thus, viewing the domestic reparations program through feminist, ethnographic lenses offers the opportunity to learn from the ways in which the system has been implemented.

COLOMBIA'S ARMED CONFLICT AND TRANSITIONAL JUSTICE SYSTEM

This book is set in Colombia, a country that continues to live with an armed conflict that started over sixty years ago and that has developed a robust, gender-sensitive, transitional justice system in the last two decades. With a national population totaling around 50 million, official records estimate the number of victims of the armed conflict at more than 9.4 million. Although such figures can never tell us about people's experiences of the conflict, in this case, they can help convey a sense of the scale of the conflict. For example, up to January 2023, official records listed 8,391,662 people as victims of forced displacement, 37,770 as victims of kidnappings, 191,060 as victims of forced disappearance, 10,459 as victims of torture, and 36,908 as victims of sexual violence.[42]

Throughout the Colombian armed conflict, but particularly during the last twenty years, sexual violence has been perpetrated by members of all armed groups: right-wing paramilitaries, left-wing guerrillas, government forces, and foreign troops. Although sexual violence has been perpetrated against women and men, it has been established that impoverished, racialized, cisgender women and girls have constituted the vast majority. Official figures show that of the 36,908 people recognized as victims of sexual violence, at least 31,300 are cisgender women.[43] Sexual violence against them occurs in militarized contexts—underpinned by racist, classist, and sexist rationales—but is also accompanied by other forms of violence such as land dispossession and forced displacement. Similarly, based on the logics of prejudice and hatred, people with diverse gender identities and expressions and sexual orientations, whose main forms of reported victimization are forced displacement and forced disappearance, have also suffered significantly as victims of sexual violence. At the individual level, armed groups have used sexual violence to punish their nonheteronormative bodies and identities, and at the collective level, it has been used against social leaders and human rights defenders to hinder political organization and activism.[44]

The armed conflict, however, is not only about the direct actions and operations of armed groups. In the case of Colombia, legal and illegal armed groups have both cooperated with and fought against domestic and international political and economic actors to gain control of land, ecosystems, and communities.[45] Throughout the duration of the armed conflict, wider society—as represented by the media, church, and education, among other sectors—has played a key role in producing and reproducing narratives that normalized and legitimized violence against certain groups of people that have been considered, at different times and under different circumstances, as threats to the patriarchal, capitalist, mestizo dominant order. Examples include peasants striving for an equal distribution of land and food sovereignty, Indigenous people and Afro-Colombians fighting against the pervasive extractive economies imposed on their ancestral lands, workers organizing in unions, students taking political action to defend access to education or showing their support of other causes, human rights lawyers fighting impunity, or people with diverse gender identities and expressions and sexual orientations trying to defend their mere existence.

As a result of pressure from victims' organizations, civil society, and the women's and feminist movements, Colombia has developed a robust, gender-sensitive, transitional justice jurisprudence. An example of this is the 2016 Peace Accord between the Colombian government and the Revolutionary Armed Forces of Colombia–People's Army (FARC-EP), which sought to end the war between government forces and Colombia's largest and oldest guerrilla group. The 2016 Peace Accord includes six points aimed at addressing issues such as FARC-EP's demobilization, agrarian reform, and the trade in illicit drugs. The fifth of these points was specifically targeted at victims and centered on the creation of the Comprehensive System of Truth, Justice, Reparation, and Non-repetition, which aims to contribute to sustainable peace building. It comprises three bodies: the Special Jurisdiction for Peace (JEP), the Unit for Searching for Missing Persons, and the Commission for the Clarification of the Truth, Coexistence, and Non-recurrence (hereafter the Commission). All of these bodies have different mandates, budgets, procedures, and time frames.

Although at the beginning of the peace negotiations in October 2012, neither the government's nor FARC-EP's agendas were informed by a gendered approach, due to pressure from the women's and feminist movements, in 2014, a gender subcommission was installed. This subcommission not only achieved some level of representation in the negotiations but also ensured the inclusion of a gendered approach throughout the accords.[46] An important example of this is the Commission, as from the moment the truth-seeking body was created, it was established that it must include a gender unit with the express purpose of guaranteeing a gendered approach throughout the proceedings. Another example is the JEP, which in 2023 opened investigations into patterns of macrocriminality regarding sexual and reproductive violence and other crimes committed as a result of prejudice, hatred, and discrimination based on gender, sex, diverse gender identity, and sexual orientation in the Colombian armed conflict.

The implementation of the 2016 Peace Accord overlaps with the enactment of previous transitional justice legislation, such as Law 975 of 2005, better known as the Justice and Peace Law, which sought to regulate the demobilization of paramilitary groups, and Law 1448 of 2011, known as the Victims' and Land Restitution Law (hereafter Victims' Law), which initially covered a ten-year period that ended in June 2021 but was subsequently extended for a further ten years through Law 2078 of 2021. The Victims' Law represented a landmark in terms of recognizing the existence of the armed conflict in the country and denoting a shift toward a more gender-sensitive, victim-centered transitional justice system. It created the National System for Comprehensive Victim Support and Reparation (SNARIV), and within its remit, the Victims' Law established the domestic reparations program, under which collective and individual victims are able to access integral reparations, including measures of compensation, restitution, satisfaction, rehabilitation, and guarantees of non-repetition.

The SNARIV, which comprises over thirty state agencies at the national and regional levels, including the Ministry of Health and the Office of the Attorney General, and sets out different permanent instances of victims' participation, "is in charge of formulating or executing the plans, programs, projects and specific actions, tending to the attention and integral reparation of the victims."[47] In order to accomplish these unprecedented endeavors, the Victims' Law established the Unit for the Assistance and Integral Reparations of Victims (hereafter Victims' Unit or the Unit) and charged it with coordinating the measures of reparations to which victims are entitled and articulating the different entities that comprised the SNARIV.

One of the groundbreaking features of the Victims' Law is its recognition of children born as a result of sexual violence in conflict as direct victims of the armed conflict. Although their inclusion has received little attention, as will be shown throughout the book, the creation of this sociolegal category offers the opportunity to examine the domestic reparations program and its implementation over the last ten years, seeking traces of the existence of the sociolegal category. Although the women I have worked with during the research that led to this book have actively engaged with different transitional justice mechanisms, based on various normative frameworks, the focus of this book is firmly on their experiences of navigating the part of the victimhood system that is concerned with access to individual and collective reparations within the domestic reparations program, particularly in relation to gaining access to reparations for their children born of conflict-related sexual violence.

Under the Justice and Peace Law, reparations to victims are provided through judicial decisions, which have generally moved at a very slow pace. Up to April 2022, more than fifteen years after the implementation of the Justice and Peace Law, 111,194 cases had been presented before the Justice and Peace Magistrates, of which 65,489 remain at the investigation stage. There had been a mere seventy-two convictions, and only twenty-five for crimes of sexual violence and related offenses, accompanied by a very low implementation rate of the reparations ordered. Under the Justice and Peace Law, victims' participation was mostly limited to hearings about the reparations process, during which they could intervene and submit requests for specific forms of reparations, which had to be accompanied by supporting evidence. Decisions were made after periods of conciliation with the defendants. Under the Victims' Law, reparations are granted not based on assessments made in court but through the domestic reparations program. This program has the potential to reach, in equal and standardized terms, a broader number of victims. Although the Justice and Peace Law continues to sanction court-ordered reparations, the creation of the domestic reparations program has provided more clarity for victims in terms of what their right to integral reparations entails and more equal access to the resources available for reparations—in particular, compensation, which is now capped according to the stipulations of the Victims' Law.[48]

The Colombian domestic reparations program has been described at the international level as comprehensive and ambitious. Despite being groundbreaking in many respects—for example, in its recognition of children born of conflict-related sexual violence as victims, inclusion of sexual violence, and creation of specialized strategies to work with women who have endured conflict-related sexual violence—these adjectives are not always used as compliments. The complexity of its administrative machinery, together with the fragmented nature of its responses, have prevented victims from receiving the reparations to which they are entitled and urgently need while creating new forms of violence by, for instance, making victims wait for years without any clear information about what the process will entail. Although more than ten years after its implementation, progress has been very slow, with only 8,370 victims of conflict-related sexual violence having received monetary compensation and 1,637 having received access to mental health care, it offers learning opportunities for similar programs elsewhere. This is because it has the potential to reach larger numbers of victims, and in more meaningful ways, than court-ordered reparations.[49]

For victims from impoverished, marginalized communities whose main relationship with the state has been through its military presence, their participation in transitional justice mechanisms often represents the acknowledgment (often for the first time) of their citizenship. Similarly, it also signifies the recognition of their experiences of war, the opportunity to have their voices heard, and the promise of accountability, redress, and non-repetition. In order to participate in the transitional justice system, however, victims are expected to familiarize themselves with and adapt to the specific administrative procedures, technical terms, practices, and time frames associated with each process. They also have to be willing to invest emotional and economic resources during the lengthy period involved and be able to take time away from their caring responsibilities and other forms of paid and unpaid work.

In the case of the Victims' Law, more than a decade after its implementation, the everyday operation of the domestic reparations program has often become part of impoverished rural communities' incomes. This derives not only from the expectation of eventually receiving individual and collective financial compensation but also from activities such as attending workshops in exchange for travel money and lunch, cooking for the Victims' Unit's activities, or offering services to NGOs involved in implementing measures of reparations.

SAN MIGUEL

The rural, Afro-Colombian community of San Miguel belongs to the municipality of Buenos Aires, which is located in the north of Cauca, one of the thirty-two departments into which Colombia is divided. Buenos Aires' average temperature across the year is 22°C, although it always seems to feel hotter than that when I've been there, and its administrative center, the town of Buenos Aires, is located partway up the mountain at 1,200 meters above sea level. San Miguel, with a population of approximately 400 people, is located on the same mountain and is divided into different rural areas that are connected by dirt roads. Buenos Aires has an estimated population of 32,645, of which only 1,863 live in the small administrative center; the remaining 30,782 live in rural areas.[50] Although over time I have witnessed improvements in the network of roads that connects the different parts of the municipality, this infrastructure is still fragile. For example, it was not until 2015 that the main road that connects the administrative center, which houses key facilities such as the hospital, to the rural areas and other parts of the country was paved. During the rainy season, landslides continue to be a major risk and cause of disruption, and the community dirt roads become inaccessible.

Since the foundation of Buenos Aires in 1536, gold mining attracted Spanish colonizers and mestizos and, with them, thousands of enslaved African men and women who were brought to work in the mines. Nowadays, Afro-Colombians are the largest population group in Buenos Aires, followed by Indigenous Nasa Páez and mestizos. Economically, gold mining remains one of the main sources

FIGURE 2. Main entrance to the community, San Miguel, 2022

of income for the municipality, together with small-scale agriculture. Whether it is multinational corporations disputing access to gold since the early twentieth century or state-led extractive projects such as the construction of the Salvajina Dam in 1985, conflicts over land have defined the history of Buenos Aires.[51] Indigenous Nasa Páez and Afro-Colombians have fought against the dispossession of their ancestral territories and for the recognition of their collective rights as ethnic peoples.

The chain of mountains stretching across the north of Cauca, and Buenos Aires in particular, has historically played host to different armed groups. Its geographical location and poor infrastructure, which makes it difficult to access the region, have also made it appealing to armed groups as a corridor for transporting war supplies and for the production chain of illicit drugs.[52] The nature of the armed conflict in the region has changed over time, and some scholars have identified at least four distinct phases.[53] The first stage, from 1990 to the mid-1990s, relates to the geographical expansion of guerrilla groups—in particular, FARC-EP and the National Liberation Army (ELN)—and the increase in coca crops for the production of cocaine. The second phase, between 2000 and 2004, was defined by the consolidation of a paramilitary regime and the arrival of the United Self-Defense Forces of Colombia (AUC), Calima Bloc. The third stage, spanning from the mid-2000s to 2016, was characterized by the overlapping activities of guerrilla paramilitary organizations that emerged after the 2004 demobilization of the AUC, Calima Bloc, and the increasing presence of civil society and grassroots organizations. The fourth phase, after the signing of the 2016 Peace Accord, initially witnessed a de-escalation in confrontations between armed groups followed by a reconfiguration of the armed conflict that is still ongoing in 2023.[54]

The end of the 1990s saw a transformation in the way in which paramilitary groups were organized in Colombia. Instead of armed groups operating at the local and regional levels, they became configured as part of a national project with political, social, and economic goals. This was evidenced, for example, by the paramilitary organization's involvement in politics, supporting candidates through local and national elections; in its increased influence in the public administration of education and health programs in various national territories; and in the geographical expansion toward the southwestern part of the country—traditionally controlled by FARC-EP and where Buenos Aires is located. This growth in the paramilitary project, together with the continued guerrilla presence across the national territory and ongoing struggles among the different groups to consolidate control over strategic paths, made 2002 the year in which the armed conflict reached its highest level of expansion.[55]

As part of the paramilitary expansion project, between 1998 and 2002, the AUC, Calima Bloc, disputed FARC-EP's control over the regional chain of production of cocaine in the southwestern part of the country.[56] On March 11, 2000, César Negret Mosquera, then governor of Cauca, received a communication from Ever Veloza (alias H.H.), paramilitary commander of the Calima Bloc, announcing the commencement of their operations in the department.[57] Some reports indicate that in May 2000, a group of fifty-four paramilitaries marched from the department of Valle del Cauca, through the town of Timba, and toward Buenos Aires to set up their training base in San Miguel's rural school, from where they ran their operations throughout the north of Cauca.[58] Between 2000 and 2004, the paramilitaries, who by then numbered around two thousand, imposed economic, political, and social control over the region and the population, causing the displacement of an estimated eight thousand people.[59]

While for many in Buenos Aires and the north of Cauca, the presence of the AUC, Calima Bloc, meant forced displacement, for the community of small farmers in San Miguel, it entailed an experience of confinement. From the moment they arrived, paramilitaries assumed ownership of the community's rural school, which was responsible for primary education, by establishing their training and storage base there. They also restricted people's mobility through curfews and checkpoints located at the main entrance to the community and along the dirt roads that connect the different rural areas. Forced nudity, mistreatment, and abuse in the form of racist language against both women and men were commonplace at the checkpoints, as were the detention, killing, and disappearance of people who did not have their national identity cards with them or were suspected of being guerrilla sympathizers.

The paramilitaries imposed regulations on the everyday life of the community. They set strict quotas for the quantity and types of medicines and groceries people could buy and bring into the community. They also ordered inhabitants to leave the doors of their houses open during the evenings so that they could come in as they pleased and make use of their facilities. People tell stories of paramilitaries sleeping in their houses, watching TV, eating their food, destroying their crops, killing their animals, and burning their fences to make bonfires. Teachers working at the school received an order not to interrupt the classes. However, they were under constant surveillance and could not do their jobs freely. Every day, teachers had to ask for permission to open the classrooms, and classes took place against a backdrop of armory and military training. Families were also forced to keep sending their children to school even though no proper classes were taking place. Not uncommonly, children were assigned tasks such as transporting weapons and other supplies, delivering messages, or watching roads. A lot of girls experienced sexual harassment and rape along the dirt roads that connected their houses to the school, and many children ended up dropping out of school. Some people managed to flee from this regime of violence, while those who stayed stopped working the land and raising animals; hunger became part of everyday life for families in San Miguel.

Women and girls, for their part, were forced to cook for the paramilitaries and wash their clothes. Different forms of sexual violence, and the threat of it, became a feature of their daily lives. It pervaded the places that had previously felt familiar and safe: inside their houses, along the dirt roads, and in the creeks where they collected water and took baths. Many women and teenage girls became pregnant as a result of the abuse perpetrated by the paramilitaries. Some are currently parenting the sons and daughters to whom they gave birth. In 2012, San Miguel embarked on the process of collective reparations under the domestic reparations program.

FEMINIST QUESTIONS ABOUT SILENCE AND UNINTELLIGIBILITY

Frequently, research is triggered by something that we saw happen or something that we experienced, and it is only in the course of the investigation that we encounter the many silences that are, at different levels and with different intensities, embedded within our work. The story of the research that led to this book starts not with something that was seen or said but with silence. Back in 2011, when stories about women's experiences of conflict-related sexual violence in

Colombia had begun to gain more attention in the national media, I was reading a newspaper article relating to the launch of a report exposing the situation of women and girls across the country. Although the particularities of the story have long escaped my memory, what I do remember is that the rape of one of the women featured in it resulted in pregnancy. It was probably not the first time that I had read about women becoming pregnant and giving birth to children after enduring sexual violence perpetrated by members of armed groups, and yet it was the first time I realized that I had never read any stories about those children and what happened to them.

Thus, this project began with questions about silence and concealment in contexts of war and political transition.[60] From the outset, it adhered to an ethnography of violence that sought to avoid revictimization by not focusing on the violent events themselves; rather, it tried to understand people's trajectories in a comprehensive way, including their experiences of survival, joy, anger, and resistance during war.[61] It also cleaved to an ethnography of silence in contexts of armed and political violence, which understands silence as a site of meaning and, instead of seeking to "break it" by extracting fragments of people's suffering, aims to read more deeply into its texture.[62] What interested me was not silence and concealment in general terms but those particular gendered silences that existed together with women's experiences of conflict-related sexual violence, which require us to be attentive to the different meanings they convey.

Sometimes, silences exist within women's own recollections and reveal much about what they dare not name out of fear or refuse to name as a way of denying power to certain events, people, and feelings by keeping them in the realm of the unsaid.[63] In other instances, silence is imposed on and expected of women by their relatives, members of their community, or political leaders.[64] But silence can also be produced by scholars, activists, and practitioners who, in their attempts to expose women's experiences of conflict-related sexual violence, not only disregard the other dimensions of women's gendered experiences during conflicts but also silence them as complex, integral persons who are not just victims.[65] When it comes to the children born of sexual violence, silence can also be a component of women's strategies to protect them from their biological fathers, from their communities, and sometimes even from themselves, as they fear what that information could trigger inside them.[66]

During the time in which I have been engaging with questions about children born of conflict-related sexual violence in Colombia, I have encountered all these forms of silence, sometimes individually and sometimes in combination. I have learned to listen to them, often missing a lot of what they were conveying and sometimes getting it wrong. The more I engaged with those gendered silences, the clearer it became that in the case of these children, there was something more configuring all that was not said about them. I learned from Cynthia

Enloe that it is not enough to bring the category of gender into our research, as "there needs to be a feminist consciousness informing our work on gender."[67] A feminist consciousness allowed me to start not only paying attention to the gendered silences that surrounded their existence but also questioning the ways in which they remained *unseen* despite having so many forms of visibility.

Learning to read, think, write, and undertake the research journey as a feminist ethnographer has taught me to be attentive to the ways in which entangled power relations of class, gender, ethnicity, sexuality, and age render certain bodies, knowledge, and experiences invisible, often to the extent that we do not even question their absence.[68] This entailed engaging with the invitation posed by feminism, in its diverse forms, to question androcentric and anthropocentric disciplinary foundations and constantly ask who the subjects I am working with, but also myself, understand as legitimate producers of knowledge or what they consider to be legitimate issues worthy of serious research.[69] It also involved understanding and identifying gender, sexuality, and reproduction as types of power relations that are constitutive of every social phenomenon, including armed and political violence, transitional justice, and peace building.[70] The research that led to this book—and for that matter, the researcher I was when I started paying attention to the unsaid—lacked such a feminist consciousness. However, that consciousness has allowed me to explore the different intersectional layers that have configured the unintelligibility of the people born of conflict-related sexual violence in Colombia, and I have the research journey itself and the relations of generosity and solidarity that I have become part of while undertaking it to thank for that.

This book also draws on Judith Butler's invitation to question which experiences of war we see, the frameworks that allow us to see them, and how we apprehend those we actually see.[71] For over sixty years, the armed conflict in Colombia has operated through an intricate economic, cultural, environmental, and social grid, permeating our language, subjectivities, and relations and constraining our ability to question the normalization of violence against "certain others," to feel and show solidarity, and to imagine futures that are not coerced by the rationales of war.[72] As a Colombian, mestiza, middle-class woman from Bogotá, unlearning this and creating other ways of being part of the complex realities of the country have not been easy tasks. The questions this book explores and the pathways it follows, in this respect, demand that alongside the quest to understand the unseen presence of people born of conflict-related sexual violence and women's gendered experiences of war and transitional justice, I must constantly examine my own positionality and ability to understand, empathize, and see.

Throughout the process that is reflected in this book, I have also learned that research is not only about understanding timings and respecting the pace that specific questions and methodological designs require but also about the location and our position within it. Although I started thinking about the lack of information relating to children born of sexual violence perpetrated by members of armed groups in Colombia around 2012, it was not until the end of 2015 that I was in a position to conduct fieldwork in the country. That was due to a particular moment in my academic career: I was embarking on my PhD project and saving enough money through several small and not-so-small grants and hours of teaching and administrative jobs at the University of Essex, where I studied for my PhD, at a time in my personal life that allowed me the freedom to travel. In 2015, after several years of negotiations between the Colombian government and FARC-EP that had been publicly announced in 2012, the situation in many regions of the country that had been severely affected by the armed conflict, including the north of the department of Cauca, was still tense but somewhat calmer due to the expectation that the parties involved would soon reach an agreement.

Although back then I had heard rumors that the paramilitaries had returned to recover weapons and money they had left in *caletas* (hidden spots across the landscape) and were commanding outsiders to leave, those rumors referred to a situation that had occurred around 2010. In the end, I was able to travel and move around relatively unimpeded, exercising caution but without encountering many difficulties. Throughout my years of visiting Buenos Aires, I have seen and heard how the dynamics of the armed conflict in this part of the country have changed and influenced, for better and for worse, people's relationships with one another and with the place in which they live. The last few years, in that sense, have been especially brutal due to the reconfiguration of armed groups and their disputes over the production chain of illicit drugs. This situation has been accompanied by the persecution and killings of former FARC-EP combatants and peasant, Afro-Colombian, and Indigenous leaders who are trying to defend their territories from extractive projects that thrive on the dispossession of land and the poisoning of ecosystems while threatening traditional agricultural ways of life. Between the signing of the Peace Accord in 2016 and the beginning of the pandemic in 2020, for instance, at least 215 social leaders and 36 former FARC-EP combatants were killed in Cauca. Between 2020 and 2022, at least forty-two massacres were perpetrated in Cauca, and in 2022, at least 25 social leaders were killed.[73]

This book is the result of the overlapping circumstances and fortuitous timing that allowed me to visit Buenos Aires in 2015 and the relationships I have built with both the people and the place. I do not feel confident that I would be able to visit Buenos Aires and move around in the way that I do if I did not have the familiarity with the landscape and the support networks I have now. Embarking on this kind of project under the current situation of armed violence and fear would be very difficult, if not impossible. One of my recent visits in late

2022 made me realize the importance of timing when conducting research. At the time, I was working with a group of women and a colleague on a photo-voice project. We had spent all day in one of the women's houses looking at the pictures they had taken during the week; we had laughed, cried a little, and even done some singing and dancing.

We had enjoyed a delicious late lunch, and then we found ourselves rushing back to the city of Cali. We were not rushing to avoid being caught out by the curfews recently imposed by one of the illegal armed groups—something I had not witnessed in my many years of visiting Buenos Aires and had not been seen at that level since the 2000s, when paramilitaries were effectively the ruling authority. This time, we were rushing because we needed to drop the picture files off at the photo shop in Cali so that they could print them in time for the next session a week later. We were in a car with Manuel, a university student I had hired to drive us around, and his girlfriend when we ran into traffic, which was unusual on those rural roads. When we asked what had happened, someone told us that we had to be patient: two people had been killed, and their bodies were lying in the road ahead. Commanders from one of the illegal armed groups had given the order to leave the bodies there, and people from the community were trying to negotiate with the commanders to let them take the bodies to their families. I am not sure how I would be able to navigate these kinds of situations emotionally and physically if it were not for the networks in Buenos Aires to which I now belong.

As for the research question and the methodological design, when I began the project, I assumed that the only way to conduct committed research was by talking directly to children born of conflict-related sexual violence and asking about their experiences. However, I quickly realized that doing so could entail all sorts of risks for them and their mothers. For one thing, many of them are not aware of the circumstances of their conception, and avoiding forced disclosure must be a priority.[74] For another, research conducted in different contexts of war has shown that approaching them as "being born of conflict-related sexual violence" can not only increase stigmatization but also create new forms of violence toward them.[75] Instead of framing my questions in a way that would require me to interact with them, I chose to be patient and simply observe when and how narratives about them emerged.

Since I started visiting Buenos Aires and San Miguel many years ago, I have found different ways of being present in the community: I have participated in the process of collective reparations that San Miguel has been undergoing since 2012, volunteered at the school, and engaged in research and storytelling training processes with girls and a photo-voice project with victims of conflict-related sexual violence. I have worked with women who endured sexual violence perpetrated by paramilitaries and other members of armed groups in relation to their right to reparations and have served as a bridge between the women and the Victims' Unit to try to advance their children's access to reparations. Clearly, the questions I can ask now are not the same ones I was able to ask (or would have thought to ask) when I first embarked on the research. Nonetheless, you will not find in these pages the voices of the young women and men born of the sexual violence that their mothers endured, who in some cases have not had conversations about the circumstances of their conception with their mothers. The time for that is yet to come.

I would like to finish this section with two notes on the language of victimhood regarding the ways in which I refer to the boys, girls, teenagers, and adults born of conflict-related sexual violence and to the people who have experienced armed and political violence in Colombia. First, the term *children born of war* was proposed to expose the situation of children conceived between members of foreign troops and local women in war contexts. Although the term did not originally focus explicitly on conflict-related sexual violence, its conceptual development during the last decade has placed the focus there, gaining visibility not only within interdisciplinary academic networks but also among activists and human rights practitioners. The term, its conceptual development, and the political visibility the people working with and for that conflict-affected population have gradually achieved have, for instance, facilitated the unparalleled international attention described at the beginning of this introduction.

Kimberly Theidon reflects on the difficulties she has encountered regarding how to refer to those children, teenagers, adults, and elderly people in her own research. The term *children born of war*, she notes, "lacks an agent or a perpetrator, and war itself does not impregnate anyone."[76] For the purpose of intersectional research, the term offers few possibilities, as it does not allow for the emergence of the stories that those people, with their diverse identity markers, may tell. The danger of the term, argues Theidon, is that it creates a single story. I identify with Theidon's difficulties, as in my own research journey, I also struggled with how to refer to them. The last few years have witnessed a shift, both in the literature and in policy documents, away from the term *children born of war* to *children born of conflict-related sexual violence*, reflecting conceptual conversations with the work that has been undertaken regarding sexual violence in war contexts and what consent means under those circumstances. Despite this continuing struggle regarding how to refer to them in my research, in this book, I navigate between two terms: *children born of conflict-related sexual violence* and *people born of conflict-related sexual violence*. I am aware that the former does not reference age, and indeed, that is not the source of my conflict. However, I have observed firsthand the problems caused by approaching them exclusively as their mothers' children. Not only has doing so contributed to their unintelligibility, but it has also played a role in hiding women's experiences of reproductive violence behind the expected labor of motherhood.

The second note on language is connected with the terms *victim* and *survivor* when referring to people who have endured conflict-related sexual violence. At the international level, the last decade has seen a shift away from the former to the latter. This is partly in acknowledgment of the fact that within the victimhood system, the term *victim* entailed an expectation of sacrifice, passivity, and unconditional forgiveness.[77] For women in particular, criticism of the term highlighted the dangers of reproducing patriarchal power relations and assuming that women in war, transitional justice, and peace-building contexts were vulnerable, agentless targets of sexual violence in need of protection by men. Seeking to acknowledge women's agency, the term currently preferred is *survivors of conflict-related sexual violence*. Although, conceptually and politically, debates in Colombia align with these criticisms of the notion of a victim, they diverge in relation to the political meaning of the term. Achieving recognition of both the existence of the armed conflict and victimhood has constituted part of long-term fights by social movements in the country against denial, impunity, and state violence.[78] In that sense, in Colombia, the term *victim* has also been claimed by the various social movements to which the diverse groups of victims belong as a potential site of power.[79] Consequently, in this writing exercise, I use the term *victim*.

LAYERS OF UNINTELLIGIBILITY: BOOK CHAPTERS

Chapter 1 introduces us to the unintelligibility of the boys, girls, teenagers, and young adults born of conflict-related sexual violence in Colombia. The first of the layers that have configured such unintelligibility relates to the frameworks through which we have become aware of their presence without really seeing them and the way in which they have fallen into a gray area between feminist political struggles. Chapter 1 shows that while the organizations that sought to fight against and seek redress for conflict-related sexual violence understood them as an adjective for women's victimization, their counterparts that were fighting for women's reproductive rights saw them as unwanted lives. In recent years, however, a transformation of those frameworks has occurred. Fueled by transnational Latin American feminisms, a shift has taken place within the feminist movement's political struggles and strategies; instead of focusing on individual campaigns, the movement is advancing interconnected issues of social justice. This has broadened the frameworks through which conflict-related reproductive violence is understood, allowing the emergence of subjects and experiences that had previously remained unseen, such as children born of conflict-related sexual violence.

Chapter 2 addresses the materialization of this phenomenon within the bureaucracies of reparations while revealing another layer in the configuration of their unintelligibility. Within the victimhood system—and in particular, the area concerned with the right to reparations—the category of children born of conflict-related sexual violence was created, thus entitling them to redress. With the commitment to respect women's own processes and avoid revictimizing them by forcing the disclosure of their experiences to their children, this category became nested within the bureaucracies of reparation set up to address the harms caused to women by conflict-related sexual violence. However, a decade after the implementation of the Victims' Law, the category of children born of conflict-related sexual violence is yet to become legible within the system; little progress has been made in terms of accessing their right to reparations, while at the same time, their mothers have been charged with the responsibility for navigating the bureaucracies of reparations and seeking justice for their sons and daughters. In order to do so, women have not been offered any specialized or sustained support and have to draw on whatever resources they alone can get hold of.

Chapter 3 explores the naturalization of the labor of motherhood as another layer in the configuration of people born of conflict-related sexual violence's unintelligibility. It follows the fading of the use of the label *paraquitos* in San Miguel to refer to the children born of paramilitary sexual violence to unveil the less obvious but entrenched gendered politics of identity and reproduction. Unlike other war contexts in which identity is transmitted through the paternal line and children are discriminated against, as they are believed to be part of an "undesirable other," in the context of Colombia, women have the power to transmit identity, and hence, their children are accepted within their communities. This does not mean that those people born of paramilitary sexual violence are not understood as problematic within those communities or that all traces of their biological fathers are gone, for they remain in the ways that their absence affects the children's identities and in the many consequences that the sexual violence they perpetrated against women have left for their bodies and lives, including the children who might physically resemble them and for whom women are trying their best despite the hardships of their own life trajectories.

Chapter 4 focuses on the process of collective reparations that San Miguel is currently undergoing and the struggles over memories of the past that occupy a central place in the bureaucracies of victimhood and redress. Although women's experiences of the paramilitary confinement, and of sexual violence in particular, played an essential role during the initial negotiations between the community and the Victims' Unit and still occupy a place within their collective memories, children born of paramilitary sexual violence remain invisible within those narratives. Chapter 4 proposes that narratives about people born of conflict-related sexual violence inhabit the space of absence that lies in between silence, with its power to conceal, and unintelligibility, with its inability to see. By exploring the trajectory of the collective reparations process in San Miguel, this chapter interrogates the logic and methodologies that the architecture of transitional justice has prioritized in the acknowledgment of experiences of violence and questions what happens within those negotiations when the mark of victimhood—in this case, the label *paraquitos*—has vanished. It conceptualizes people born of conflict-related sexual violence as impossible witnesses: They emerged from the violent past but did not inhabit it. They cannot reconstruct, firsthand, their communities' narratives of the armed conflict or the distinct form of violence by which they became, according to the Victims' Law, officially recognized as victims.

This book is not about victims' participation in transitional justice mechanisms. However, during the time I have spent visiting the community and working with women in San Miguel, I have seen the toll that participation has taken on people, on their relationships with one another and their sense of solidarity, on the imagination of what justice or injustice is, and on their individual and collective ability to think creatively about the future on their own terms. This is to say not that transitional justice should not be victim centered but that the terms on which participation is expected have entailed severe consequences for people's political imaginations of themselves and their interpersonal relationships. Women are exhausted by fighting for accountability and their right to integral reparations and by navigating the system of victimhood and its various bureaucracies. They do want and demand justice for their children, but most importantly of all, they want and demand a better life for them. It does not matter if it is achieved through reparations; they will do anything within their power to protect those children from being dragged into the victimhood system and the new forms of institutional violence it produces.

A NOTE ON NAMES AND TRANSLATIONS

Throughout the book, I have used pseudonyms, in line with the preferences of the people I interviewed and had conversations with. The only exceptions are for individuals with a notable public presence, such as certain government officials or activists speaking publicly at events like the Colombian National Congress or United Nations meetings. All my fieldwork was conducted in Spanish, and I have personally translated interviews, conversations, and documents into English.

1 · BETWEEN POLITICAL STRUGGLES
Gendered Victimhood and Unwanted Lives

On September 27, 2021, during her opening remarks at the Global Survivors Fund (GSF) side event to the seventy-sixth session of the U.N. General Assembly on Reparations for Survivors of Conflict-Related Sexual Violence, U.N. Special Representative of the Secretary-General (SRSG) on Sexual Violence in Conflict Pramila Patten started her presentation with the following words: "We meet today with the knowledge that reparations are what survivors of conflict-related sexual violence request most, and yet still receive least." The opening session consisted of a short welcoming speech from each of the parties involved in organizing the event: Denis Mukwege, Nobel Peace Prize winner and president and cofounder of the GSF; SRSG Pramila Patten; Jean-Yves Le Drian, Minister for Europe and Foreign Affairs, France; Uto Takashi, State Minister for Foreign Affairs, Japan; and H. E. Choi Jongmoon, Second Vice Minister of Foreign Affairs, Republic of Korea. During her four-minute presentation, Patten talked about children born of conflict-related sexual violence: "As wars grind on, they grind down the hopes of entire generations, including children born of rape. My Office has been mandated to produce a special report on this subject to address the neglect and knowledge gap that hampers our response, and to ensure specific attention is paid to this voiceless category of victims, who risk being relegated to the shadows of society, marginalized, undocumented, and sometimes left stateless. Children conceived through rape and their mothers face unique and pronounced challenges in societies polarized by war."[1]

These words reflect a historic moment at which unprecedented international attention became directed toward the situation of people born of conflict-related sexual violence. In 2019, the U.N. Security Council adopted the landmark

Resolution 2467, an instrument designed to strengthen the prevention of and response to conflict-related sexual violence through a survivor-centered approach. For the first time ever, the Security Council talked about women and girls who become pregnant as a consequence of conflict-related sexual violence and their children born of those abuses. It was recognized that both mothers and children may experience "life threatening and enduring risks and harms . . . including economic and social marginalization, physical and psychological injury, statelessness, discrimination and lack of access to reparations."[2] The resolution urges states, in accordance with their obligations set out in the Convention on the Elimination of All Forms of Discrimination against Women (CEDAW) and the Convention on the Rights of the Child, to recognize children's rights under national legislation. Finally, the Security Council requested the secretary-general to report on these issues and for the SRSG on Sexual Violence in Conflict and the SRSG on Children and Armed Conflict to collaborate in achieving this end.

Following Resolution 2467, in January 2022, the SRSG on Sexual Violence in Conflict produced a report entitled *Women and Girls Who Become Pregnant as a Result of Sexual Violence in Conflict and Children Born of Sexual Violence in Conflict*. Building on the annual reports presented to the Security Council by the SRSG on Sexual Violence in Conflict since 2009 and quantitative and qualitative information collected from U.N. field officers, national authorities, local and international civil society organizations, and victims, this report sought to address an important issue that has been highlighted by a growing number of interdisciplinary scholars and human rights activists across the globe since the 1990s: there is a knowledge gap regarding children born of conflict-related sexual violence, with severe implications in terms of a lack of public policies and normative frameworks to guarantee their rights and well-being.[3] This gap, however, is accompanied by the awareness that due to the circumstances of their conception and the identities of their biological fathers, these people face enduring discrimination and inequalities that could affect their access to land, education, and citizenship as well as their social status and opportunity to have a loving family.[4] They also face unique risks that could jeopardize their well-being, even endangering their lives and making them vulnerable to other forms of violence such as recruitment, trafficking, and sexual exploitation.[5] Questions about who should assume leadership on these matters and how to proceed in a way that fills the knowledge gap but does not entail further risks for either the children or their mothers have been very much at the heart of these debates for decades.[6]

In a globally groundbreaking decision, Colombia became the first country to recognize children born of conflict-related sexual violence as victims of the armed conflict and thus entitled to integral redress. Law 1448, which was passed in 2011, known as the Victims' and Land Restitution Law (hereafter Victims'

Law), represented a political achievement and a landmark in terms of recognizing the existence of the armed conflict and its devastating consequences for Colombians across the country. It established the legal framework for identifying individual and collective victims, advancing the process of land restitution, and delivering integral reparations to victims. The Victims' Law was given a period of ten years in which to accomplish these unprecedented endeavors, which came to an end in June 2021. Amid acute political polarization, at the end of 2019, the Colombian Constitutional Court ordered that the law be extended for at least ten more years.

Despite the creation of the sociolegal category of children born of conflict-related sexual violence, the attention paid to this population has fallen into a gray area between the agenda that seeks to address the impacts of the armed conflict on women and that which focuses on children affected by war. This chapter addresses the tensions that have shaped that gray area and the frameworks that have resulted in children born of conflict-related sexual violence remaining unseen. Although the legal category was included within the section of the law devoted to conflict-affected children, this in itself did not reflect the advocacy and interests of the children's rights networks, whose resources were directed toward tackling child recruitment. Instead, it was the result of international and local women's and feminist movements' struggles against conflict-related sexual violence. While this inclusion was part of efforts to advance issues of gendered justice, for the broader women's and feminist movements, children born of conflict-related sexual violence were understood through the lens of the fight to achieve legal and safe abortion. More than ten years after the implementation of the Victims' Law, these political struggles have so far left women and their children in limbo, without justice or redress.

According to the records held by the Unit for the Assistance and Integral Reparations of Victims (hereafter Victims' Unit or the Unit), the governmental agency in charge of articulating measures of redress, over thirty thousand people have been recognized as victims of conflict-related sexual violence in Colombia.[7] Considering that pregnancies are a possible outcome of sexual violence, it would seem reasonable to expect the presence of a significant number of people born as a consequence of such practices, and yet the official records show a total of just 965.[8] It is not my intention to introduce these figures in order to discuss the problems of underreporting and the inability of official figures to represent the reality of conflict-related sexual and reproductive violence. Rather, I do so because they reflect the tensions and dynamics involved in configuring those people born of conflict-related sexual violence as victims of the armed conflict in Colombia. For the most part, this is not a story of silence, because silence requires knowledge and the power of concealment. The story of the sociolegal category of children born of sexual violence perpetrated by members of armed groups in Colombia is one of *unintelligibility*. Despite their unquestionable physical presence across the country, references to them in their mothers' testimonies, and the creation of the sociolegal category that recognizes them as victims in their own right, people born of conflict-related sexual violence remain invisible as independent subjects to the institutions that seek to name, write about, understand, and address the consequences of the armed conflict.

This chapter is about the unintelligibility of the people who are born of conflict-related sexual violence. Unintelligibility, however, is not neutral, because everything we see, hear, and perceive reflects the frameworks through which we apprehend the world.[9] Unintelligibility, in the case of people born of conflict-related sexual violence in Colombia, is not so much about a commitment to denying their existence or an intention to conceal it. It is more about the entangled ways in which power relations, such as those connected with sexuality and gender, have rendered certain bodies and experiences of violence invisible, such as people born of conflict-related sexual violence and forced motherhood (or fatherhood, in the case of transgender men). The dominant frameworks through which we have *seen-without-really-seeing* people born of conflict-related sexual violence in Colombia have cast them as secondary characters in the narratives about the victims of sexual violence. However, fueled by feminist struggles, in the last few years we have witnessed and been part of a transformation that has taken place within those frameworks, and with that transformation, we have started to see the emergence of these people, who are no longer children, and have started to pay attention to their mothers' stories of reproductive violence.

LIVING IN THE SHADOWS: "THE SILENT ISSUE OF CHILDREN BORN OF RAPE"

In a groundbreaking decision, the 2011 Victims' Law included "children conceived as a result of wartime sexual violence" in its definition of victims of the armed conflict. Through this normative framework, the state of Colombia acknowledged that due to the circumstances of their conception, they experience specific harms and types of violence, and as a result, they are entitled to integral reparation measures including economic compensation, satisfaction, and rehabilitation. Despite this legal recognition and the efforts of some human rights practitioners working on conflict-related gender issues to seek the necessary political interest and resources to start filling the knowledge gap, people born of sexual violence perpetrated by members of armed groups continue to be marginalized by transitional justice initiatives. Although they have been recognized as victims since 2011, there has been no progress in terms of public policies, and attempts to understand the particular forms of violence they experienced while growing up have been almost nonexistent.

On November 2, 2018, when Colombia was still the only country in the world to recognize people born of conflict-related sexual violence as victims within its domestic reparations program, Charo Mina-Rojas addressed the U.N. Security Council regarding the plight of that population in Colombia. Mina-Rojas, a well-known social leader of the Afro-Colombian peoples' network fighting for collective and territorial rights in Colombia, Proceso de Comunidades Negras, spoke about the significance of the legal developments that had taken place regarding victims of conflict-related sexual violence and their children born of these abuses. However, the main emphasis of her presentation was on the silence and impunity that still characterizes access to their rights. To illustrate this point, Mina-Rojas noted that until 2018, almost seven years after the implementation of the Victims' Law, "no children born of rape during the Colombian conflict have yet received reparations." She finished her presentation by suggesting some future recommendations that the Security Council could present to the Colombian government. The first of those directly addressed the aforementioned knowledge gap: "For the Colombian government to urgently fund a UNICEF/UN Women proposal to conduct an ethically informed needs assessment on children born of sexual violence during the Colombian conflict to promote a greater understanding of the dimensions of the protection gap and help remove barriers to the implementation of reparations for children born of sexual violence under the 2011 Victims Law 1448 and decree-laws 4635 and 4633 for Afro-descendant and Indigenous victims respectively."[10]

Throughout the many years I have devoted to researching the tensions around people born of conflict-related sexual violence, the words *silence, hidden,* and *marginal* have characterized the conversations I have had about them with human rights and transitional justice practitioners, activists, and scholars. Often, thinking out loud as we converse, these people reflect on the many times during the course of their work—mostly in rural, militarized parts of the country—that they have met women with children born of conflict-related sexual violence or have heard of children without fathers or of ethnicities different than those of their mothers who were treated with suspicion among their communities. This is frequently followed by the realization that they did not pay any attention to them, that they did not *see* them. In line with this, Zainab Hawa Bangura, the former U.N. SRSG on Sexual Violence in Conflict, during her visit to Colombia in 2015, expressed her serious concern about what she called "the silent issue of children born out of rape."[11]

In Colombia, as in other contexts around the world, naming practices made the existence of people born of war-related sexual violence visible outside their communities.[12] However, neither women's organizations nor organizations working to protect children's rights have included them in their agendas. In relation to victimhood, the former have concentrated their efforts on sexual violence in war contexts, while the latter have constructed their networks and infrastructure around child recruitment. In between these two political endeavors, the situation and needs of people born of conflict-related sexual violence have fallen into a gray area. In a 2016 interview with representatives of UNICEF Colombia, while talking about the different challenges involved in providing psychosocial support to war victims, a child protection officer, Rocío Mojica, mentioned one conflict-related issue in particular that has often been overlooked: "The topic of children born of war seems to be the most hidden one."[13] This scenario has translated into the idea that the situation of people born of conflict-related sexual violence is a matter that needs addressing urgently; however, there is an almost complete absence of debate and collaboration from governments and private initiatives. During that same conversation at the UNICEF offices in Colombia, a former child protection officer, Esther Ruiz, addressed precisely this lack of initiatives and proactive efforts to support these war-affected people: "We've been trying to propose a project for over a year now, but it's proven to be very difficult. Our idea was to assess at a national level the extent of the presence of children born of war—of course, without stigmatizing them, but acknowledging that the first problem we need to solve is the institutional invisibility of these children."[14]

Despite Colombia being the location of the longest active armed conflict in the region and the fact that several peace processes have been held with armed groups since the 1980s, for decades, the Colombian government's official position was one of denial. It was not until 2011 that, through the Victims' Law, social movements achieved the official recognition of the armed conflict that they had been seeking and, in doing so, asserted the political status of their historic battles against denial, impunity, and state violence.[15] The recognition of victimhood in Colombia, which did not start with the Victims' Law, legitimizes interconnected claims of truth, justice, redress, and non-repetition and thus represents a potential site of power.[16] The inclusion of the category of children born of conflict-related sexual violence as victims, however, was not a response to these people's own historic struggles or to the networks addressing the impacts of war on children. Rather, it was grounded in the work of the feminist and women's movements against conflict-related sexual violence. María Eugenia Morales, the former director of reparations of the Victims' Unit, described the fact that this group was now recognized as victims as a great achievement. However, when I asked her about the continuing lack of attention that these people receive, she replied, "The inclusion of these children in the definition of the category of victims happened at the very last moment of the debates [about the Victims' Law]. It was not part of the previous discussions and was not foreseen. It was the UN Women representative [Julissa Mantilla], who had also been part of the

Peruvian Truth and Reconciliation Commission, who pushed the topic onto the agenda. She kept insisting . . . Before that, the topic was completely invisible. I would say that, in part, explains why the topic has had so little diffusion."[17]

Looking at the broader context, the lack of information about and attention paid to the situation of people born of conflict-related sexual violence is by no means unique to Colombia. This conflict-affected population has historically been largely ignored by the international community and official global human rights discourses.[18] Although they have been the focus of a growing interdisciplinary field of research and advocacy, such as the War and Children Identity Project (WCIP), the International Network for Interdisciplinary Research on Children Born of War (INIRC), the Children Born of War H2020 Marie Curie Innovative Training Network, and the European Research Council–funded EuroWARCHILD project, people born of conflict-related sexual violence have not featured within the official remit of children's rights or women's rights. When the subject appears in public discussions, however, it usually does so in the language of conflict-related sexual violence.[19] A notable example of this is that even at this moment of unprecedented international attention, and although the U.N. Security Council asked the SRSG on Sexual Violence in Conflict and the SRSG on Children and Armed Conflict to collaborate on the report mentioned previously in this chapter, the 2022 report was in fact produced by the office of the former.

Regarding war-affected children in general, since the early 1990s, various transnational networks have raised awareness about the impact of war upon children and have succeeded in placing the issue on the international human rights agenda.[20] In that sense, the emergence of the "child combatant" category is understood within human rights frameworks as an achievement in the struggle to protect children in contexts of war. Interdisciplinary efforts have achieved a more comprehensive understanding of child recruitment, challenging initial conceptions that focused exclusively on boys who were captured, abducted, and forced to handle weapons in combat.[21] In that regard, the use of boys and girls by armed groups—not only for fighting but also for other purposes such as passing information, cooking, cleaning, or sexual slavery—now forms part of what we understand as child recruitment, allowing more comprehensive, gender-sensitive processes of disarmament, demobilization, and reintegration to take place.[22] In a similar way, the binary perception of those people who, through various means, were forced to become part of armed groups as either "victims" or "perpetrators" has been challenged, and conceptual approaches now exist that allow them to be viewed as "complex political perpetrators."[23] This nuanced approach to the experiences of these people has enabled us to question what justice, truth, redress, and guarantees of non-repetition could mean in these cases.[24]

In conversation with international debates, in Colombia, academic, legal, and public policy developments about war-affected children have focused specifically on child recruitment. The Colombian Truth Commission found that between 1990 and 2017, there were at least 16,238 cases of child recruitment across the country, but it estimated that the actual figures could be as high as 30,000.[25] In terms of the legal acknowledgment of this situation, in 2008, the Colombian Constitutional Court stated that the recruitment of children from impoverished backgrounds had been a systematic practice among all armed groups throughout the national territory and that it was closely connected to forced displacement. For its part, the Special Jurisdiction for Peace (JEP), one of the three bodies created via the 2016 Peace Accord between the Colombian government and the Revolutionary Armed Forces of Colombia–People's Army (FARC-EP) that investigates thematic or geographic macrocases within which individual cases of human rights violations are grouped, opened a macrocase on the recruitment and use of boys and girls in its first round of prioritization.

With each macrocase, the JEP seeks to become more effective in investigating large-scale human rights violations by creating patterns of macrocriminality. In the first round of prioritization of cases, between July 2018 and March 2019, the JEP opened seven macrocases, each of them devoted to the investigation of crimes such as kidnapping, the killing of civilians presented as combat casualties by state agents, and child recruitment. Following the 1997 Cape Town Principles' definition of child soldiers, and in a move that goes beyond the binary victim-perpetrator paradigm, the JEP recognizes that boys and girls were forced into joining armed groups to perform various roles, including cooking and for sexual purposes. Within this macrocase, the JEP is also investigating intraparty sexual violence, sexual slavery, forced abortion, and forced contraception.

The Commission for the Clarification of the Truth, Coexistence, and Nonrecurrence (hereafter the Commission), which presented its final report in 2022, has also broadened political conversations about war-affected children and produced a volume of its final report about the impacts of war on boys, girls, and teenagers.[26] In addition to investigating child recruitment and displacement, which remains the key focus of the volume, the Commission builds on the knowledge of interdisciplinary networks of scholars, practitioners, and grassroots organizations who have made strenuous efforts to show the severe adverse consequences that war has had on various aspects of life, particularly in racialized communities that have to endure economic and ecologic violence.[27] The Commission's investigations have included examining issues such as the way militarization has affected urban and rural learning communities, with tremendous transgenerational impacts for entire social groups. It has addressed aspects like the role teachers have played in resisting armed and political violence and the profound damage armed groups have caused by using schools as training and storage centers. The Commission has also explored how other dimensions of war affect children's lives, such as the consequences of growing up without parents and grieving their absence after they had been killed, kidnapped, or disappeared.[28]

In this volume, for the first time in a Commission report, there is a section entitled "Sons and Daughters of Combatants, Ex-combatants, and Members of the Armed Forces," which sheds light on aspects of their experiences such as loneliness, stigmatization, and exile.[29] It also includes some reflections on children born of conflict-related sexual violence. Unlike the different experiences addressed in this section, these three pages do not include any testimonies from children and draw mostly on academic literature and three reports on gender-based violence submitted to the Commission by scholars and women's organizations. This situation, in part, responds to methodological difficulties the Commission faced during the COVID-19 pandemic; as no previous work had been done with this population, conducting interviews with them would have required the children and their mothers to be approached under conditions that were not possible during the period of travel restrictions and social distancing.[30] The focus, then, was placed on introducing some of the ways in which children born of conflict-related sexual violence been singled out within their communities, primarily through naming practices.

Despite these conceptual and political transformations, child recruitment continues to be the dominant reference whenever the impact of the armed conflict on children and teenagers is discussed. Throughout the many years of research I have undertaken since 2012, I have found myself navigating around and across this category, which is commonly used to understand the link between childhood and armed and political violence. During the early years of my research, in my interactions with practitioners, scholars, and public policymakers working to support children's rights, I would usually introduce my work as relating to the category of "children born of war" or "children born as a result sexual violence committed in the context of the Colombian armed conflict." Very often, I found myself in the middle of the interview or conversation before realizing that the person I was talking with, sometimes even after weeks of email exchanges, assumed that my research focused on child recruitment. Time after time, I found myself trying to steer conversations away from the framework of recruitment, and interviewees often reminded themselves as they were speaking that *that* was not what the conversation was about.

In a similar way, in regard to my interactions with practitioners, scholars, and public policymakers working with war-related gender-based violence, the category that featured prominently in the conversations was "sexual violence," as they often assumed that my work focused on children, particularly girls, who were the direct victims of war-related sexual violence. This book, however, is also the result of the way in which my own frameworks have broadened, shifted, and transformed. During the last few years of conducting research, I have noticed how my interactions with people have changed since I started framing my work through the lenses of reproductive violence, even if that category also remains to be filled with meaning.

GENDERED VICTIMHOOD AND THE BODIES IN BETWEEN THE STORIES

Since the 1990s, international efforts to raise awareness about the existence and plight of people born of conflict-related sexual violence have been accompanied by questions about their invisibility within human rights agendas.[31] Seeking to understand why they have been unseen as independent subjects of concern within international human rights agendas, Charli Carpenter noted that, although at first glance they might appear to fit within the "victimhood scheme" of the child protection network, there was something about this particular issue that had historically "convinced activists at many locations in the child rights network that the political and normative risks of advocacy outweighed the possible benefits."[32] One perspective that has been put forward within the global advocate network is that raising awareness about the situation of these children could put them at further risk—that is, by creating this specific category of concern, children could be singled out and face stigmatization and discrimination.[33] In addition, there are concerns about the fact that in many cases, children do not know the circumstances of their conception.

Although these are legitimate and pressing matters, they do not explain why, despite the multiple forms of violence these children experience across war contexts, their present and future well-being has been neglected. First, there is a counterargument that maintains that if the category is not clearly established and discussed, it is impossible to design public policy and programs to effectively address their situation and the risks they face.[34] Furthermore, although it is true that in many cases, children do not know the circumstances of their conception during the early stages of their lives, research has shown that this reality is often presented to them through practices of discrimination and labeling within the community.[35] Finally, the risk of increasing stigmatization applies to other populations that have already gained a prominent position within human rights advocacy networks such as children affected by HIV/AIDS or child soldiers.[36] The president of the Inter-American Commission on Human Rights, Julissa Mantilla, who as a representative of U.N. Women advocated for the inclusion of the category of children born of conflict-related sexual violence in the Victims' Law, talked about these risks in an interview I conducted with her in 2016:

> There is a risk of stigmatization, which is true, but because of this risk, one cannot say "Well, I will not investigate" because it is also difficult to investigate sexual violence and all [other] human rights cases. Investigating a case of torture is not a walk in the park, but all the necessary mechanisms have been developed—the Istanbul Protocol—and people continue to work on the issue. That is to say, the way torture testimonies are taken nowadays, compared to how they were taken twenty years ago, well, there has been a whole learning process. And probably the first interviews were terrible, and people were stigmatized, but you cannot use that argument to avoid working on an issue. Rather, what the state should do is invest a lot of its resources in anthropologists, lawyers, archaeologists, [and] psychologists to find the answer.[37]

People's embodied experiences of violence and the institutional knowledge of those experiences are not one and the same. Institutional silence and a lack of conceptual or methodological tools with which to understand the complex and diverse experiences of people born of conflict-related sexual violence do not stop or transform the discrimination, ostracism, and other forms of violence that they already experience in their everyday lives, with profound implications for their well-being in both the present and the future. For people born of conflict-related sexual violence and their mothers, not being included in institutional agendas does not equate to a life free of hostility and discrimination based on the context of their conception and who their biological fathers are. As Kimberly Theidon observes, in their communities, these children "are hidden in plain sight."[38] While people, including their mothers, might not talk about them loudly, with everyone, or in terms that are legible within human rights frameworks, violence manifests in their bodies and in their presents and futures in very concrete ways. The lack of public policy does not change this; in fact, if anything, as time goes by and children grow older, their situation could worsen, particularly in racist, militarized contexts of extreme economic violence. With reference to this point, Mantilla continued in our 2016 conversation,

> I do believe that the state has an obligation to make this issue visible. When U.N. Women raised this issue, I remember that the speakers [about the Victims' Law] said, "No, because we are going to stigmatize those children with that," and we told them, "Well, in the case of the *paraquitos*, they are already stigmatized." I do believe that the argument clearly goes in the direction of establishing the obligation of the state. Now, the state does not know how to solve it, that is true.

Because neither the state nor anybody knows. But that is a different issue. But we cannot say "Then we better leave this matter."[39]

Not only do these children exist in their communities and in the everyday lives of their mothers, but mentions of them within institutional structures outside of their communities are often related to forms of violence directed toward them that tend to get lost in translation. In the case of conflict-related sexual violence and people born of these abuses, actors such as the media, human rights agencies, and academia have played a significant part in producing and disseminating discursive realities that reproduce patriarchal notions of gender, identity, and reproduction. Patricia Weitsman argues that paying attention to the language and narratives of such discursive constructions allows us to identify the notions behind practices of conflict-related sexual violence toward specific groups of people in tangible contexts and the legitimization of violence toward children born of that violence.[40] The war that took place between 1992 and 1995 in Bosnia and Herzegovina, for example, is emblematic not only in terms of the international coverage of the systematic sexual violence committed against women but also in terms of the women who gave birth to children conceived in this way.

In fact, part of that coverage focused on the stories of infanticide and rejection of the children by their mothers. Despite this, the international community remained passive and took no action to support the women or the children. In her work, Charli Carpenter shows how this absence of concrete actions was not due to a lack of information about the horrifying situations that both women and children were living through; rather, it was due to how this information was circulated and the narratives that were produced about them.[41] Coverage of the war by the Western global media produced storylines that included children born of wartime sexual violence. However, the ways in which they were portrayed did not create an impression of them as war-affected children. Instead, as Carpenter shows, they became symbols of crimes against women, genocide against ethnic and national groups, and diversions from the path toward an imagined civilized global community. In the mass media and news coverage, those children were referred to as "children of atrocity" rather than human beings who deserved solidarity and empathy and were entitled to rights and protection. This scenario was presented as a conflict of rights between the child and the mother, on one hand, and between the child and the mother's community, on the other. It also created ambiguity about what kind of organization or network should have taken up their cause.

In Colombia, media coverage of the situation of children born of conflict-related sexual violence has been very limited and grounded in the coverage of sexual violence in the context of the armed conflict. As a result of the campaign and pressure exerted by the women's and feminist movements, since the 1990s, the Colombian press has increased its coverage of the effects of the armed conflict on women living in conflict-affected regions and, in particular, of sexual violence.[42] However, the attention devoted to sexual violence in online and print media is accompanied by an almost total silence about the children born of those forms of violence. A couple of years ago, Sergio Lo Iacono, a colleague and friend of mine, and I embarked on a project to explore the emergence of narratives about children born of conflict-related sexual violence in Colombian online media in a more systematic way. We carried out a mixed-methods review that combined extensive content analysis and ethnographic content analysis of articles published in *El Tiempo*, one of the two national newspapers in Colombia, between 1990 and 2015.[43]

The almost total absence of these children from the storylines was evidenced by the fact that out of the 1,101 articles we included in our analysis, only 11 included mentions of children born of conflict-related sexual violence. Throughout these 11 articles, we found that children appeared as what we called "secondary characters" in the storylines within the explanatory framework of the discourse of "sexual violence as a weapon of war." References to children born of conflict-related sexual violence were included in the newspaper coverage only in relation to and to reinforce the representation of women—the main characters in the storylines—as passive victims of sexual violence or, in a few cases, empowered survivors. In relation to the former, mentions of the children served merely as a "symbolic adjective to stress the victimization of women" and their endless suffering.[44] With regard to the latter, references to the children were used to illustrate women's coping strategies or abilities to overcome their war experiences and, in particular, to reinforce the idea of their resilience through motherhood. To a lesser extent, references to the children were also used to contribute to the representation of perpetrators of conflict-related sexual violence, the other main characters in the storylines, as permanent presences in the lives of women and communities or as absent fathers, almost disregarding their role as perpetrators.[45]

In the absence of established frameworks with clear concepts, methodologies, resources, and devoted networks of scholars, advocates, and policymakers to make sense of information about children born of conflict-related sexual violence, their existence was approached through the lens of the discourse of "sexual violence as a weapon of war." In the 1990s, a strong feminist and women's movement succeeded in attracting international attention to sexual violence in war contexts. Based on the systematic recollection of testimonies, particularly from victims of the war in the former Yugoslavia and the Rwandan genocide, the movement transformed the way that sexual violence in those contexts was understood; war-related sexual violence against women went from being completely invisible, to being understood as regrettable but unavoidable, to being recognized as a systematic practice used to achieve military and political objectives.[46] Drawing on a notion of gender that understood sex as the main way in which men exercise oppression over women, subjugating them across different contexts, the discourse of sexual violence as a weapon of war became the dominant framework with which to understand, think, and write about gendered experiences of war.[47] In Colombia, where the feminist and women's movements also adopted it as a strategy for advocating and organizing domestically, this discourse has been effective in the movements' fights to challenge the normalization of sexual violence against women in the context of the armed conflict.[48]

The recognition of the positive transformations achieved across the world through the discourse of sexual violence as a weapon of war has also been accompanied by revisions to this explanatory framework with which to approach gendered victimhood. Maria Eriksson Baaz and Maria Stern have pointed out that while it has created methodological, conceptual, and advocacy tools that can be used to address wartime sexual violence, it has also reproduced patriarchal power relations and static roles: women are understood mostly as vulnerable victims of sexual violence, and men, through militarized masculinities, are viewed as either perpetrators of sexual violence or protectors of *their* women.[49] At the same time that this framework has created static subjects, it has silenced other subjects and experiences, either because they exist outside the borders of the discourse—such as cisgender men who experience wartime sexual violence, women as combatants or peace builders, or people with diverse sexual orientations, gender identities, and expressions—or because they are explained only in relation to their role within the narrative of women as victims and men as perpetrators, such as the case of children born of war-related sexual violence.[50]

Victims of conflict-related sexual violence have always talked about their children born of these abuses—sometimes not loudly, not explicitly, or not in terms that are legible within human rights frameworks. References to their sons and daughters often get lost in the testimonies of their experiences of sexual violence and in their stories of the journeys they have undertaken in order to endure and overcome those experiences. The trained human rights lenses that have predominantly focused on identifying stories of sexual violence in war contexts—particularly, those perpetrated for strategic purposes—have often filtered and rendered invisible the more comprehensive accounts of gendered victimhood that women share.[51] This includes aspects like the sexual violence they experience in contexts unrelated to war, the nonsexual violence they have endured in militarized contexts, and the various forms of armed and political violence that have not only deprived them of their reproductive autonomy but forced entire communities to live in contexts of reproductive injustice.

FROM UNWANTED LIVES TO REPRODUCTIVE JUSTICE

The center of Bogotá had turned into a massive party. "Es legal, es legal, el aborto en Colombia es legal" was the chant that, among tears of joy, drums, and hugs, burst out and filled the city's main square and the streets around the Colombian Constitutional Court. After eight hours of debate and over two years since the beginning of this phase of the fight for reproductive freedom, on February 21, 2022, the Constitutional Court decriminalized abortion up to the twenty-fourth week of pregnancy. While thousands of *cuerpas* kept their collective party going with cumbia, hip-hop, and reggaeton blaring from the sound system, the doctor and international reproductive rights expert and activist Ana Cristina Gonzalez addressed the crowd. As one of the emblematic leaders of the social movement to legalize abortion in Colombia and pioneer of the lawsuit that led to the court's decision, Gonzalez declared that this was a historic celebration, but an incomplete one. Although the landmark decision placed Colombia at the forefront of abortion rights in Latin America and the Caribbean, with the longest deadline for people who can become pregnant to access legal abortion services in the region, it still meant that for those people, there were limits to their citizenship. In Gonzalez's words,

> Although this is a massive advancement, and has put Colombia at the forefront not only in Latin America and the Caribbean, the Court missed a historic opportunity to reduce, with the total elimination of the crime of abortion from the criminal code, discrimination against us. And it did so, because there are still those who seek to impose on us the fate of forced motherhood. The same forces that were previously against divorce, against the 8-hour law, against women having a bank account and owning land. But the road is open. And with it, the possibility for women to enjoy their rights and the freedom that today has been recognized, making them more equal. Freedom will make us full citizens, whose capacity as moral subjects will be respected. We, women citizens, will continue to fight until the crime that in this century continues to punish us for being women is eliminated. In the meantime, we will make a reality the new regulatory framework that today allows us to choose the destiny of our lives and write our biographies. For all girls, adolescents, and women in Colombia! So that they will never again be forced to carry pregnancies and endure forced motherhood, let's continue the party of freedom![52]

The fight to achieve safe, legal, and free abortion has been at the core of the women's and feminist movements for decades across the world. However, within these movements, birth control has entailed both progressive reproductive rights and class-biased racist strategies of population control.[53] The history of the birth control movement in the United States has reflected some of these tensions since the late nineteenth century. Led by privileged white women involved in the movement for political equality, the "voluntary motherhood" campaign advocated for women's right to refuse their husbands' sexual demands as a way of controlling their reproductive lives. For those women, planning their pregnancies and not having the burden of constant childbirth and miscarriages was the only way they could enjoy the political rights they were fighting for. For women without the economic and social privileges of the middle and upper classes, those goals were completely outside the realm of what they could identify with. The campaign presented birth control as a path to a new form of womanhood whereby women could vote, pursue higher education, and have financial independence. Birth control advocates, however, also fostered the argument that birth control was a means to prevent the propagation of groups outside those of privileged white society. For impoverished racialized women, birth control was presented as a moral obligation on the basis that their large families were a burden on the tax system and charities, and their children did not belong to the "supreme class."[54]

During the twentieth century, these debates assumed different shapes through the proliferation of neo-Malthusian ideas, which were popular even among socialists who saw birth control as a means to stop the flow of new workers into the labor market. Eugenics also established a stronghold within the birth control movement, advocating for the protection of U.S. society by preventing the reproduction of the "unfit sectors."[55] The history of the movement translated into a deep mistrust within the 1970s women's and feminist movements that were advocating for abortion rights through an individual choice rhetoric.[56] While mass sterilizations were forced upon Black, Puerto Rican, Chicana, and Native American Indian women, Angela Davis points to the failure of the white mainstream feminist movement to "provide a voice for women who wanted the right to legal abortions while deploring the social conditions that prohibited them from bearing more children."[57]

With the aim of shifting the emphasis of the debates about reproduction away from individual choice toward social justice, in 1994, Black feminists in the United States proposed the framework of reproductive justice.[58] Reproductive justice, as an intersectional alliance between scholars and activism, follows three main principles: "(1) the right *not* to have a child; (2) the right to *have* a child; and (3) the right to *parent* children in safe and healthy environments."[59] These principles are accompanied by a claim for sexual autonomy and gender freedom. From a reproductive justice perspective, it is impossible to imagine safe and dignified fertility management, childbirth, or parenting without women having access to "community-based resources including high-quality health care, housing and education, a living wage, a healthy environment, and a safety net for times these resources fail."[60] As an intersectional framework of scholarship and political action, one of the departure points of reproductive justice is that people's reproductive lives exist within entwined racist, sexist, classist, and colonial systems that underlie practices, laws, and policies that deprive people of control over their bodies and reproductive autonomy. In this sense, women's reproductive destinies are closely linked to the conditions of the communities that they belong to and live in.[61] For women and communities living in war contexts, those conditions are also defined by the policies, economies, logics, and practices of war.

In Colombia, as in so many places around the globe, the abortion rights campaign was central to the 1970s women's and feminist moments. With the goal of transforming legal frameworks, women's organizations appealed to the National Congress, advocating for the legalization of abortion. In 1975, for the first time, a liberal party senator presented a bill in Congress to legalize abortion within the first twelve weeks of gestation under two circumstances: fetal malformation and when the pregnancy represented a risk to the health or life of the woman. Following this, in 1979, the liberal party congressperson Consuelo Lleras de Samper presented three bills seeking to achieve the same change in the law, adding sexual violence as a third circumstance under which women could access abortion services. These four abortion bills were not passed by Congress, and neither were the other almost forty bills that were presented prior to 2017. In the 1970s, around 20 percent of maternal mortality in the country was due to abortions. Asserting that abortion is also a matter of public health, toward the end of the 1970s in Cali and Bogotá, some health practitioners' organizations started offering safe, clandestine abortion services. In the 1980s, these organizations extended their services to other cities like Medellín and, in doing so, continued to risk not only prison but also armed violence from drug cartels and paramilitary groups.[62]

As was the case with international debates more widely, in Colombia, access to safe abortion was approached differently by different sectors of the women's and feminist movements—namely, those who talked about women's sexual and reproductive freedom and those who focused on gaining the right to abortion. From a women's sexual and reproductive freedom perspective, the fight to decriminalize abortion took place within the larger campaign for women to gain complete control over their bodies, sexuality, reproduction, and lives. From a rights approach, the emphasis was placed on achieving the legalization of abortion by changing legal frameworks and, through that, forcing the state to guarantee access to sexual and reproductive health services. From within the former movement, feminist collectives like Mujeres en la Lucha (Women in the Struggles), which was formed in the late 1970s, advocated for the *libre opción a la maternidad* (freedom of choice for motherhood)—the right for women to freely choose whether they wanted to have children or not and, if so, how many children, in dignified conditions, with economic autonomy. In the words of Olga Amparo Sanchez, a historic feminist beacon in Colombia who was a member of Mujeres en la Lucha, this meant "that women could have dignified conditions in which to have their children, such that they would not die from abortion or childbirth. That women could have options available to them not only in terms of contraceptive control methods but also access to fertility treatments."[63]

As was the case at the international level, the fight to include abortion in legal frameworks, which was central to the feminist struggles, also received substantial support and legitimization through a Malthusian agenda and the so-called war on poverty.[64] Across Latin America, the "war on poverty" provided the context through which governments and international organizations disguised Malthusian policies behind fertility control programs.[65] The strategy of blaming poverty on the number of children born by racialized impoverished women—and not on exploitation, oppression, and unequal distribution of wealth—legitimized the imposition of eugenic policies such as forced sterilization on women with disabilities and Indigenous women[66] It also increased the urgency of demands to legalize abortion, which were unrelated to reproductive autonomy, targeting specific groups of women whose reproduction was treated as problematic for the development of the dominant, class-structured, white and mestizo order.

The first Feminist Latin American Congress, which took place in Bogotá in 1981, showed the transformation that the women's and feminist movements in the region had undergone in the previous decades. With the acknowledgment that normative changes had been achieved to gain educational, voting, and inheritance rights, the emphasis switched to the patriarchy's colonization of women's bodies, sexuality, and reproduction. Reflecting the tensions about how to approach abortion and the role it played in women's struggles, population control policies occupied a central place in the discussions held during the three-day-long congress.[67] For the Colombian movement in particular, the centrality of reproductive autonomy and the right to abortion were accompanied by discussions about its role regarding the exacerbation of political and military oppression that the country had endured since the late 1970s. As political and armed violence increased in the 1980s, 1990s, and 2000s, rendering visible the differentiated impact of such violence on women became a key aim of the women's and feminist movements' agenda.[68] The crisis of internal mass displacement that occurred between the late 1990s and the first half of the 2000s became entangled with stories of conflict-related sexual violence against women across the country.[69] The Colombian feminist movement's strategy to render visible the violence that women and girls were enduring across the country grounded its conceptual, methodological, and political action in the international-led discourse of sexual violence as a weapon of war.[70]

During the first half of the 2000s, the feminist and women's movements in Colombia made significant advances in relation to both the fight against conflict-related sexual violence and the right to abortion. The context was extremely hostile on both fronts. On the one hand, the early 2000s saw the highest levels of conflict-related sexual violence perpetrated during the armed conflict to date, and on the other hand, conservative, religious, and anti-rights movements were a strong force in Congress.[71] In response to these circumstances, feminist and women's organizations acted on several fronts. Regarding sexual violence, they organized themselves to influence the Justice and Peace Law, which is regarded as the first piece of transitional justice legislation in the country and was, at that time, being discussed in the Constitutional Court. In this context, feminist and women's organizations made visible the occurrence of conflict-related sexual violence and its differentiated impact on women and girls across the country. They advanced strategies for strategic litigation and representation of victims of sexual violence during the paramilitary hearings.

Regarding the right to abortion, since the early 2000s, the feminist and women's movements had recognized in the Colombian Constitutional Court a path through which to make progress.[72] Women's Link Worldwide led and presented a lawsuit to the court requesting them to declare the criminalization of abortion under any circumstances to be unconstitutional. This lawsuit led to the Constitutional Court decision C-355 of 2006, through which the court overturned the absolute ban on abortion, allowing the procedure to be used in three circumstances with no limits in terms of the stage of the pregnancy: when the pregnancy constitutes a danger to the life or health of the pregnant woman, when there are serious malformations that make the fetus nonviable outside the womb, and when the pregnancy is the result of sexual violence, incest, or artificial insemination or embryo transfer without consent.

Although decision C-355 represented a significant advancement in terms of reproductive rights not only in Colombia but in the region as a whole, people with the capacity to gestate and who wanted access to their right to abortion faced multiple obstacles—in particular, racialized, impoverished people living in the most war-affected or rural areas of the country were likely to encounter cultural, economic, institutional, and bureaucratic barriers that endangered their well-being, health, and life. In those contexts, abortions outside the law involved a huge risk. For example, one in three women who had a clandestine abortion experienced complications that required medical attention—or that should have received medical attention—often with lifelong consequences. This resulted in an estimated seventy women per year dying from unsafe abortions.[73] In 2020, over one hundred organizations and activists from diverse sectors of the women's and feminist movements in Colombia joined forces in the Causa Justa movement. In September of that year, Causa Justa filed a lawsuit before the Constitutional Court, requesting the complete decriminalization of abortion. After more than two years of hard, committed work on the streets, in court, in the classrooms, and in the media, the Constitutional Court made the landmark decision that decriminalized abortion until the twenty-fourth week of pregnancy.

Instead of talking about women in abstract terms, the arguments presented in the lawsuit involved an intersectional analysis and highlighted the overcriminalization of racialized young women from impoverished and rural contexts in the country. In terms of age, for instance, it was shown that out of the 2,290 women who were criminalized in 2017, 75 percent were under twenty-four years old, and 42 percent were between fifteen and nineteen years old. In addition, there were thirty-eight cases of fourteen-year-old girls and three cases of girls aged between eleven and twelve.[74] One of the main arguments presented in the lawsuit was that because abortion was still considered a crime by the penal code, resulting in a sentence of between sixteen and fifty-four months in prison for whoever assisted with the abortion and for the person who interrupted the pregnancy, the law was inefficient and allowed fundamental rights to be violated—in particular, those of women who could not afford and had no nearby access to private and safe abortion services. The persistence of obstacles to accessing abortion services was closely associated with health professionals' and institutions' interpretations of partial decriminalization, which allowed them to arbitrarily set deadlines and requirements. The lawsuit showed that despite the C-355 decision, 99 percent of abortions in the country were still performed outside the law.[75]

The lawsuit linked the total decriminalization of abortion with social justice and structural issues beyond individual choice. For instance, it framed the full recognition of women's reproductive autonomy as essential to peace building. Acknowledging that armed conflict radicalizes the conditions that interfere with women's autonomy over their sexuality and reproduction, the lawsuit argued that the total decriminalization of abortion would contribute to redress for the victims and guarantees of non-repetition regarding conflict-related sexual and reproductive violence.[76] The lawsuit noted that the overlapping existence of the armed conflict and state violence in rural regions of the country translated into very limited access to basic health services for the local population. It also showed that compared to areas where armed groups did not have a strong presence, in the most conflict-affected regions, maternal mortality was 7.6 times higher, pregnancy rates among girls between ten and fourteen years old were twice as high, and reported cases of sexual abuse were ten times lower.[77] Under these circumstances, the supply of gender-sensitive specialized services for women, and even more so for people with nonheteronormative gender identities or expressions, was very limited. There was a lack of adequate infrastructure for carrying out abortions safely and an insufficient number of properly trained health workers to provide unbiased sexual and reproductive services.[78]

While in the United States, we are currently witnessing threats against and setbacks for women, girls, and gestating people's reproductive rights, in the Latin American and Caribbean region, the *marea verde* (green tide) that started in Argentina has spread over the whole region. On June 24, 2022, the U.S. Supreme Court overturned the 1973 landmark *Roe v. Wade* decision that guaranteed the federal constitutional protection of abortion rights. This decision, which formed part of a broader conservative and right-wing pushback against the rights of cisgender women and people with diverse sexual orientations and gender identities and expressions, not only affects access to safe and legal abortion services but might also jeopardize other rights that were protected by the right to privacy from governmental interference, such as the use of contraception or same-sex marriage.[79] By contrast, in the last few years, the Latin American feminist movement has achieved significant victories that have advanced gestating people's reproductive rights within the region and beyond.[80] This is a transnational movement that is no longer unidirectional and guided by white, mainstream types of feminism from the global north; it is a diverse movement that works together to advance reproductive justice issues within patriarchal, colonial, and capitalist systems.

Since the 1980s, Latin American feminisms have worked toward internationalizing the movement through the development of regional collaboration and agendas. Since the 2000s at least, three elements have characterized the Latin American feminist movement's struggles regarding not only the decriminalization of abortion but also real access to reproductive services based on domestic legislation: forging alliances between actors from diverse backgrounds and social movements to advance a sexual and reproductive rights agenda; developing transnational strategies within the human rights framework that, despite taking place at the local level, have progressed regional and global struggles; and offering support to women who want access to abortion services in free or affordable, safe, and dignified conditions.[81] Framing the criminalization of abortion as a violation of fundamental rights, such as health and equality, has proved an effective strategy for urging states to comply with their obligations under international human rights laws.

At the same time, in the last few years, there has been a shift in terms of how abortion has been introduced and apprehended in public debates beyond the legal sphere. On one hand, systematic efforts to collect interdisciplinary evidence regarding who is most affected in contexts of the criminalization of abortion, as shown by the Causa Justa lawsuit, have served to foster informed debates about reproductive care beyond the arguments about individual choice within the sphere of social justice. On the other hand, there have been strategic efforts by grassroots movements to advance reproductive claims and through the coordination of different sectors of the feminist movement in various urban and rural spaces such as the streets, classrooms, courts, and media. This means not only that the fight for the decriminalization of abortion exists within the context of broader claims for social justice for cis women and people with diverse sexual orientations and gender identities but also that these legal changes require cultural transformations—the "social decriminalization" of abortion not only by lawmakers and health practitioners but within society at large.[82]

Drawing on, thinking about, and unlearning from frontier feminisms, the contemporary Latin American feminist movement has achieved transborder interpellations and repercussions by pursuing interconnected struggles instead of individual campaigns.[83] In its scholarly and politically active dimensions, this diverse feminist movement is—at its core and not without opposition and backlash—anti-capitalist, anti-racist, and trans-inclusive. It draws on diverse bodies and sites of enunciation to produce knowledge, strategic alliances, and forms of struggle to subvert entangled systems of oppression. Veronica Gago argues that challenging the normality of those systems has had the effect of expanding and creating new frameworks with which to redefine subjectivities, connect struggles, and produce knowledge through a new vocabulary based on emerging sensibilities. While the decriminalization of abortion remains one of the common causes among the diverse feminist movement in the region, Gago notes that it has served as a motive and a platform for the coordination of political forces, struggles, and political performances across borders.[84]

In Colombia, the transformation of the frameworks through which reproductive care and sexual and reproductive rights are understood has also permeated the fields that seek to address the armed conflict. Through those transformations, understandings of gendered victimhood have moved beyond the strategic use of sexual violence against women, and experiences of war-related reproductive violence such as forced parenthood, forced contraception, and abortions are becoming not only visible but part of the interconnected struggles to advance gendered justice. Within the transitional justice system, different sectors of the feminist movement—including victims' organizations, scholars, and civil society organizations, most of which are the same ones behind the fight for the decriminalization of abortion—have been working together and are succeeding in broadening transitional justice's understanding of gendered victimhood. For instance, after years of coordinated domestic and international advocacy from the feminist movement, in 2023, the JEP opened a macrocase to investigate sexual and reproductive violence and other crimes committed as a result of prejudice, hatred, and discrimination based on gender, sex, and diverse gender identities and sexual orientation in the armed conflict.

The Colombian Truth Commission, for its part, was the first truth-seeking mechanism worldwide to include reproductive violence in its investigations and recommendations for reparations and non-repetition. The transformation of these frameworks has also created cracks through which the embodied existence of people born of war-related sexual violence and their mothers' stories of reproductive violence can start to be rendered legible.

FILLING THE KNOWLEDGE GAP: THE CREATION OF THE LEGAL CATEGORY

The ombudsman's office in Popayán, the administrative capital of the department of Cauca, is crowded throughout the year. There are always people queuing outside the gate, most of whom are Indigenous or Afro-Colombian or from peasant communities, waiting to talk with a representative of the state in order to present a new case of human rights violations, check on the current state of their file, provide new documents, or as was often the case with the gender team with whom I worked, receive psychosocial or legal assistance. During the time that I was conducting fieldwork in 2016, the gender team was composed of two women: a psychologist and a lawyer. The office they shared was constantly busy, with women and people from other offices bringing new files to pile onto their already overcrowded desks. Amid the constant bustle, they made a space for me on one of their desks—whoever was less busy that day or whoever was out visiting communities and thus would not be requiring the desk. For weeks, I sat and reviewed documents containing the testimonies that the gender team had collected from wartime sexual violence survivors from Buenos Aires. Those testimonies form part of the legal process and the bureaucracies that women have to navigate in order to access reparations under the 2011 Victims' Law.

While reviewing those testimonies, one aspect that captured my attention was that women were asked about pregnancies immediately after being asked about sexually transmitted diseases. In reference to the implied burden associated with the collection of testimonies, Julissa Mantilla stated,

> I believe that in regard to this topic, what is missing is a previous debate. The interviewer knows that he has to ask about pregnancies, but he doesn't know why. I mean, he might know that he must ask in order to find out how many children [a woman has], but there was no previous discussion about why we care about that. Is it because otherwise, the feminist will yell? No! Why do we care? Is it because it will contribute to redress, to guarantees of non-repetition, to understand the harm caused? Only when you understand the purpose of a question do you understand where to include it and how to express it.[85]

The way in which the category was included in the Victims' Law reflects the knowledge gap about children born of conflict-related sexual violence. This gap does not just constitute a lack of information about them, because at the moment the law was drafted, information about them had been circulated in the forms of, for example, naming practices and the testimonies of their mothers. The knowledge gap refers more to the frameworks and infrastructures through which we seek, see, make sense of, and act upon the information we have—for instance, what concepts and methodologies are being developed to think, write, and develop concrete actions regarding children born of conflict-related sexual violence; what institutions and actors are producing and engaging with that work; and how is that work being funded. On September 27, 2010, the draft of the Victims' Law was presented for the first time in the Colombian Congress.[86] This document contained a section devoted to conflict-affected children (Chapter XIII) and asserted their right to truth, justice, and integral reparations (Art. 107). Although it referred to all child and teenage victims of human rights and international human rights law violations, the document highlighted the right to integral reparations only for some categories of war-affected children: those who became orphans as a consequence of the armed conflict (Art. 114), victims of landmines and unexploded ordnances (Art. 115), and victims of recruitment and use by armed groups (Art. 116). There was no mention of children born of war-related sexual violence, as was the case throughout most of the debates that preceded the final version of the Victims' Law.

The first draft that included the category of children born of conflict-related sexual violence was published on March 1, 2011, during the final stages of the debates and a couple of months before the law came into effect on June 10, 2011. As a result of the advocacy of former U.N. Women representative Julissa Mantilla, the recognition of children born of conflict-related sexual violence as victims was reflected in the section devoted to conflict-affected children, as follows:

TITLE VII. INTEGRAL PROTECTION OF BOYS,
GIRLS, AND TEENAGE VICTIMS
Article 174. Rights of boys, girls, and teenage victims. This law will understand as a boy, girl, and teenager every person under the age of 18. Boys, girls, and teenage victims of Human Rights' violations and violations of International Human Rights Law will enjoy all of their social, cultural, political, and economic rights, and in addition they will have access to:

1. Truth, Justice, and Integral reparations
2. The restitution of their rights

3. Protection against all forms of violence, damage or physical and mental abuse, ill treatment or exploitation, including recruitment, forced displacement, landmines and unexploded ordnances, and sexual violence.

Paragraph. For the effects of this Title, boys, girls, and teenagers conceived as a consequence of sexual violence in relation to the internal armed conflict will also be considered.[87]

In that final paragraph, children born of conflict-related sexual violence were acknowledged in the Victims' Law. Their inclusion was different, however, to that of other categories of conflict-affected children like orphans or victims of recruitment; children born of conflict-related sexual violence were not defined in a separate article but simply added without any development of the category itself or elaboration on the way in which they were going to be addressed. As for the other categories of conflict-affected children, their addition to the document at an earlier stage, together with the work of existing networks in producing knowledge and advocating on their behalf, facilitated their more comprehensive inclusion in the final version of the Victims' Law. Articles designed to address those conflict-affected children sought to cover the particularities of each category's experiences by providing normative definitions of types of harm and showing an understanding of aspects such as the entities designated to address their situation and technical guidelines for how to do so. In the case of orphaned children, for instance, the law states that any national, regional, or local authority that receives information about children who have lost one or both of their parents due to the armed conflict has an obligation to immediately inform the Colombian Family Welfare Institute (ICBF) so that they can initiate the process of reparation (Art. 188). In the case of child victims of landmines, the law talks about their integral rehabilitation; it states that on the basis of scientific assessment, the victim has the right to receive medical treatment, prosthesis, orthoses, and psychological assistance free of charge and for as long as necessary (Art. 189).

If the women's and feminist movements won the political battle to gain legal recognition of this population affected by the armed conflict through their fight against sexual violence, it was the language of the struggle for women's reproductive autonomy that defined the category. As mentioned previously, Article 181, Paragraph 1 of the Victims' Law states, "For the effects of this Title boys, girls, and teenagers *concebidos* [conceived] as a consequence of sexual violence in relation to the internal armed conflict will also be considered." It is noteworthy that the word *conceived* is used rather than *born*. I highlight *concebidos* because, despite this paragraph being included in the section about conflict-affected children, the description of the category frames it within debates about women's sexual and reproductive rights. When asked about this wording, Julissa Mantilla, who has raised awareness about this from the moment the law was published, noted, "Our proposal was 'children *born* as a result of sexual violence,' and those were the terms we used throughout the debates. However, when the law was approved, they changed *nacido* [born] to *concebido* [conceived]. That modification went unnoticed, and no one called attention to it."[88]

Despite the fact that when the Victims' Law was published, abortion was already legal for victims of sexual violence, through this linguistic change, the recognition of the right of redress was granted to the fetus instead of the born child. Thus, the frameworks for understanding the experiences of those subjects born of conflict-related sexual violence shifted from a child-centered approach to one that sought to enforce control over women's sexuality and reproduction. Mantilla highlights two aspects that could be turned into institutional violence against women's reproductive autonomy. First, the way that the definition of the category is worded could be used by health practitioners to create even more obstacles that make it difficult for women to access their right to abortion on the basis that, under the Victims' Law, the fetus is also considered a victim and therefore entitled to redress. Second, the argument about receiving "double reparations" if a woman gives birth to the child could be used as a deterrent to prevent women from accessing abortion services in an effective and timely manner.[89]

In the case of Colombia, the wording of the legal category of children born of conflict-related sexual violence and the place in the document where it was included reflect both the tensions surrounding the category itself and its unintelligibility—on the one hand, the tensions among the relevant fields whose job it is to fill the knowledge gap regarding children born of sexual violence and their access to justice and, on the other hand, the frameworks through which we seek to render them legible. The former shapes the gray area in which the category is situated, failing to gain a proper place on either children's or women's rights political platforms. The latter describes children born of conflict-related sexual violence through the language of violence against women and, in particular, wartime sexual violence and sexual and reproductive rights. Debates about gendered victimhood are grounded in broader understandings of gender, sexuality, and reproduction, and they are permeated by the historic battlefield over women's sexual and reproductive autonomy. For instance, at the same time that the Victims' Law was being debated in Congress, the Colombian Conservative Party, supported by some sectors of the church and Opus Dei members within the government, led an initiative to dispute the C-355 ruling by the Constitutional Court and return to the complete criminalization of abortion in the country.[90] Although this initiative was unsuccessful, it illustrates the constant battle that was waged over women's bodies and reproductive freedom.

In practice, neither the wording of the category of children *conceived* through conflict-related sexual violence nor their recognition as victims entitled to redress has been used against women's right to abortion. In that regard, Mantilla, who continues to follow this topic closely, told me that she has asked people working in the Victims' Unit about this, and they have not encountered any cases. She notes, "So far, the argument about the *concebido* has not been used to interfere with legal abortions or with reparations, or at least those situations have not been documented." I believe, however, that the fact that the argument about the *concebido* has not been used in relation to legal abortions or to access "double reparations" says less about achievements in the context of women's reproductive autonomy and more about the absence of public debates and negotiations seeking to understand the situation, needs, and roles of people born of armed conflict-related sexual violence.

CONCLUSIONS

On June 28, 2022, the Colombian Truth Commission presented its final report: *Hay futuro si hay verdad* (There is a future if there is truth). With the Jorge Eliécer Gaitán Municipal Theater in Bogotá packed to its full capacity of over fifteen hundred people and thousands more watching the live stream not only across the country but across the world from their houses, offices, and public squares in rural and urban areas, the president of the commission, Father Francisco de Roux, walked onto the stage with ten of the commissioners who had led this truth-seeking journey. Two of the commissioners, the much-loved Alfredo Molano and Angela Salazar, had passed away during the period of the commission's mandate, and Commissioner Carlos Guillermo Ospina, a retired army major, had resigned from his role a couple of months earlier.

As the compere of the event welcomed the president and commissioners to the stage by announcing their names, the whole theater greeted them with a standing ovation, one that we all joined in, independently of our own backgrounds and experiences: Victims of paramilitaries, guerrillas, the armed forces. *Campesinos* and *campesinas*, Indigenous people, Afro-Colombians, *raizales*, mestizas and mestizos. People of all ages, with diverse sexual orientations and gender identities and expressions; international and national representatives of social movements and grassroots organizations; former combatants; diplomats, journalists, scholars, and politicians from a wide political spectrum. The recently elected President Gustavo Petro and Vice President Francia Márquez were also there, unlike the then president who was still in office, Ivan Duque, who refused to attend and instead embarked on a twenty-day European tour.

After almost four years of effort and commitment, Father Francisco de Roux stood on the stage with the ten commissioners seated behind him to honor the victims, to hand in the final report to the government, and to address the country as follows: "Why did we Colombians let this tearing apart of ourselves continue for years, as if it had nothing to do with us? Why did we watch the massacres on television day after day as if it were a cheap soap opera? Why was the security surrounding politicians and big property not security for the people and the *resguardos* and the popular sectors that were on the receiving end of the landslide of massacres? How can we say that we are human when all this is part of us?"[91]

The audience present in the theater, and the victims in particular, were there not only to witness this historic moment for the country. They were also there—as they have been throughout decades of resisting the entanglement of state, economic, political, patriarchal, and armed violence—to challenge power relations, to show their joy and anger, and to honor those who were no longer with us. Throughout the event, the audience booed whenever the name of the absent president was mentioned and cheered for the elected president and vice president. People shouted after the compere had finished introducing the commissioners, demanding that the names of the much-loved Alfredo Molano and Angela Salazar be included in the introduction: "And Alfredo Molano and Angela Salazar, who are no longer here but always in our hearts!" People called out in memory of left-wing presidential candidates who had been killed, of political movements that had been systematically annihilated, and of union leaders and defenders of their territories who continue to be murdered. Someone seated in front of me screamed, "For the trees that are falling every day in the Amazon. It is a genocide against our brothers the trees and our brothers the animals!" Every time it happened, Father de Roux paused his speech and listened. In response to some of them, he amended his words while he nodded and sometimes smiled at others. With their voices, people opened windows into aspects of this decades-long war, and others clapped and cheered.

At some point, a woman seated near the stage stood up and demanded Father de Roux's attention. "Father Franciso, Father Franciso!" she called out several times until he stopped speaking. "Where are our sons and daughters born of the crime of sexual violence?" she asked loudly and clearly. I was unable to hear what she said after this, as the cheers and clapping from the audience, which I joined in with great excitement and surprise, drowned out the rest of her claim. Despite not hearing what she said next, I knew that her words resonated with the transformation of the frameworks through which we understand, name, and think about reproductive violence. This transformation, which is the result of decades of feminist struggles fought in the streets, in the courts, in the classrooms, in households, in health centers, and in the everyday lives of urban and rural women and people with the capacity to gestate, has not only helped make a conversation about people born of conflict-related sexual violence possible but also helped make it legible within transitional justice mechanisms, such as this truth-seeking endeavor.

We are witnessing a moment of unprecedented international attention being directed to the situation of people born of conflict-related sexual violence. Since the 1990s, a growing number of interdisciplinary scholars and human rights practitioners have advocated for the inclusion of children born of conflict-related sexual violence across the globe on human rights agendas. The understanding that due to the circumstances of their conception and the identity of their biological fathers, these people experience different forms of human rights violations that endanger their well-being and lives has long existed, together with the recognition that there is a knowledge gap about them. That gap—which entails aspects such as methodological questions about how to approach them, how much they know about their mothers' experiences of violence, what justice could mean in their cases, and what kind of resources and institutions are adequate to address their needs—has prevented the urgent formulation of policies and normative frameworks to guarantee that people born of conflict-related sexual violence are able to develop in safe and loving contexts, with the full enjoyment of their fundamental rights. It has also prevented broader social conversations about the normalization of the reproductive care and labor imposed on their mothers.

Although the United Nations and other international bodies and policy-makers have more recently turned their attention to these issues, Colombia has been attending, in practice, to the same questions for over a decade. Despite the lack of strong social movements or human rights practitioners advocating on behalf of people born of conflict-related sexual violence, in a globally ground-breaking decision, the 2011 Victims' Law recognized them as victims of the armed conflict who are entitled to redress. The creation of the legal category, however, has not been accompanied by the development of concrete policies or strategies to better understand their situation and needs as they grow older. This lack of attention is not so much the result of institutional or social denial regarding their existence or complex situations represented by the label *paraquitos*. Rather, it is a story of *unintelligibility*. For years, there has been a lack of frameworks that can be used to *see* them as independent subjects whose lives are entangled with war, particularly in relation to their mothers' experiences, but who are not defined by that. Instead, their existence has been approached through frameworks designed to understand conflict-related sexual violence and women's reproductive autonomy. Through the former, they served as an adjective for their mothers' victimization, and in regard to the latter, they were understood as unwanted lives. In the last few years, however, feminist and women's movements' campaigns for social justice have developed a more nuanced understanding of reproductive violence and gendered victimhood. Through this, people born of conflict-related sexual violence have also started to become more visible to the gaze of human rights and transitional justice.

2 · THE BUREAUCRACIES OF VICTIMHOOD IN THE MAKING

A Record of the Unintelligible and the Uncertain

I have witnessed quiet moments in San Miguel. In the early mornings when the fog is drifting down the mountains, unveiling the dark-orange dirt roads, and the air is still cool and crisp. In the afternoons after the kids have come home from school but before people return from working on the land, while the hot sun is still high in the sky, inviting people to use the shade as shelter from the heat. In the moments after the rain, especially one of those windy storms that force people to pause and wait patiently to resume their work tending the crops with their *finca* animals. When the sound of raindrops pattering loudly on tin roofs ceases, there is a certain sense of relief in the air, and chirping birds, dogs, cockerels, and hens announce that activity is about to resume. But those quiet moments, in my experience, never seem to happen on a day when there is a meeting or one of the many workshops—and there are many—being held by the Unit for the Assistance and Integral Reparations of Victims (hereafter Victims' Unit or the Unit), a nongovernmental organization (NGO), or any other government agency. No matter how sensitive the issues on the agenda, those days always come with their own soundtrack of curious passersby yelling their greetings or asking whether there will be lunch provided later, loud music blaring from neighboring houses and stores, and children and teenagers throwing footballs, guavas, or whatever they have to hand on the roof of the community kiosk where most of the meetings take place.

On August 24, 2021, one such meeting with the Victims' Unit was being held. No one really seemed to know what the meeting was about, but as I was around at that time, working with victims of conflict-related sexual violence who were seeking access to their right to reparations, the women invited me to join them: "You like those meetings, don't you? Join us on Tuesday!" The meeting was supposed to start at 9:00 a.m., so I arranged for a trusted driver to pick me up from the hotel in Santander de Quilichao at 7:00 a.m. It is supposed to be an hour's drive, and I have never known one of those meetings to start on time, but I wanted to arrive early so that I could say hello to people I hadn't seen since the pandemic started almost a year and a half ago. In the corner store that Doña Carmen's family runs, which they had recently opened with money that one of her sons had been sending from Chile, there was a group of young men listening to music—very loud *vallenato*—and drinking beer. They were sitting outside the store by a speaker, using a low wall as a table on which they were carefully arranging a tower made of cans of beer. At first I didn't recognize any of them, but as I was walking to the community kiosk, which was just across the dirt road from the store that the community had built a couple of years earlier with resources from their collective reparations, one of them shouted, making his voice heard above the words of *vallenato* singer Diomedes Díaz: "You don't say hello anymore? I didn't know you were here! Come and toast with us; we are celebrating the birth of my baby girl!"

I approached the group of men to say hello and to congratulate Omar, the man who was celebrating his newborn baby girl and whom I've known for years as one of the community leaders in the implementation of the collective reparations. Four days before that, after a high-risk pregnancy, Omar's wife had gone into labor. As there is no health center in the community, they had to go to the hospital in Buenos Aires, half an hour away, up the mountain from San Miguel by rural bus, only for her to be told on arrival that due to the level of risk, she would have to go to the hospital in Santander de Quilichao. Omar asked one of his neighbors who owns a car to drive them there, an hour and a half away from Buenos Aires, down the mountain. Due to COVID-19 protocols, she had to go inside the hospital on her own. For hours, he waited outside for news until she called him to tell him they were sending her to a hospital in Cali, another hour's drive away from Santander, farther into the valley. Omar hired a driver, an expense that most people cannot afford. The following day, his wife gave birth to a healthy baby girl, whom they named Origin in the hope of new beginnings, something for which Omar had been fighting for years and something that, for the community, came with the promise of individual and collective reparations delivered through the domestic reparations program created by the Victims' and Land Restitution Law (hereafter Victims' Law) of 2011.

The Bureaucracies of Victimhood in the Making   57

Globally, Colombia's domestic reparations program is the first of its kind to recognize children born of conflict-related sexual violence as direct victims of the armed conflict based on the circumstances of their conception. Although this means that they are entitled to integral measures of reparations, ten years after the program's implementation, not much has happened regarding access to their right to redress. This chapter addresses the production of the sociolegal category of children born of conflict-related sexual violence within the bureaucracies of reparations, with its numerous measurements, standards, protocols, and instruments. There was no previous experience or expert knowledge that the Victims' Unit, which was also created by the Victims' Law, could draw on regarding how to deliver reparations to children born of conflict-related sexual violence. Throughout the first decade since the program's inauguration, various attempts have been made to render the category legible within this system. In the negotiations that this process has entailed, the category of children born of conflict-related sexual violence and the bureaucratic maze through which it moves have been nested within the system designed to redress the effects of conflict-related sexual violence on women. Instead of assuming clear boundaries and meaning, the category became lost, mired within indicators of conflict-related sexual violence and the static logics of the architecture of transitional justice that remain rooted in the past. Within these negotiations, questions about how to render the category legible are yet to penetrate deeper debates about what reparations—and in broader terms, justice—mean in these cases. This chapter fits together pieces of a journey in which women seek to navigate the bureaucracies of reparations with and through their sons' and daughters' visibilities and invisibilities, always in the hope that reparations, in whatever form they take and whenever they come, mean a better future for their children.

On that day in August, when the Victims' Unit meeting ended after a two-hour workshop led by a social worker, the music playing was no longer *vallenato* but a more cheerful (and equally loud) reggaeton. During those two hours, people were invited to think about their pasts—about the things they could not change and everything that they felt proud of. A couple of times, the social worker mentioned that the workshop was part of the collective reparations measures and that it was connected with guarantees of non-repetition. "What was that thing the social worker said about guarantees of non-repetition?" I asked one of the women I was chatting with after the workshop outside the kiosk. "I don't really know," she admitted. "I've missed a couple of these workshops, so maybe they explained it there. But we had a fun morning, didn't we?"

In 2012, when the community of San Miguel embarked on the process of obtaining collective reparations for the paramilitary confinement that they had endured and people began giving testimonies about their individual experiences to be included in the Unified Registry of Victims, they also started to familiarize themselves with the language and bureaucracies of reparations. The expectations people had regarding not only the direct remedy for the harms caused to them by armed groups but also the potential transformation of other issues like unequal distribution of land, neoliberal policies threatening their traditional agricultural economy, and the precarious public health system were quickly matched by the nonofficial requirement for them to master the complex legal and institutional system through which reparations were accessed and distributed.

Many of them had already taken part in transitional justice activities before 2012. For example, after the demobilization of the paramilitary bloc that confined San Miguel, some women participated in a hearing on sexual violence that took place in the context of the Justice and Peace Law. However, with the passage of the 2011 Victims' Law, the promise of integral reparations appeared as a political achievement through which the state recognized the existence of the armed conflict (and what people had endured as a result of it) and sought to redress it through integral reparations: measures of rehabilitation, restitution, satisfaction, compensation, and guarantees of non-repetition. For the victims, however, integral reparations were significant not only in relation to the past and their experiences of victimhood but also in terms of hope for the future; the promise of integral reparations meant hope for a different future unblemished by the tangled web of colonial, patriarchal, and economic violence.[1]

While we were standing outside the kiosk and three sweet elderly women were updating me on the latest gossip, Clemencia joined the group and asked if I had a moment. During the many years that I have been conducting research in San Miguel, I have found different ways of being present in the community while seeking to trace the different shapes that information about people born of conflict-related sexual violence assumes. I have been part of the process of collective reparations, I have volunteered in the school, I have worked with victims of conflict-related sexual violence, and I have engaged in processes of research training and storytelling with girls. I have always been transparent about my research, and yet it is not surprising that after all these years, only a small group of people, of which Clemencia is one, remember the reason for my arrival all those years ago: women whose children were born out of paramilitary sexual violence. Those are the women whose pasts, presents, and futures are entangled in the fears and hopes they have for their children—the ones who are constantly looking for new beginnings for themselves and for their sons and daughters, trying to find a sliver of an opportunity to live a life not defined by the impositions of armed groups and by the relentless expansion of sugar cane monocrops, nontraditional mining, and other economies of war.

After laughing about some very confusing moments that occurred during the workshop, which included some dancing led by Omar, Clemencia started talking about her son. He had recently turned eighteen years old, a keenly anticipated age in Colombia, as people become legally old enough to vote, buy alcohol, and in his case, receive the financial compensation that he is entitled to as part of his right to reparations. Eighteen is also an age that is dreaded by men, particularly men from rural and urban impoverished communities whose families cannot afford to buy them out of the twelve to eighteen months of mandatory military service that they have to undertake, which often involves being sent to active combat areas. Clemencia, like most parents, has always worried about her son's well-being and future. As he was growing up, she could not sleep for thinking about the possibility of her son being taken away by any of the legal and illegal armed groups operating in the area, but now that he had turned eighteen, she worried about military service. Although she knew that he was exempted from it because he was a victim himself, it didn't stop her from worrying. "Men his age have very few options around here. And things are getting worse and worse with all of the old and new armed groups recruiting young people and forcing coca crops on us," Clemencia said. "I don't want him to do military service. Nothing to do with arms," she emphasized. "He rides his motorcycle everywhere to hang out with friends and girlfriends. I'm worried that one of these evenings, *they* will take him. Or maybe *those* who are already here."

Her son dropped out of school several years ago, but she convinced him to take accelerated courses in Santander de Quilichao so that he could finish his high school education. She told me that she keeps telling him that the Victims' Unit has an obligation to guarantee that he can study anything he wants, but he doesn't want to study. She insisted that he is entitled to receive financial compensation and that, together with education, what she would really like is for him to get psychosocial support. I asked her then what had happened with his reparations. "Who knows? I was just talking about that with Gloria—let me call her!" Clemencia declared enthusiastically as she went to look for her cousin, whose son is also eighteen, was born of paramilitary sexual violence, and like Clemencia's son, hasn't yet received any reparations. However, despite being exempt from military service and against his mom's will, Gloria's son had left to join the army a couple of months ago.

THE REPARATIONS PUZZLE

The 2011 Victims' Law, as the legal framework for the domestic reparations program, created the Victims' Unit and gave this agency the huge task of creating and implementing the program. Although there were some preexisting resources that the Victims' Unit could draw on, such as a census of forcibly displaced people, the overwhelming majority of this massive victimhood system had to be created from scratch. This entailed aspects like creating a registry of the victims, designing the tools to take the testimonies, defining how such tools would feed the registry, establishing the bureaucracies that victims of different types of violations had to navigate to access their reparations, and planning the content of the various different measures of reparation for each type of victim. In undertaking this task, the Victims' Unit built on previous experience and pools of knowledge at both the domestic and international levels, and throughout the decade during which the program has been in operation, it has benefited from various types of interdisciplinary and grassroots expertise. However, this was not the case for the specific category of children born of conflict-related sexual violence, because before they could ask any questions about how the measures of reparations should be implemented, the Victims' Unit had to fill the category with meaning and learn how to make it legible within the bureaucratic system of reparations. This section describes the complex reparation system as it appears in the legislation and some of the cracks through which the category of children born of conflict-related sexual violence has appeared.

In Article 25, "Right to Integral Reparation," the Victims' Law states, "Victims have the right to be repaired in an adequate, differentiated, transformative and effective manner for the harms that they have suffered. . . . Reparation includes measures of restitution, compensation, rehabilitation, satisfaction and guarantees of non-repetition, in its individual, collective, material, moral and symbolic dimensions. Each of these measures will be implemented in favor of the victim depending on the violation of their rights and the characteristics of the victimizing event."

Victimizing event is the term used to refer to those violations such as forced displacement, torture, and kidnappings that the law recognizes in order to grant someone victim status, which is a requirement for the person to access their reparations. Different victimizing events entitle victims to different measures of reparation. For instance, only some events grant victims the right to compensation, and the amount varies depending on the event. Although the law is clear that reparations are integral and not limited to compensation, financial compensation tends to be central to victims' needs and interests, and most of the information available in public documents produced by the Victims' Unit focuses on the route through which administrative compensation can be accessed. Each measure of reparation has its own route. However, in this section, I focus specifically on the aforementioned type of compensation, because that is the measure where I have found the most developments in relation to children born of conflict-related sexual violence.

According to the compensation route, victims are entitled to financial compensation if they have experienced any of the following victimizing events: forced displacement, homicide, forced disappearance, kidnapping, torture, harms that caused permanent or temporary disabilities, forced recruitment, and sexual violence, including cases of children born of conflict-related sexual violence.[2] Each of these categories has been assigned a specific amount of compensation. For instance, in cases of homicide, kidnapping, and forced disappearance, direct victims (or their relatives when the person in question cannot receive the compensation) are entitled to a lump sum of forty times the current monthly legal minimum wage, whereas victims of forced recruitment are entitled to a sum amounting to thirty times the monthly legal minimum wage. In cases of forced displacement, compensation of a lump sum totaling either seventeen or twenty-seven times the current monthly legal minimum wage will be equally distributed among the members of the family unit that was displaced.

If people experience more than one victimizing event, they are entitled to a lump sum of up to forty times the current monthly legal minimum wage. Victims of conflict-related sexual violence and their children born of this abuse are entitled to the equivalent of thirty times the current monthly legal minimum wage. In 2022, the minimum wage was COP 1,000,000—approximately USD 260—meaning that in the aforementioned case, they are each entitled to an amount totaling around USD 8,000 for crimes related to sexual violence. With regard to the children born of conflict-related sexual violence, as for anyone else under eighteen years old who is recognized as a victim, the Victims' Law states in Article 185, "Establishment of Trust Funds for Boys, Girls and Teenagers," that "the sum of money will be given to them once they reach the age of majority."

For victims to be able to access their compensation, the Victims' Unit has established a prioritization method, which has changed throughout the period since the law was implemented in 2011. This follows the acknowledgment that given the mass scale of the conflict, there is not enough budget to compensate all victims at the same time. In a 2017 Constitutional Court decision, the court stated that it is "reasonable that massive administrative reparation programs, typical of contexts of generalized and systematic violence, are not able to fully indemnify all the victims at the same time. In this type of situation, the Court found that it is legitimate to define reasonable terms for granting the administrative compensation and accept in that regard, certain criteria that allow them to prioritize the delivery of the corresponding measures."[3]

During the first few years after the implementation of the law, prioritization included victims of sexual violence. However, that situation changed in 2017, and currently, those who are prioritized in terms of access to compensation have to fulfill three main criteria: to be aged seventy-four years or older, to have a catastrophic or high-cost disease, or to have a disability certified by the Ministry of Health. Resolution 1049 (2019) also created a prioritization tool, which is "a technical tool that allows the Unit to analyze various characteristics of the victims through the evaluation of demographic and socioeconomic variables; characterization of the victimizing event; and progress along the reparation route."[4] Through this prioritization tool, which is applied in the first half of each year, victims are allocated a score that places them within an order of delivery. There are four phases involved in the procedure that allows victims to gain access to the compensation measure: application, analysis, reply, and delivery of the compensation to the victim (Art. 6, Res. 1049). In order to apply, Article 7 (Res. 1049) specifies that victims have to do the following:

a) Request the scheduling of an appointment through any of the channels of attention and citizen services provided by the Victims' Unit. Upon scheduling the appointment, the Victims' Unit will inform and guide the victim about the procedure provided in this administrative act, as well as the relevant and pertinent documents that must be submitted in each case.

b) Attend the appointment on the date and time indicated, and additionally:

1. Submit the request for indemnification with the required documentation according to the victimizing event for which the administrative indemnification is requested.

2. In the case of not submitting the requested documentation, the victim must then complete it, for which the Victims' Unit will grant a new appointment.

3. Once all the required documentation has been submitted, the victim must fill out the administrative compensation application form, in collaboration with the Victims' Unit and exclusively with the human resources available for such purpose.[5]

Although victims are expected to do everything in person at the Victims' Unit's offices, in cases where this is not possible, Resolution 1049 states that the Unit will make other means available, such as mobile units on specific dates that will be made public in advance. During the COVID-19 pandemic, other communication channels such as a twenty-four-hour phone line and online chat were strengthened. The last stage of the application phase consists of the Unit sorting the applications into two categories, general or priority, according to the three criteria regarding age, disease, and disabilities mentioned previously. As for the analysis and reply stages, Articles 10 and 11 (Res. 1049) specify that after verifying the veracity of the submitted documents and checking the status of the victim in the Unified Registry of Victims, the Unit will decide whether the application can be accepted. In affirmative cases, the Unit will decide whether the victim will be allowed to pursue the general or priority route. In each case, the Unit has 120 working days from the end of the application stage to come to a decision regarding the application, after which the victim must be notified of the outcome.

With regard to the last stage—delivery of the compensation—payment times will depend on the order allocated via the priority tool and the Unit's budgetary capacity for the current fiscal year. According to Article 14 (Res. 1049), the Unit will inform the victim of the relevant payment times. In those cases where the victim was underage when they were included in the Unified Registry of Victims and a fiduciary assignment was created, Article 18 (Res. 1049) states that the Unit will deliver the compensation within a year after the person's eighteenth birthday. For this to happen, the victim must update their records in the Unified Registry of Victims by submitting an enlarged copy of their national ID. In relation to the times and order allocated through the prioritization tool, the section about compensation on the Unit's website states the following:

> The turns for the disbursement of administrative compensation will be granted to those victims who, according to the application of the method, obtain a higher score per person, always taking into account the budgetary resources available to the Unit for the delivery of such reparation measures, during the corresponding fiscal year. Victims who are not prioritized through the application of the method, for the respective fiscal year, must wait for the next application of this tool in the following year, and so on until they obtain the necessary score that will allow them to access a turn for the payment of administrative compensation. This may take several years.[6]

On May 22, 2019, during a public hearing in the Colombian Congress about the state of the implementation of the Victims' Law, Yolanda Perea, a representative of the National Committee for Victims' Participation, raised deep concerns about the lack of institutional attention that children born of conflict-related sexual violence had received throughout the almost ten years since the law was introduced. Later that year, on September 9, 2019, the Colombian Congress Monitoring Commission for the Victims' Law convened a meeting to address this situation. During that meeting, which was attended by victims of sexual violence and various institutions such as the Victims' Unit, the Colombian Family Welfare Institute, the ombudsman's office, the Ministry of Health, the Ministry of Education, the attorney general's office, and the Institute of Legal Medicine and the Special Jurisdiction for Peace (JEP), women highlighted the need for children born of conflict-related sexual violence to be able to access integral reparations promptly, including psychosocial support, mental and physical health services, and education. In this regard, Yolanda Perea declared, "The Victims' Unit cannot be the sole body responsible . . . for guaranteeing all rights; it is a matter not only of compensation but of integral reparation."[7] In that same meeting, while recognizing that there was a lot of work still to be done regarding reparations for children born of conflict-related sexual violence, Ramón Rodríguez, then director of the Unit, described some of what he claimed had been the Unit's achievements to date: "The Victims' Unit has included 943 sons and daughters born as a result of the crime of sexual violence [in the Unified Registry of Victims]. For these people the Unit has activated the entire assistance and reparation route. In that way, it has provided humanitarian aid for the value of up to two minimum wages and has provided reparation measures in relation to psychosocial care through a specialized program for these victims, so that they can rebuild their social fabric and overcome this victimizing event."[8]

Pressure from victims drew some attention to the lack of progress that had been made regarding reparations for people born of conflict-related sexual violence. Questions about this situation rang alarm bells within the National System of Attention and Integral Reparation for Victims, particularly at the Unit's national level, whose director was asked to report on this matter to Congress. In this way, for the first time since the Victims' Law was introduced in 2011, the 2021 Congress monitoring report on the implementation of the law included information about reparations for children born of conflict-related sexual violence. On page 381 of the report's 480 pages, the first mention of this population highlights the deep concern expressed by the National Committee for Victims' Participation about the lack of attention they have received so far. The committee also issues a warning about the future, as there were no clear strategies for making progress on these matters in the government's plan of action for the next year.

In this report, the Victims' Unit revealed that 759 women had registered 783 sons and daughters born of conflict-related sexual violence in the Unified Registry of Victims. Between 2012 and 2021, only 63 of the children had received economic compensation.[9] The information compiled in this report differs from the information presented by the Unit's director in September 2019 not only in terms of the actual figure, which I discuss in the next section, but in terms of the assistance and reparations route that the subdirector claimed the Unit had created for children born of conflict-related sexual violence, of which there is no mention at all in the report.

An initial interpretation of the implementation of the Victims' Law with regard to children born of conflict-related sexual violence clearly highlights a massive gap. The highly regulated reparation routes for victims to access their right to integral reparations contrast with the uncertainty surrounding reparations for this group of victims. However, this is not surprising, particularly if we compare it to the way in which the law has been implemented more generally, which is highly ambitious and aligned with international law but, ten years later, has achieved very limited progress in terms of victims' access to reparations.[10] For victims of conflict-related sexual violence in particular, access to reparations has not been very timely, adequate, or dignified. For example, between 2015 and 2022, out of the more than 30,000 victims of conflict-related sexual violence, only 2,907 women had received psychosocial care. Between 2011 and 2021, only 8,267 had received financial compensation. Far from being transformative, the process for accessing any of the measures of reparations, including rehabilitation, has often been described by victims as revictimizing and constituting a new source of violence in itself.[11] The gap in the implementation of the law regarding people born of conflict-related sexual violence is not surprising because there is always a gap between the law as it is set out on paper and the law as it is implemented in practice; the existence of legal frameworks does not mean that people have access, or equal access, to them.[12]

A closer examination of the way in which the law has been implemented regarding children born of conflict-related sexual violence, however, shows us that for the last ten years, we have witnessed the creation of a new sociolegal category. As elaborated in chapter 1, unlike most of the other experiences of victimhood recognized under the law—for example, forced displacement—the category of children born of conflict-related sexual violence represented a different kind of challenge. It was a blurred area that not only had to be filled with meaning but also was required to be legible within the bureaucracies of reparations that were being created. For the category of children born of conflict-related sexual violence, these challenges have been characterized by constant but changing tensions. Such tensions encompass the blurriness of the category, women's experiences of conflict-related sexual and reproductive violence, and the embodied existence of people born of conflict-related sexual violence, not only as rights bearers but as people who are growing up faster than the slow pace of the domestic reparations program.

Neither Clemencia's nor Gloria's sons are among the sixty-three people mentioned in the monitoring report. Despite their mothers' quest for their sons' rights, a quest that began after the women themselves testified in 2012 to be included as victims of sexual violence in the Unified Registry of Victims, they haven't received any humanitarian aid or any other measure of reparation. Like most of the women I have met throughout my years of research—at least those who know that their children have the right to reparation—both Clemencia and Gloria have invested considerable resources in navigating the mazelike structure of the domestic reparations program. They have learned the vocabulary, and by attending workshop after workshop and meeting after meeting, they have taken notes about pieces of information that could help their sons and daughters get the reparations to which they are entitled. With each new interaction with people wearing the Victims' Unit vest, they have sought to add one more piece to the changing normative framework—for example, with regard to prioritization—and the complex bureaucracies of the reparations puzzle.

Throughout the years, and as their sons grew up, they have received fragments of information that mostly led to a black hole of often contradictory information or referred to other information they needed, places they had to go to, or documents they had to provide and future times that they had to await: "You have to call the Unit," "You have to go in person to the offices," "You have to wait until your son is eighteen years old," "Make sure to bring all the documents." There is a limit to how much people can do with this ambiguous information, especially when direct communication with the Unit is a challenge.[13] For example, women have reported calling the Unit and being put on hold until they get bored of waiting or the call ending abruptly before they got to talk to anyone. They have been repeatedly told to bring "*all* the documents" without any clear instructions about which documents those are. Piecing together all the steps that have to be followed and the relevant documents that have to be provided and knowing where to go is a significant part of the process of accessing reparations. Victims need to become familiar with the requisite practices, language, and techniques, which requires a great deal of resource investment and some level of professionalization in regard to the bureaucratic process on the part of the victims.

Along the way, victims learn to find translators who can decipher the illegible structures of the state.[14] This can prove to be an even greater challenge in the case of the reparations route for children born of conflict-related sexual violence because this structure is still being developed. Sometimes translators are people wearing the Unit's uniform vests either because it is their job to offer guidance to help people navigate the system or because their commitment makes them go above and beyond their normal duties (within the boundaries of the law).[15] In other instances, those translators are *tramitadores*: people who make a living by charging people money to run state errands for them. Sometimes *tramitadores* charge victims a few pesos for telling them which documents they need and a couple more for queuing on their behalf if victims want them to save their place so they can file the required documents. However, in some cases, those *tramitadores* are con artists who are after a percentage of the victims' compensation.[16] An acquaintance who works for the Unit at the national level once told me, "You learn to be careful when you share information with victims, whether it is about the reparations route they have to follow or how to find out about their individual cases, because you must make it very clear, both in words and in practice, that *that information* is a right that they *all* have. Not just those who are in front of you; otherwise, we will become *tramitadores!*"[17]

On August 24, 2021, the day after Origin was born and after the meeting with the Victims' Unit, Clemencia, Gloria, and I were standing outside the kiosk talking about their sons' futures and their high expectations of what the reparations could do for them. The beautiful voice of the queen of Tejano music, Selena, could be heard issuing from the speakers at the store where Omar continued to celebrate his new beginnings—"Si una vez dije que te amaba, y que por tí la vida daba"—when the two people from the Victims' Unit who led the workshop approached us to say goodbye. As they drew closer, Clemencia asked

The Bureaucracies of Victimhood in the Making   67

them—not for the first time in the many years they have known each other, I'm sure—what was happening with their sons' reparation processes.

"Are they registered?" one of them asked.

"We assume so!" replied both women.

Offering an example of how, for victims, so much of the process to access reparations involves receiving new pieces of information, learning new vocabulary, or finding out about new steps they still have to take, one of the two people replied, "Well, first thing you have to do is call the Unit to make sure they are actually in the Unified Registry of Victims."

"And if they are not?" I asked.

"In that case, all you have to do is call the Unit to make a *novedad* to update the information. Before you had to testify again, but not anymore!"

A RECORD OF THE UNINTELLIGIBLE

To gain access to reparations, people need to be included in the Unified Registry of Victims. For that to happen, each person's experience of the armed conflict needs to be translated into the terms of the Victims' Law and be legible within the bureaucracies of reparations. To this end, the Victims' Unit has created a series of measurements, protocols, and instruments that standardize the process for accessing reparations while responding to the particularities of each of the victimizing events. In general terms, the creation of measurements and standards builds on previous models, which are already in place and serve as a means of understanding and governing the world. It requires what Sally Engle Merry calls "expertise inertia"—skills, legitimacy, and experience in dealing with elements of the task at hand in order to adapt, refine, and expand the operating system.[18]

As mentioned earlier, the delivery of reparations to children born of conflict-related sexual violence presented different challenges, as there was no specific previous knowledge to draw on in this regard. The pool of available knowledge, including the women themselves, which was found in the networks of conflict-affected children's rights and those working with victims of conflict-related sexual violence, called for caution to be exercised in regard to approaching the children. This was due to the great uncertainty about the possible harms they could suffer through their inclusion in the bureaucracies of victimhood and because women who were already dealing with the consequences of conflict-related sexual violence could not be forced into naming their children as victims, disclosing information about their conception, or breaking silences they believed could protect their sons and daughters.[19] The Victims' Unit's response to these political and ethical negotiations was to nest the category of children born of conflict-related sexual violence within the bureaucracies of reparations for conflict-related sexual violence. While this responds to the lessons learned

68   BORN OF WAR IN COLOMBIA

over the years of seeking to address the consequences of conflict-related sexual violence, the category of children born of the abuses has not gained a clearly defined place within the victimhood system, and therefore, the people within the category have yet to see what redress actually means and what it could do for their lives. This section addresses the inclusion of children born of conflict-related sexual violence within the Unified Registry of Victims and the ways in which the category became lost within the victimhood system.

The information that is publicly available about the Unified Registry of Victims, published on the Victims' Unit's website, shows an updated and constantly changing total number of officially recognized victims of the armed conflict in Colombia. As of August 31, 2022, that figure was 9,342,426, and it is divided into two categories: subjects of attention, showing a total of 7,422,484 people, and subjects of no attention, showing a figure of 1,919,942 people. The former refers to "Victims who meet the requirements to access the measures of attention and reparation established in the Law" and the latter to "Deceased victims, direct victims of forced disappearance, homicide and not active for attention. Victims who because of different circumstances cannot effectively access attention and reparation measures."[20]

The registry is in constant motion, because the Victims' Unit never stops receiving and assessing the testimonies through which people request inclusion in the registry, and when they meet the eligibility criteria, the Unit has to confer recognition of their status as victims, which entitles them to redress. In Article 155, the Victims' Law establishes that people who have experienced any of the victimizing events listed in the law between January 1, 1985, and before the law came into effect on June 10, 2011, had four years in which to testify, starting from the moment they experienced the event. If the events took place after the day that the law came into effect, people were given two years in which to testify. Within these time frames, the law also takes into consideration circumstances beyond people's control that could have interfered with their request to be included in the registry. People who experienced victimizing events before January 1, 1985, can request to be included in the registry, but they will not be granted access to integral reparations. In those cases, they appear as subjects of no attention. For those victims, explained someone from the Directorate of Reparations at the Unit's national level, "their reparation is the recognition, because the law is not retroactive. They are recognized as victims but won't have access to any of the measures. Their measure is the recognition."[21]

In cases of sexual violence, these timelines do not apply. This means that people who have experienced forms of conflict-related sexual violence can testify and request their inclusion in the registry at any time, and so can their children born of the abuse. The registry is also in a constant state of flux because as people die, they are recategorized as subjects of no attention. In an interview with Gabriel, one of the heads of the Assessment and Registry Subdirectorate, he noted, "The registry is always increasing; the registry never stops. It adds people every day, every single day. The registry can't stop, shouldn't stop. Unless there is peace, unless there is no more armed conflict. But on the contrary, as things are, the registry keeps expanding. But the registry is also aging because people are dying."[22]

The registry also frequently changes because it is the site of constant negotiations. Those negotiations involve pressure from victims' organizations and other civil society organizations but are also shaped by internal advocacy from different teams within the Unit—for example, the Gender and Differential Approach team (before it was dismantled in 2021), the Psychosocial team or the Assessment and Registry team itself. For instance, Gabriel told me that after several years of reading statements by victims of sexual violence, the Assessment and Registry team identified that women often described how armed groups forced their children to witness the abuse they endured. This experience of victimhood, however, was not included in the registry. The registry team presented the case inside the Unit and succeeded in getting those children included in the Unified Registry of Victims.

Negotiations about the registry can be seen in its demographic descriptions. Nowadays, the Unified Registry of Victims offers some level of demographic description of the total number of people recognized as victims. Under the label "Gender," for instance, the information is presented as 4,644,189 men, 4,692,987 women, 4,559 LGBTI, 305 did not report, and 386 intersex.

"What happens about the overlap between the *I* in *LGBTI* and the 386 people included under intersex?" I asked Gabriel, who had been patiently explaining how the registry worked.

While looking more closely at his computer screen, on which the website showing the publicly available Unified Registry of Victims was open, he exclaimed, "Oh, yes! We must remove that *I* and just leave *LGBT*. All this is a work in progress."

"And if we want to see, let's say, lesbian women, where would we find them? Under women or within LGBTI?" I asked.

"They would be under LGBTI, because we haven't disaggregated the information," Gabriel replied.

"That [the registry] has tons of serious flaws!" added Alejandra, a member of the Psychosocial team at the national level who had joined the conversation. She then told me about an occasion when her team had asked Gabriel's team for the "LGBT database," which she made clear was still referred to in this way despite all their advocacy efforts to get the acronym changed so that it reflects more inclusive and less rigid approaches. Alejandra's team needed to call people listed in the database to let them know about a psychosocial care strategy oriented toward people with diverse gender identities and expressions and sexual orientations. That strategy was part of the Unit's measures of rehabilitation offer, and so people needed to be made aware that they could join it. As it happened, once they started calling, they realized that some people who were in that database were cisgender heterosexual. "How embarrassing! There were not thousands, but even if there were ten cases, that's terrible. We were scared to call!" Alejandra said.[23]

A different kind of transformation that has taken place within the registry is connected with the categories under which people are recognized as victims: the victimizing events. Originally, there were eleven victimizing events: terrorist acts, threats, harms against people's freedom and sexual integrity (sexual violence), forced disappearance, forced displacement, homicide, antipersonnel mines, kidnapping, torture, child recruitment, and land dispossession. Over the years, other categories have been added to the list of victimizing events: property loss, physical personal injury, psychological personal injury, and the most recent addition, confinement.[24] The Unified Registry of Victims shows the number of victims recognized under each of the victimizing events, with the largest number of victims being allocated to the category of forced displacement, with a total of 8,317,718 up to August 31, 2022.[25] As the list of victimizing events gets updated, so does the Unified Registry of Victims and the information that is publicly available on the website. Confinement, for instance, has already been included in the list, and up to August 2022, a figure of 101,216 victims were listed under this category.

"Look!" Gabriel exclaimed, turning to Alejandra. He was navigating the public Unified Registry of Victims from his computer so he could tell me about the different parts of the registry when he reached the victimizing events. "They have already added confinement."

"But we haven't managed the addition of the sons and daughters [born of conflict-related sexual violence]," replied Alejandra in a tone of cheerful resignation.

The first time I heard a reference to a figure claiming to represent the number of people included within the category of children born of conflict-related sexual violence in the Unified Registry of Victims was in 2016 in a conversation with Diana Tamayo, then team leader for the Victims' Unit's Gender and Differential Approach team, and María Eugenia Morales, former technical director of reparations at the national level. Diana mentioned that up to 2015, the Directorate of Reparations hadn't received any cases of children born of sexual violence, so they started an active discussion inside the Unit to try to understand why this was. They created a working group, which included the Gender and Differential Approach team, the Directorate of Reparations, and the Area of Registry. From those meetings, it emerged that the Area of Registry had been creating a database of children born of conflict-related sexual violence, but they were unsure what to do with it. Up to that date, the database included 533 people.[26]

A couple of years later, in November 2019, during a public event in Bogotá, then director of the Victims' Unit, Ramón Rodríguez, announced an updated number: 965.[27] A year after that, following the public hearing in Congress and the meetings mentioned previously in which the National Committee for Victims' Participation raised concerns about the lack of attention paid to children born of sexual violence, I found the first figure in an official document. In the eighth report produced by the Monitoring Commission of the Implementation of the Victims' Law, the Victims' Unit cited 783 people as being included in the Unified Registry of Victims as children born of conflict-related sexual violence.[28]

"Where are the sons and daughters born of conflict-related sexual violence in the registry?" I asked Gabriel.

"They are all *here*," he said while moving the pointer over the figure of 35,853, which corresponded to victims of "crimes against freedom and sexual integrity in the context of the armed conflict."

"They are all there, but the register won't let you see them," added Alejandra. Gabriel and Alejandra explained that the 35,853 were not all direct victims of conflict-related sexual violence but victims acknowledged within that category. As children born of conflict-related sexual violence were included in the registry in conjunction with their mothers' victimizing event, that's where they were.

"But that's not something that the figure [of victims of sexual violence] shows you, and neither does the registry. You can only see that in the database," Gabriel noted enthusiastically, shrugging to indicate the quandary that this represented. The database, as they explained, is in fact the "root" of the registry, to which very few people, even within the Unit, have access. It is the database of the entire population of victims of the armed conflict in Colombia, including the census that was in place before the Victims' Law.[29]

This "root" database is fueled by every single testimony that, after assessment, has been accepted and translated into standardized Excel language. The registry is a further translation of this database. As our conversation continued, Alejandra exclaimed with admiration, "And it's a database that Gabriel and his team do manually in Excel!"

"In that database," Gabriel explained, "you find all sorts of things. And, well, it's not surprising—it's a registry of over nine million people! I'm sure there are more sons and daughters [born of conflict-related sexual violence] that we haven't identified. The only way to find them, to identify that population, is through the testimonies or through the Excel database, because that's something that right now you cannot do with the registry."

To this, Alejandra complemented with a tone of frustration in her voice, "We have asked for it [the inclusion of the category of children born of conflict-related sexual violence in the registry], but that's very expensive, and they have paid no attention to us."

The database, however, is also subject to revision. For example, Alejandra told me that on one occasion, her team needed to contact victims as part of the policy of integral psychosocial care for women who are victims of conflict-related sexual violence. They asked Gabriel's team for the database of participants, which they had to filter through the database of the entire victim population. When they received the database, they noticed that there were nine men on it, despite the policy being exclusively directed at women. They checked all the information recorded in the database for each case and realized that four of those people were actually transgender women. In those cases, Alejandra explained, they amended the records manually so that they no longer appeared as men. "Checking and cleaning nine entries is nothing, but imagine doing that for nine million people!" she said.

The bureaucracies through which people seek inclusion in the registry start not with the registry itself but when they apply to be recognized as victims.[30] For people to be included in the database, they had to request to be recognized as victims of the armed conflict and provide testimony. For that purpose, the Victims' Law ordered the Unit to create a form to standardize the process through which testimonies were taken. It also decreed that the attorney general's office, the ombudsman's office, the municipal *personerías*, and when abroad, the consulates must oversee the taking of testimonies after receiving appropriate training from the Victims' Unit. Each of the individual testimonies is recorded on the standardized form, and that form is then sent to the Unit's national offices. Once there, a team is tasked with assessing the request and issuing the official communication letter, in which the person is notified as to whether the request has been accepted. For that purpose, Gabriel explained, "[they] do not consider the armed actor at the time of assessment. It is the violation of international humanitarian law, or the violation of human rights, and whether it [the event] has a 'close and sufficient relationship with the armed conflict.'"

Unlike the registry and the database, the Unified Form for Testimonies (FUD) has hardly changed since it was created following the implementation of the law. The FUD is composed of four pages and twelve annexes, one for each of the victimizing events plus an extra one for extended narratives. On those pages, the public service employee who takes the testimony must enter "the basic data that will allow the necessary information to be obtained for a correct assessment, using a differential approach, and will assist in the determination of measures of assistance, care and reparation that are appropriate to the harm suffered and the needs of victims."[31] The first page, entitled "Basic Information," requires information that ranges from the "place where the testimony was taken" to the demographics of the person giving the testimony. At the end of the page, there is a table containing three columns. The first one is labeled

"Annex" and is already populated with numbers from one to eleven. The second column is labeled "Event" and lists each of the eleven victimizing events that were originally recognized within the Victims' Law framework. Next to each of the events is a column labeled "Number of Events," where the person taking the testimony must enter information about the number of times each of the victimizing events occurred. The third victimizing event listed in the table is "Harms against People's Freedom and Sexual Integrity," which refers to conflict-related sexual violence.

The second page of the FUD, entitled "Characterization," asks for a list of people who were affected by the victimizing events referenced on the first page. Regardless of whether they are relatives, the form requires information about each person to be completed, such as their date of birth, relationship to the direct victim, gender identity, ethnic group, and any disabilities. The third page, entitled "Account of the Facts," is blank, as it is intentionally left open for a narrative about the victimizing events to be provided.

If the statement is longer than one page, it must continue in annex 12 of the FUD. The fourth page, "Procedure Verification," presents a list of questions relating to the procedure itself. This checklist also has space to provide the number of annexes included with the testimony, the relevant supporting documents attached to the request (for each of the victimizing events), an indication of whether anything has been amended on the other pages, and at the end, space for signatures and fingerprints. The latter applies to the person who is requesting to be recognized as a victim, the testimony taker, the legal representative in the case of underage applicants, and the interpreter in the case of people who provided their statement in any language other than Spanish. As mentioned previously, the full application form includes an annex for each of the victimizing events. For example, in the case of a woman whose son was killed and who was herself forcibly displaced and raped, the application would need to have at least three annexes. Each of these annexes must be completed at the same time as the statement-taking procedure, a process that not only is extremely emotionally taxing for the two people involved in the process in different ways but demands significant training and knowledge of the law and the bureaucratic process embedded in taking the statement and completing the different subsections of the FUD.

Annex 3, "Harms against People's Freedom and Sexual Integrity," contains fourteen questions. It starts by asking for basic information about the date and location of the event(s) and then asks about the type of impacts suffered, with a list of fifteen options from which to choose. It also inquires about the type of sexual crime experienced—in response to which, there are five different options—and whether the person received any medical attention or if they had previously reported these events. Question 2 in annex 3 asks, "Find out if there is any child born of the sexual abuse: If so, register the details of the child in the following space. Make sure that this information is also recorded in the characterization table (page 2)."

"Has this question been part of the FUD since the law was first implemented?" I asked Gabriel.

"From the very beginning," he replied. "But they [children born of conflict-related sexual violence] got lost in the database."

During the first few years after the Victims' Law was passed, every single child born of conflict-related sexual violence who was included in the registry database was recorded under the category "Harms against People's Freedom and Sexual Integrity." In the process of translation from the FUD to the database to the registry, they were all assumed to be direct victims of sexual violence. Thus, these children were lost and were only discovered when a group of people from within the Victims' Unit noticed their absence and started looking for them.

There are three key moments within the time frame of the implementation of the law that reflect some of the tensions between the existence of the legal category of children born of conflict-related sexual violence and their unintelligibility within the system. Specifically, these are moments when their absence has been noticed and attempts have been made to render their existence legible within the bureaucratic infrastructure of the law. The first moment occurred a couple of years after the law came into effect, around 2015, when people from the Directorate of Reparations, the Gender and Differential Approach team, and the Area of Registry became aware of the lack of information about children born of conflict-related sexual violence and began to speculate about it. Based on an extraordinary understanding of the Victims' Law, they noticed that despite the already large number of victims of sexual violence recorded within the registry, there had not been any requests submitted for reparations for children born of conflict-related sexual violence. When the registry team started scrutinizing the Excel database, they found that there were approximately one thousand entries for women who had experienced sexual violence that mentioned the existence of children born of the abuse in annex 3 of their FUD, but there was a limit to how much the database could tell them without referring back to the original statements.

Although the category of children born of conflict-related sexual violence was included in the law, it did not gain a defined place within the bureaucracies of reparation because of a lack of clarity regarding its content and boundaries. It was included in the FUD, but in such a way that no one knew what to do with it or what its inclusion actually meant. It was included in the hope that the question of how to deal with it would be answered by a group of *experts* that was still in the making. The realization that children born of conflict-related sexual violence had been lost in the database was also accompanied by one of the greatest fears that surrounds their presence within the reparations bureaucracies. Not only had they not received any of the integral measures of reparation to which they were entitled while growing up, but the moment they would reach the age of eligibility for their compensation was getting closer. This triggered several alarm bells. As there were no clear protocols regarding the recognition of their victimhood or how to interact with them, there was a risk that once they turned eighteen, they could receive a call from the Unit that could potentially cause serious harm. First, the Unit did not know whether the person was aware of the circumstances of their conception or how much knowledge they had about the reason behind their inclusion in the Unified Registry of Victims. Second, there was a chance that they could receive a call telling them that the compensation to which they were entitled, as *direct victims of conflict-related sexual violence* themselves, was ready.

Through a strategic alliance, the International Organization for Migration (IOM) paid a consultant to sit in the Victims' Unit's archive for six months. Their job was to read the one thousand statements from women whose FUDs mentioned children born of the abuse. This person had to verify that the three steps that, by then, the Unit had agreed upon regarding how to proceed with the inclusion of children born of conflict-related sexual violence in the Unified Registry of Victims, had been completed. In the process, the Unit consulted the two sets of expert knowledge that could advise them on how to imbue the category of children born of conflict-related sexual violence with meaning: organizations working with children's rights and organizations working with survivors of conflict-related sexual violence. As a result of those debates, it was established that the route for children born of conflict-related sexual violence to be included in the Unified Registry of Victims would be through their mothers. In their case, their mothers were required to have explicitly stated during their own testimonies that they wanted their sons or daughters born of conflict-related sexual violence to be included in the Unified Registry of Victims. In accordance with this decision, the IOM consultant had to retrospectively read all the relevant FUDs and check the following: first, that annex 3 clearly stated that the woman had a child born as a result of the abuse; second, that the child mentioned in annex 3 had also been included on page 2 of the FUD; and third, most importantly, that the mother had clearly stated in the descriptive narrative her desire to include her child in the Unified Registry of Victims. "That's how we found the nine hundred and something cases that we know of," explained Gabriel.

"How much easier if, instead of having to do all that in the FUD during the testimony taking, we already had the option to include the sons and daughters within the list of victimizing events [on page 1]," said Alejandra, her frustration showing in her voice. "Of course! That's why they were all lost and misplaced.

It doesn't make anyone's life easier by making it a requirement to complete all three things [in the FUD] for them to be included. But to change that [in the FUD] is *la muerte*. We'll see the end of the [Victims'] Law before we achieve any modification to the form. I've tried. It has to be done eventually."

"Doing it is very expensive, it's very challenging, but there is also a lack of will to do it," replied Gabriel.

"The form is very good because it standardized something that before [the Victims' Law] people did without any consistency. But it [the form] is obsolete now. We need, for example, the sons and daughters [born of conflict-related sexual violence] to be added so that they [the statement takers] don't have to go all the way down [to annex 3] to do it!" exclaimed Alejandra.

There were two other noteworthy moments at which negotiations have been held to render the legal category of children born of conflict-related sexual abuse legible within the bureaucratic infrastructure of the Victims' Law. Unlike the instances previously mentioned, these have involved active attempts to create standardized protocols for interacting with them throughout the process of recognizing their victimhood, including them in the Unified Registry of Victims, and offering forms of reparation. To this end, around 2017, the Unit formed an alliance with the JEP to hold focus groups with women who had given birth to children as a result of conflict-related sexual violence in different parts of the country. The idea behind it was to ask them about their sons' and daughters' situations and needs, to ascertain how much they knew about their origins, and to gain a better understanding of how to approach them without endangering the children, the women, or the relationship between them.

This effort connects with the present moment, in 2022, during which time some very committed people within the Unit, without much institutional support, are drafting some of those protocols based on insights from the focus groups while trying to learn from other women who have also given birth to children born of conflict-related sexual violence. For now, and while the protocols for how to interact with people born of wartime sexual violence are being created, Gabriel's team has marked them in the database. They still appear within the category of sexual violence, but the mark beside their names indicates that any interaction with them requires the assistance of the Directorate of Reparations Psychosocial team. To date, this still hasn't happened. The creation of the new protocols remains at the stage of finding a place to nest them within the entanglement of existing protocols and bureaucracies of reparations.

REDRESSING THE UNINTELLIGIBLE:
TURNING RIGHTS INTO LUCK

Gloria's son was not included in the registry. We found out a week after Origin was born and several years after Gloria's request to be included as a victim of sexual violence in the Unified Registry of Victims. She had mentioned her son during her original statement, and so for years, she assumed that he had also been included in the registry. With the assistance of Alejandra, Gloria filed a *novedad* so that the registry could be updated. In this case, filing a *novedad* was quite a straightforward process, as I managed to work out after hours of interviews, calls, and observations. Previously, if women wanted to include their children in the registry, they had to go through the entire process of testifying again. However, since 2017, if they want their children to be included in the registry, women must only file a *novedad*: update their own statement with a copy of their national ID, their child's birth certificate, and a copy of the child's national ID. The documents can be submitted in person or at one of the Unit's offices or mobile units. More recently, women have also been allowed to upload them through the Unit's website. However, it remains challenging to find out the information they need—information about whether the child has been included in the registry, what procedure they must follow to include them, and how to do so.

This is partly because women often assume that their children have been included, as they mentioned them in their own testimony, and when they have asked about their children's reparations, they have been repeatedly told that they would have to wait for their children to turn eighteen. That answer is most likely to have come from someone in the Victims' Unit who had no real information about reparations for children born of conflict-related sexual violence other than that for them to receive financial compensation, they have to wait until they reach the age of eighteen, as is the case with all children who are classified as victims. For these women, many of whom have been waiting for an answer from the state for most of their child's life, the *novedad* and obtaining inclusion in the registry mark only the beginning of an uncertain journey to get access to reparations. For so long, women's resources have focused on battling with the system to find out the initial information they require regarding their children's access to reparations that questions about what those reparations entail have been postponed. Although the women are often quite familiar with the intricacies of this bureaucratic journey, as they have been navigating it on their own account for many years, their children's odyssey is accompanied by a whole new level of uncertainty, as no one really knows what to expect as a result of it.

On August 26, 2022, a year after Gloria found out that her son had not been included in the registry, Alejandra and I traveled to Buenos Aires to meet with a group of ten women. Most of them came from San Miguel, while some lived in other communities in Buenos Aires and others lived in Cali, where they had stayed after being forcibly displaced by paramilitaries at some point between 2000 and 2004. Among the things they all had in common were the years they had spent knocking on doors, asking loudly or quietly (but always extremely cautiously to avoid drawing unwanted attention to their children) about their sons' and daughters' reparations. Their sons and daughters who were born of different forms of paramilitary sexual violence, who were now reaching the age of eighteen, and who were facing—like most people their age living in impoverished and heavily militarized contexts—a great deal of uncertainty with regard to both their present and their future. The other two things they all had in common was the belief that their children had already been included in the registry, as they had mentioned them in their testimonies many years earlier, and now that their sons and daughters were becoming adults according to the law, they were waiting for the Unit's call to inform them that their compensation was ready.

We agreed to meet at the headquarters of the Association of Afro-Colombian Women of the North of Cauca (ASOM), a collective composed of approximately two hundred women who for twenty-five years have withstood the entangled advances of armed groups and the extractive industries. One of the women who had helped me with the logistics of the meeting arranged for us to use a tin-roofed open space on the second floor at the back of ASOM's offices, a relatively quiet place the organization uses for workshops that could host this group of women away from prying eyes. It was so close to the creek that we saw two iguanas hanging from trees, and I came under attack by the *jejen*. Also known as black fly, the *jejen* is an aggressive type of mosquito, such that in seasons like this one, if you are by bodies of water, you can only effectively protect yourself from them with military-strength repellent or, as I learned that day after the women took pity on the state of my arms, neck, ears, and ankles, using shampoo as if it were body lotion.

"What do you expect from this meeting?" asked Alejandra to get the ball rolling with the group of women.

"I'm here for my son's future," said one woman.

"I came because I'm looking for solutions," added another.

Clemencia, who was sitting in front of me, explained the following while the other women endorsed her words by nodding and muttering in agreement: "I'm here because I don't want my son to go through everything I've been through. Ever since I testified in 2012, I have been to so many different spaces! We have been to endless workshops, we've queued for hours hoping for answers, we've called the Unit and been put on hold. I've signed hundreds of attendance sheets. And I don't want that for my son. I know that he has rights, and I want to understand what those are."

The Bureaucracies of Victimhood in the Making 79

Together with the bureaucracies of victimhood, the government has also created devices, practices, and mechanisms through which to show that progress is being made while concealing its lack of implementation in practice. Valentina Pellegrino has described this phenomenon as *incumplir cumpliendo* (complying incompliantly).[32] The production of documents containing strategically chosen categories, measures, and spent budgets, Pellegrino notes, creates an impression of action, of compliance, and of movement toward closing the gap between the law as it is expressed on paper and the effects that the law is supposed to have on people's lives. Clemencia's words reflect the everyday aspects of this phenomenon. Every workshop that victims have attended, every attendance sheet they have signed, and every call they have made through which they have received a piece of relevant information during the many years that they have been seeking access to reparations has been translated by the government into figures that supposedly prove their compliance with the law. The government has specialized in turning institutional violence into compliance reports. For so many years now, women who are victims of conflict-related sexual violence have been embedded in the bureaucracies of victimhood. During all that time, instead of integral reparations, they have received fragmented measures of reparations—for example, through sporadic psychosocial care workshops or individual appointments with inexperienced psychologists employed on short-term contracts. Those measures, very often, have been inadequate as well as untimely and undignified: the uncertainty surrounding what to expect and when to expect it "means that the reparation process itself is not reparative" but revictimizing.[33] Clemencia's words, in this sense, represent a call for the children of conflict-related sexual violence not to be dragged into the same victimhood paradigm that women like herself have endured, in the hope that it will translate into new beginnings for themselves and their families.

"How many children born of the crime of sexual violence do you think are included in the Unified Registry of Victims?" asked Alejandra before introducing the purpose of the meeting. The women looked at one another, but no one offered an answer. The figure of "around 970" was followed by a collective expression of surprise. The woman sitting in front of me covered her mouth with her hand while someone else shouted, "That many?" It seemed that, for a moment, the loneliness of their journeys was accompanied by the loneliness of many other women and their children. "And we are sure there are many more across the country," said Alejandra. She then continued,

As you know, children born of the crime of sexual violence were included in the Victims' Law, but back in 2011, no one told us how to include them in the registry. Ever since that moment, we have struggled to understand how to do it in a way that protects you [women] and the child and what reparations should look like in those cases, and that's why I am here. Because we know that there is a lot of uncertainty regarding your sons' and daughters' reparations, but also because we know we must guarantee their access to integral reparations. They are entitled to compensation, but also to the other measures of reparation, like psychosocial support. We haven't done it because we do not know how to do it. We need your help to understand how to do it. We need you to be the voice of women across the country.

Out of all the women who attended our meeting that day, there were three whose children had not been included in the registry. For one of them, initiating the process would be simple enough, as all she had to do was file a *novedad*, and Alejandra herself could bring the relevant documents to the Unit. However, the situation of the other two was different. Neither of them was recorded in the registry as victims of sexual violence, and therefore, it was impossible for their sons and daughters to be recognized as children born of conflict-related sexual violence. They were included as direct victims of forced displacement and, in one of the two cases, also as an indirect victim of homicide. In their cases, Alejandra explained, they would have to give their testimonies again and make sure that they included the crime of sexual violence. "The good part," Alejandra reassured them, "is that sexual violence is not prescribed, and you can still declare it."

On the day that the meeting was held, the Unit's prioritization compensation algorithm rang for Lucia, the daughter of one of the women who had attended the meeting, named Cecilia. While Alejandra was explaining how the prioritization process worked, Cecilia received a call from her daughter. I couldn't believe that I was witnessing that moment. "What a coincidence!" I told Cecilia. "How extraordinary that on precisely the day you meet with the Victims' Unit to have this conversation about your daughter's reparations, she gets the call."

"What I can't believe," said Cecilia, "is the bad luck that Lucia had her ID stolen a couple of days ago!" The excitement about the news that the compensation was ready was matched by the concern about how she would be able to withdraw the money. For Lucia to withdraw the money, the caller explained that she had to bring her national ID to the offices of a specific bank. No one else could go on her behalf, and only the original ID would be accepted; no copies were allowed. She had a week in which to do it; otherwise, the money would be sent back to the Unit's national offices. What, from our perspective, felt like a series of fortunate and unfortunate events occurring simultaneously was, from the Unit's perspective, a sophisticated system that had run the prioritization compensation algorithm, in combination with the standardized protocols and norms described in the first section of this chapter, that shaped the bureaucracies of reparations. A decade after the implementation of an ambitious domestic reparations program, the intricate bureaucratic system had turned rights into a matter of luck.

Cecilia, who was still waiting to receive her own compensation, gave the phone to Alejandra so that she could talk to Lucia. "It's more common than you think," explained Alejandra. "That's why there is a procedure for when people can't claim their compensation because of a lack of national ID. You must reschedule the delivery. It will take some time, but at least you know that your compensation is ready." After Alejandra had hung up, she told Cecilia and me that what she couldn't understand was who made the call and why no one had contacted the psychosocial team within the Unit to support the process. Three days later, Cecilia left me a message in which she shared the happy news about Lucia's good fortune: the bank had paid Lucia's compensation despite her showing them only a copy of her ID. "The weird part," explained Cecilia, "is that instead of the lump sum of thirty times the minimum wage she was supposed to receive, she received twenty-six! We'll have to call the Unit to find out about that." In practice, it's hard to know what happened to all the established protocols, and those still in the making, that should have been followed and were not. Cecilia and her daughter, for their part, will keep hoping that luck is on their side as they continue to navigate the bureaucracies of reparations.

Gloria also came to the meeting. Unlike the other women, she was not there to ask whether her son had the right to education, financial compensation, or psychosocial care. A lot had happened in the year since she filed the *novedad* asking for him to be included in the registry and since he became officially recognized as a victim of the armed conflict who was entitled to integral redress. In December 2021, just a few months into his year of military service, he came back home because he could no longer endure the harsh conditions and constant mistreatment that it entailed. In doing so, he was classed as having deserted the military. Not only did his legal situation become uncertain, but he was also facing a possible prison sentence of between eight months and two years. Gloria's anxiety escalated as the presence of old and new armed groups grew around them. Instead of giving communities in that area a break from the imposition of war, the early stage of the COVID-19 pandemic in 2020 was used by armed groups to strengthen their operations. Massacres and killings of community leaders, human rights defenders, and demobilized former combatants had a more devastating impact in Buenos Aires than COVID-19.[34] Peasant economies, already under a constant state of siege due to the expansion of the extractive industries and neoliberal policies, day by day, became less of a realistic possibility for young people to earn their livelihoods. Instead, the economies of war—whether in the form of armed groups managing coca crops, working in the processing labs in the bushes, or joining an armed group—were constantly and aggressively knocking on young people's doors.

One hot morning in late July 2022, Gloria and I were sitting by a creek in a spot that Gloria chose because no one could see or overhear us there. Gloria needed to share the deep sorrow she was feeling in her heart. After having deserted from the military, her son had been recruited by one of the illegal armed groups that were trying to gain control over that part of the country. First, he started working on one of their coca crops, for which he was paid COP 60,000 a day (approximately USD 14), instead of working for small peasant farmers on their *fincas*, which paid COP 30,000 (USD 6) a day. He then joined the armed group, where he was promised a monthly salary of COP 1,000,000 (USD 215). She didn't know how to get him back. "When he joined the army," Gloria told me, "he said that at least with them, if something happened to him, they had to bring me back his body. But with these people, I don't know where he is; I know nothing of his whereabouts."

"He left the army before; don't you think there is a possibility that he will also leave them now? It's only been a couple of weeks," I said naively.

"He can't," replied Gloria. "Once someone joins, leaving is no longer an option. If he does, they will chase him, and they will chase us all. But hope is the last thing that I will lose. That's why I pray, and I don't tell people *they* took him. I pray he'll find his way out back to me." Gloria attended the meeting, but instead of asking about reparations, she really wanted to talk about justice.

CONCLUSIONS

For the last decade, the Victims' Unit has had the very challenging job of filling the sociolegal category of children born of conflict-related sexual violence with meaning and creating a bureaucratic system of reparations in which it can exist. There was no formula for doing this, no pool of expert knowledge, and the task was made even more complex by the mass scale of the ongoing armed conflict in Colombia. Drawing on developments that have occurred within the fields that work with conflict-affected children and conflict-related sexual violence, the category of children born of conflict-related sexual violence became nested within the system to redress the consequences of sexual violence in contexts of armed and political violence. Through this process, however, the category became lost, hidden, and diluted within the measures, standards, and practices that were introduced to address sexual violence. For now, it is a category lost within another category. Its boundaries are blurred and so is its content.

Since the beginning of its development in the 1990s, the model of transitional justice has adopted the goals of achieving truth, justice, and reparations as its pillars.[35] The understanding that redress is paramount within a victim-centered approach that seeks justice is, by now, unquestionable within this paradigm.[36] The notion of redress and the measures of reparation within this model respond to specific experiences of armed and political violence forced upon people and translated into legal categories of harm.[37] In that sense, they reference the past in order to reimagine the future. This includes the past of the victim before the specific events occurred, the past of the context that allowed the events to happen, and the future that the victim was deprived of due to the events. For victims of conflict-related sexual violence, measures implemented to remedy the impacts of sexual violence on their bodies and lives have involved, for instance, specialized health care to reconstruct their reproductive systems or treat sexually transmitted diseases and mental health support to deal with suicidal thoughts and feelings of constant fear, mistrust, and guilt.

Throughout the past few years, the bureaucracies of reparations for children born of conflict-related sexual violence, embedded as they are in those created for their mothers, have followed the harm-centered logics behind ideas about rehabilitation, satisfaction, compensation, and guarantees of non-repetition. Attempts to render this category legible within the system have so far focused on producing knowledge with which to shape and label it. These negotiations have been guided by questions about the place it should occupy within the system and how to involve people born of conflict-related sexual violence in the bureaucracies of victimhood. However, what does not seem to have received much attention yet is the question of what reparations—and in broader terms, justice—should look like in their cases.

Individuals inside the Victims' Unit have negotiated to render the category of people born of conflict-related sexual violence legible within the victimhood system. These attempts have translated into a number. From an institutional perspective, a number, as ambiguous as it is, serves to buy time in terms of accountability. By offering an official figure, the Unit reveals at the same time as it conceals.[38] Being able to quantify their existence not only within the population of victims but, to an extent, within the reparation process (i.e., how many people have received compensation) means that it has something to show when asked about the knowledge gap regarding children born of conflict-related sexual violence. It confirms that they exist within the realm of victimhood with its architecture of transitional justice. However, questions about their legibility must be accompanied by deeper debates about what kind of reparations they need and what justice entails for people like Gloria's son. They have the right to reparations, but above all, they have the right to access education, health care, and decent housing. They should be able to enjoy life in nonmilitarized contexts without the constant worry about whether there will be running water to cook with, electricity to keep the fridge working, or even enough food for themselves and their families.

The negotiation to fill the legal category with meaning and render it legible within the bureaucracies of victimhood and reparations is a process that continues to evolve. The creation of this system nests within the more standardized bureaucracies that have been developed to address wartime sexual violence, with similar strengths and shortcomings, but it is also imbued with the same language and terminology. As with their mothers' quest for redress, the timescales within which these bureaucracies operate do not correspond to these people's actual needs and expectations, and the painfully slow pace is, in itself, a source of institutional violence. Not only does the state "always arrive late," but the different ways in which it has historically been present in peasant communities and communities of Afro-descendant and Indigenous peoples have also served to create racialized landscapes of discrimination.[39] For people who live in militarized contexts of colonial and economic violence, like Gloria's son, to dream of a future is a privilege. Redress, in the case of people born of conflict-related sexual violence, is not necessarily about the victimizing events that they have experienced. Instead of being grounded in the paradigm of justice that addresses the victimizing events of the past, redress should be grounded in a paradigm of justice that views it as "a process that continuously reaches toward a future not defined by conflict in which younger generations can thrive."[40] Reparations, in their case, should lay the foundations for them to dream of a future that belongs to them.

3 · CONTESTED IDENTITIES
Reproductive Violence, Reproductive Labor, and War

"I don't know if you've heard about that boy who attacked his little brother with a machete," Doña Libia asked me while we were taking a break from the hot midday sun under the shade of a mango tree in front of the school in San Miguel. Against a background of the cacophony coming from a group of boys and girls who were engaged in what seemed to be a game of simulated and real pushing, screaming, laughter, and tears, Doña Libia told me a story that would soon become recurrent during the first few months of my stay in San Miguel in 2016. It was the story of a teenager who was "out of control," according to Doña Libia. During the end-of-year festivities in 2015, at one of the evening cookouts that the neighbors organize with their relatives who are visiting from other towns and cities, the live music was interrupted by screams coming from one of the houses near the school. "I wasn't there," Doña Libia continued, "but people say that they saw the little brother running out of the house as if he was being chased by all the souls in purgatory. It turned out that he was actually being pursued by his older brother wielding their mom's machete!" Their mom, who was taking part in the evening celebrations, ran after them and stopped what could have been a tragedy from occurring. Other than a badly scratched leg sustained from tripping over as he fled, the little brother was more or less unharmed. Several months after this event, people were still in shock. "It was only a matter of time before something like that happened," Doña Libia remarked as I went back into the school, where a group of kids was waiting for me to resume the drawings we had been working on that morning.

Only after hearing more than a couple of different versions of this event did I come to understand that the biological father of the teenager with the machete was a paramilitary and that the teenager belonged to the group of young people

85

who—at some point in their lives, mostly when they were still children—had been associated with the label *paraquito*, a term that is rarely heard nowadays. Astrid, then spokeswoman for the community during the negotiations with the government about collective reparations and with whom I was working closely in 2016, told me how young people in San Miguel had better access to primary and high school education than their predecessors, and yet their opportunities for making a living seemed to be more restricted. As she reflected on the younger generations, she brought up the story of the teenager. "It backfired on her, you know?" Astrid added after a short pause. "All this time his mom has been yelling at him, mistreating him, telling him to stand up for himself against the world, and now it has backfired. She's been telling him to defend himself because he is the son of a *paraco* [slang for 'paramilitary'], and now we can see the consequences."

In this chapter, I explore the gendered politics of identity and reproduction that have contributed to the unintelligibility of people born of conflict-related sexual violence. In San Miguel, I encountered a fracture in the narrative about those young men and women born of paramilitary sexual violence. Stories about the *paraquitos* receded, only for the less obvious but entrenched gendered politics of identity and reproduction to be revealed. Despite the term having fallen into disuse, they are understood as still being problematic for the community. In these social negotiations, women have been blamed for failing to raise their children according to the gendered expectations and values of the community. The biological and cultural input of the mothers—completely absent from the label *paraquito*—has assumed an active role in the configuration of a subject who is shaped no longer by the terror that the father represented but by the violence rooted in gendered expectations of care.

As I will show, narratives about people born of conflict-related sexual violence in San Miguel have emerged in the tensions between local frameworks for understanding gender, sexuality, and reproduction and frameworks for understanding violence against women. At the intersection, women's experiences of the armed conflict have been denied and judged through patriarchal values, and their sons and daughters have been configured as problematic subjects. Through the normalization of paramilitary sexual violence during the community's confinement and the naturalization of patriarchal expectations of gender roles, women have been blamed both for the paramilitary abuse of their bodies and for having endured it. In this context, their sons and daughters born of this abuse are understood through the labor of motherhood and not through the experience of war and survival.

FIGURE 3. A woman on her way to run errands, San Miguel, 2017

ON THE PRESENCE OF THE FATHER

Clemencia did not have an easy childhood. She has loving memories of her dad from when she was a young girl, but after he died when Clemencia was just seven years old, she stayed with her two sisters, her brother, and her mom, who, in Clemencia's opinion, "doesn't have it in her to be loving." After Clemencia's dad passed away, his family refused to allow Clemencia's mom access to their land. She was then left with four children to raise without much support, as her own parents had died when she was very young and left her with no inheritance, the main way in which land usually passes from generation to generation among this Afro-Colombian peasant community. Clemencia's memories of her mom are mainly of beatings and mistreatments. "I don't blame her; that's the only language she knew. That's the language I learned from her," Clemencia recalled. One day, Clemencia, two other women, and I were talking about the scars we had sustained during our childhoods. We all had stories of childhood games that involved climbing trees or playing hide-and-seek that left our skin permanently marked in a way that reminded us of fun times. We were all laughing, but Clemencia had still not shared any stories, which was unlike her. One of the women questioned Clemencia's uncharacteristic silence. "You must have a hundred stories! What's the story behind that scar across your arm, for example?"

Clemencia was around nine years old, and she was collecting fruit from a neighbor's trees to sell without the neighbor's knowledge, something that she was good at. She was agile and stealthy, so people never caught her climbing their trees. This time, however, she slipped. As she fell, a branch pierced her arm, creating a deep gash in the skin of her forearm, all the way from her wrist to her elbow. As best she could, she grabbed the bag of fruit she had already collected and dragged it all the way to her house. When her mom saw her, she went crazy, Clemencia recalled: "She was so mad, she clutched me by the hair and shoved me out of the house, screaming that I was a good for nothing." Clemencia sneaked around to the back of one of their neighbor's houses, where there was a stone basin for storing rainwater, and used their laundry soap to clean her wound. She then went to the house where one of her cousins lived and asked her to stitch the broken skin back together. "Growing up like that," Clemencia told us, "I became a matchstick, ready to set everything on fire." She was tough, always ready to punch her way out of any situation, but also lonely because she felt that she was all alone against the world. In a voice tinged with sadness, she once told me,

> I created this shell so that no one could get close to me, so that no one could hurt me. For years, I always carried my knife in my bra and was ready to use it. I've stabbed five people in my life. I stopped carrying it after I stabbed someone at a party. I was wearing a beautiful red dress and was having so much fun! This guy came up behind me and touched my shoulder. Something snapped inside me. Next thing I knew, I turned round, knife in hand, and stabbed him in the arm. To think that all he wanted was to dance!

When the paramilitaries arrived in 2001, Clemencia was fifteen years old. She had never seen a camouflage uniform in her life. Like everyone else in the community, she knew that guerrillas were in the area, but she had not seen them. She also knew about the army, but she hadn't seen them either. By the time the paramilitaries had established their storage and training base at the school, Clemencia had already grown accustomed to the constant mistreatment and physical abuse she received from her mom, but nothing could have prepared her for what was to come next. If Clemencia's family had struggled to survive before the paramilitaries arrived, things became much worse afterward. The whole community was confined, and mobility both within and outside San Miguel was very restricted, even if it was just to work on the crops, attend to the farm animals, go to the health center, or do grocery shopping. Food was scarce, and fear and uncertainty were common currency. The occupation took its toll on women and girls in particular; they were forced to cook for the paramilitaries and do their laundry, and they were also obliged to entertain them. Clemencia remembered the first time she was raped. She recounted that a friend found her crying behind a tree. She was crying because she was scared, because the man who raped her pulled her hair, kicked her in her stomach, and punched her in the back—because he hurt her, and she didn't know what to do. "I'm not even sure how I became involved with the father of my son," Clemencia commented while recalling her first memory of the paramilitary who would later become the biological father of her child. She continued,

> One day my mom sent me to the store to run some errands. A man [paramilitary] greeted me very politely. And I replied, pretending to be calm, but I was trembling inside. I'm telling you that I don't know when I started to be with him. I don't know how that happened. What I can tell you is that, honest to God, that was very good fortune for me, because the rest of them stopped looking for me. Before him, I would be in my house, and someone would come and bring word that one of them wanted me. And no matter what time of day it was, I had to get dressed to go and meet them. Thank God that stopped!

By the time the paramilitaries underwent their demobilization in December 2004, Clemencia was not the only woman in San Miguel and the surrounding communities who had given birth to children conceived through sexual violence. In her close circle alone, her sister and her cousin Gloria also have children born of the abuse endured by women during that period. It did not happen immediately after the paramilitaries left, but at some point in time, after the community's initial disbelief as to whether the paramilitaries really had gone, people started calling the children *paraquitos* (little paramilitaries). When this happened, some women took their children and fled to the cities to work as maids or in any other form of employment they could find. They were terrified that people would try to hurt their children as a form of revenge for all the pain and suffering that the paramilitaries inflicted on them. Some women chose to stay and sought to protect their children as best they could. "Back then, everyone was very ignorant. It's not like that anymore," Gloria recalled. "Sometimes you would see people jokingly calling the children *paraquito*, as if it were a game, and the children, all innocent, would come and high-five them! There were also people who harassed them. People told them that they were going to grow up to be just like their fathers." In response to that, Clemencia remarked, "I used to beat the hell out of everyone who I caught talking to my son like that. Even his little brother, my younger son, would do it every now and then."

In Colombia, children born of conflict-related sexual violence became visible to people outside their communities through naming practices. Although sexual violence in the context of the Colombian armed conflict has been committed by all armed groups—and therefore, there are children fathered by paramilitaries, guerrillas, the military, and foreign troops across the country—it was the label *paraquitos*, in particular, that spread in the form of a shocking rumor among human rights organizations. The clear association that the label suggested between the children and their biological fathers was taken up by outsiders, particularly those working in areas that have claimed expertise in the understanding of war and its consequences, as a sign of stigmatization imposed on these boys and girls by their communities. It was regarded as a distinguishing mark attached to their identity, most likely to be internalized in a way that shaped their behavior or at least people's expectations of it.[1] As they had already been labeled as an "evil other" by their communities, it was generally assumed that these boys and girls were going to be ostracized, discriminated against throughout their lives, and mistreated.[2] "What do you think is going to happen to those children people call *paraquitos* as they grow up?" I asked someone from a human rights organization based in Bogotá in 2015 before I came to understand that the label was now mostly a thing of the past. "No one knows, but if you ask me, I think it might be too late for them now," they replied.

Driven largely by naming practices, in interdisciplinary international scholarship, the notion of stigma has been used to conceptualize the plight of children born of war-related sexual violence as people who, based on the circumstances of their conception and the identity of their biological fathers, experience different forms of discrimination throughout their lives. Naming practices, in that sense, have served to unveil some of the complex relations that these people embody for their mothers and their communities. The following are examples of the broad diversity of experiences that labeling practices have revealed: children born of rape during the Rwandan genocide were referred to as *les enfants mauvais souvenir* (children of bad memories), while in northern Uganda, children fathered by members of the Lord's Resistance Army (LRA) have been registered with names by their mothers that convey their experience of the abduction, such as Komakech (I am unfortunate), Anenocan (I have suffered), and Lubanga Kene (only God knows why this happened to me).[3] In Peru, children born of rape perpetrated by soldiers have been called *los regalos de los soldados* (the soldiers' gifts).[4] In Colombia, as well as the label *paraquito*, children fathered by U.S. troops have been called *niños del Plan Colombia* (Plan Colombia's children), and children born of sexual violence perpetrated by soldiers have been referred to as *niños verdes* (green children).

Thus, the concept of stigma has been helpful as a red flag for anticipating the connection between naming practices and the legitimization of actions and policies that could jeopardize these children's well-being—in some cases, even leading to infanticide—and deprive them of access to food, land, housing, education, health, or citizenship.[5] Kimberly Theidon, however, argues that "stigma" provides a narrow frame within which to reflect on the identities and experiences of these people; the concept of stigma does not account for the gendered power relations that are anchored in specific systems of meaning, which are both reproduced and contested in the context of war and the repercussions during its aftermath.[6] Naming practices offer insight into the social negotiations about memory and memorialization as well as theories of transmission between parents and children.[7] Both the emergence of the label *paraquitos* in San Miguel and the way in which it has since faded illuminate some of these negotiations.

Its emergence provides a snapshot of a moment when people attempted to name and rename the world that, in the case of San Miguel, remained after years of paramilitary confinement—years in which the paramilitaries rigorously imposed a social order that deprived people's imagination of a present or future that was not governed by them, and these children embody clear traces of the paramilitaries' years of governance. Its vanishing, as I explain further in the following sections of this chapter, reveals the underlying gendered politics of reproduction in which children born of conflict-related sexual violence are understood not as "other" but as their mothers' responsibility. Questions about the biological and cultural reproduction of the community are, after all, questions about who belongs and the social negotiations that belonging entails. In San Miguel, after several years of paramilitary confinement, the dynamics of the armed conflict have changed. It is not simply that people are living in the aftermath of war, as war has taken on different reconfigurations since the paramilitaries demobilized in December 2004, but the experiences of the paramilitary occupation now lie in the past, and consequently, there has been a transformation in people's experiences of the present and in the possible futures that they can now imagine. This has also been accompanied by a transformation in the ways in which people name the world around them.

By using a label that refers to the children's fathers—the label of the father—people in the community, but mostly those outsiders who reproduce the stories they have heard or witnessed as if they were still happening in the present, grant those paramilitaries the power to continue being present (even if only symbolically) in the communities they had tormented, even after they had left and the communities themselves had stopped labeling the children as *paraquitos*. By reproducing narratives associated with the term, outsiders from the media, the academy, and human rights organizations have contributed to keeping alive the idea of a permanent paramilitary presence in those communities. In doing so, they reproduce the symbolic weight of the father, through which biological fatherhood is imbued with the power to reproduce not only life itself—the population—but also the social body and the wider political community.[8]

Neither Clemencia's nor Gloria's sons, nor those of any of the other women I have met in San Miguel and the surrounding communities, are referred to as *paraquitos* anymore. Members of their families and communities do not mistreat them on the basis of who their biological fathers are and the violence they imposed. They are not ostracized or understood through the notion of "otherness," and yet they carry in their bodies traces of their biological parents, of the cultural meaning of both of their identities, and the experiences of violence that led to their conception. The disappearance of the label, therefore, does not mean that their biological, cultural, and social inheritance has been erased. The question that remains, then, is about the ways in which that presence manifests and materializes in the identities and lives of the children and their mothers. In relation to the continuing presence of their biological fathers—perpetrators of war-related sexual violence—Theidon explains that "theories of transmission are another sphere in which biological fathers, although physically absent, may be omnipresent in the symbolic register."[9]

Margaret Lock's concept of local biologies refutes the assumption that the physical material body is universal to argue that embodiment is constituted by both the biological and the cultural, which in turn are coproduced and reproduced in the self that is experienced by each individual and represented by the individual and others.[10] The coproduction of biology and culture, claims Lock, configures subjective embodied experiences and discourses about the body. At the same time, this coproduction is internalized and individualized, creating embodied experiences that are shared among groups of people. Building on Lock's concept of local biologies, Theidon conceptualizes biology as a system of signification that—in this case, through sexual reproduction—is capable of producing not simply life itself but also meaning that goes beyond a static notion of stigmatized individuals.[11] Reflecting on the identity of people born of conflict-related sexual violence and the places they are granted within their communities, therefore, requires an understanding that their biological bodies represent the cultural reproduction of their parents' own identities and roles. Genes, which in this sense involve the coproduction of biology and culture, cease to be a distinct sequence of nucleotides inside a chromosome and instead become the vehicle for transferring forms of social meaning from parents to offspring, thereby shaping the way in which they are rendered visible within their communities.

The case of Nigeria is illustrative of a system of transmission within which biological fathers are imbued with the power to define their children's identities, while their biological mothers are disregarded. In the context of the ongoing conflict in northeast Nigeria, hundreds of women and girls have been abducted, forcibly married, enslaved, and raped by Jama'atul ahl al-sunnah li da'awati wal jihad (JAS) fighters, known as Boko Haram. Amid disputes over territories held by JAS, large numbers of men, women, and children have either escaped or been rescued. They have been placed in camps for internally displaced people either in host communities or in their local government areas. Many of the women and girls who were abducted are now leaving with their children born of war-related sexual violence. Discrimination against them and their children has been largely driven by fear that the women had been indoctrinated and radicalized in captivity and that the children contain, inside them, dormant *juju* (charms) that could be activated at any time by the group in order to turn the child into a militant. Rumors of abducted women returning to their families and murdering their parents have spread among communities. These women have been referred to as "Boko Haram wives," "Boko Haram blood," and *annoba*, which means "epidemics" and reflects the belief that their supposed radicalization can be spread to others.[12]

The children, for their part, are referred to as "hyenas among dogs," and the notion of "bad blood" is commonly used to describe the deterministic relationship between the biological father and the child.[13] Women are more likely to be accepted back into their communities, as there is an assumption that they can be "cleansed" and former relationships can be restored. Women's identities are assumed to be susceptible to being erased and rewritten. Children, on the contrary, are believed to carry what is commonly referred to as Boko Haram's genes in their blood. Within this system of local biologies, the identity of the father is transmitted to the children and is seen as defining who that child is, whereas the mother's genetic and social inputs are regarded as having no power to shape the children's identity. It is at the intersection between local biologies and violent regimes in which sexual violence has been used that we find the reproduction not only of the population but of the fear and suffering that the perpetrators embody. It is not simply that the child shares their father's biological genes that could, for instance, make them look alike; in contexts such as Nigeria, the child "belongs" to the system of violence that the father represents.

In San Miguel, despite outsiders' preconceptions (based on naming practices) that the children carry their biological fathers' identities, children are not associated with "otherness" in the community. And yet, as the story of the teenager who chased his little brother with their mom's machete illustrates, those people born of conflict-related sexual violence are understood as problematic. The labeling that associates them with their biological fathers, both through its presence and its fading, plays tricks in relation to the way in which the identities and situations of people born of conflict-related sexual violence are perceived. First, the label's visibility remains so apparent that it has made it easy for outsiders to keep narrating the label as though it were still happening in the present, thereby reproducing the idea of children as stigmatized people. The second trick played by this labeling practice is that once it is gone, it creates the illusion that those boys, girls, teenagers, and young adults are no longer part of their mothers' lives and communities. The waning of the label could also trick us into forgetting how they were conceived—that their biological fathers abused their mothers and that their mothers, regardless of what they did with the baby once it was born, were forced into that position.

Clemencia proudly talks about how she has played the role of both mother and father to her son. Sometimes when she describes the great efforts and sacrifices that raising him on her own have entailed, she pats herself on the back with a smile on her face. "I have taught him to be good, to be caring. It hasn't been easy because I was broken. I've had to put my pieces back together," she proudly declares. For women like Clemencia, even once the label has vanished and beyond the genetic traces that are sometimes apparent in the children's physical characteristics, the presence of the biological father remains active in at least two ways: in women's experiences of sexual violence and its various physical, emotional, and psychological consequences and in the implications of their sons and daughters not having a biological father to trace.

ON THE ABSENCE OF THE FATHER

The story of Rosa is no different from the stories of many women in San Miguel. She met the father of her son at the community's rural school when she was a child. They were classmates, and at some point before graduating, they started dating. "I was very young, and he was very sweet and handsome. I was very attracted to him. Next thing I knew, I was already pregnant!" Rosa tells me, laughing. As her mom and dad refused to send her back to school, Rosa had to start working to pay for her expenses and to save money for the baby. Despite the family's disapproval of her situation, she continued living in the family home with her parents, sisters, and boyfriend, who moved in with them soon after she started working. After the baby was born, Rosa and the father of her child—who at that point in her recollection, she started calling her husband—stayed living with her parents until one day, before the baby was even six months old, he left to start dating another woman. "He got tired of my mom nagging all day long, and who wouldn't?" Rosa emphatically added.

For some months after he left, he brought her milk and food for the child, but by the time the baby had turned one year old, he no longer offered any kind of emotional, moral, material, or economic support. Instead, Rosa remembers how painful it was for her to see him dating another woman, who was one of her close friends, and subsequently having a child with her. Although Rosa's son has his father's surname and they refer to him as "Dad" (but no longer as "husband" for Rosa), he is never around and plays no active role in their lives. "Sometimes when my son needs to buy things for school, I tell him to ask his dad. 'What for?' he says. 'He is very stingy!' Around here you see a lot of irresponsible fathers. They impregnate a woman and then they don't want anything to do with them.

Around here so many of us [women] are both mother and father." Later in the same conversation, I asked Rosa about the children born of the paramilitary abuse. "I feel very sorry for them," she said. "They have no father to look after them, just a mom, and that makes me very sad." Time and again, I encountered that reference to the absent father in relation to people fathered by paramilitaries. In a context where, in general, the presence of biological fathers seems to be flexible, the constant references to "a lack of dad"—when that dad is a paramilitary who participated in the occupation of the community and perpetrated sexual violence—linked to the child's identity offers valuable insight into negotiations about local gendered politics of reproduction.

Clemencia remembers the last time that she saw her son's father. He was not around San Miguel in those days, as he had been moved to a different area of operations by the paramilitary bloc to which he belonged. A couple of months before Clemencia's last encounter with him, she had had a row with her mom that led to her fleeing San Miguel. Clemencia was already pregnant and living with her mom. They were staying on someone's land in exchange for keeping it clear of weeds. She related that one day, she came back to the house from burning charcoal and started cooking rice. Clemencia was exhausted and had forgotten to run an errand her mom had asked her to do. When her mom came back from picking up oranges, bananas, and mangoes to sell, she became very upset by Clemencia's forgetfulness and started yelling and throwing things at her. "She started choking me and at the same time was kneeing me in the stomach. Can you believe it?" Clemencia exclaimed, the disbelief still apparent in her voice. "Next thing I knew, I bit her on the hand. It was years ago, but I can still kind of taste it! As soon as she let go, I ran and didn't stop until I reached my aunt's house, who lived nearby."

Later that day, Clemencia was outside her aunt's when a paramilitary commander approached her: "What's this story that you hurt your mom? She came to see me earlier to complain about you. She said you've been hitting her." Clemencia told me that this took her so much by surprise that it was not until after he had left that she understood the danger her own mother had put her in. "I explained what had happened," Clemencia told me, "and I guess he believed me because he just left. But after he left, I realized that I had been lucky. I didn't even know what I had saved myself from." Clemencia described how, for days, all she could do was cry. She did not know what to do and felt lonely and lost. She was terrified that the commander would change his mind and have her punished or killed. It was then that a friend of hers told her that she knew of a family near Cali who were looking for a live-in maid. Her friend, who was already working as a live-in maid for another family, helped Clemencia get out of San Miguel and start her new job. Clemencia recalled that her friend would call her every day to tell her how to do all the household chores, as all Clemencia knew how to do was to work the land. On Sundays—her day off—Clemencia has fond memories of being taken to the park by her friend and a couple of other women from around San Miguel who were working similar jobs. "I owe them so much. I was falling apart. They would even buy me ice creams," Clemencia recounted. "I didn't even have money for that!"

One day, Clemencia got a call from a friend who was in San Miguel. Her friend said that a paramilitary who had recently arrived was asking for Clemencia. "He looks a lot like *yours*, but I can't really tell if it's him," Clemencia remembered her friend saying. Clemencia isn't sure why, but she left her job without telling anyone and headed to San Miguel. "I didn't even get paid," she said, laughing. Once she saw him and they started talking, he asked her if it was true that she was pregnant. "I told him that it was true, that I was pregnant. And he started crying and couldn't stop. He said that he didn't want to leave me alone with the child. He said, 'If I don't go back to my job, they will kill me. Come with me; I'll leave you with my family.'" Clemencia explained that this conversation took place in early 2003, when her son's father's paramilitary bloc was already preparing for their demobilization in December 2004. He offered to take Clemencia to live with his family, who were from a different part of the country, and come back for her after his release from prison eight years later. "I didn't even consider it. What was he thinking? I wanted nothing to do with him. I know that with all the abuse, the rapes that I was enduring back then, he helped me, but I wanted nothing to do with him!" Clemencia exclaimed emphatically.

At first sight, Clemencia's son and the other children born of the paramilitary abuse are no different from other young people of the same age. It is not uncommon to hear adults or older people in the community talking about the younger generations, in abstract terms, as lacking in energy, interest, and enthusiasm and as not being part of the solution to the many problems that San Miguel has to deal with. However, among the younger generations, the young men and women born of paramilitary sexual violence occupy a distinct place. Time and again in my conversations with people in San Miguel, the lack of a father was identified as *the* issue associated with them. In cases like the story about the teenager wielding the machete, it was offered as an explanation for what people described as their unacceptable behavior, their aggressive and reckless attitudes, their poor performance at school, and their lack of interest in working the land. However, as was the case in my conversation with Rosa, the lack of a biological father was also used to describe feelings of pity and sympathy toward them, sometimes as an exoneration for behaviors that were frowned upon or features of their personalities such as shyness or absentmindedness: "You can't blame them [children born of paramilitary sexual violence], without a father to show them the way. They don't know any better!"

During World War II in countries such as Norway and Denmark, children fathered by the Allies or German soldiers were discriminated against not just because of who their biological fathers were but also because they were sons and daughters of single mothers. Those children were labeled "bastards."[14] The story of Rosa and her son's father, which is shared by many other women in San Miguel, suggests that in this community, neither women nor their children are judged based on the biological father's lack of involvement in their lives, not even in cases when the biological father refuses to acknowledge his paternity; being a single mother in San Miguel is culturally accepted. Absence, in relation to the biological father who was a paramilitary, does not necessarily refer to their role in the child's life, and as introduced in the first section of this chapter, it has nothing to do with granting the child a place within the community either, because identity in San Miguel is transmitted through both parents. An example of other systems of transmission in which both parents had the power to transmit identity to their children can be found in the German policies of reproduction during World War II. While sexual relations between Germans and groups of people considered to be of an inferior race were forbidden, they were encouraged with groups of people considered to be of racial value—for example, with Norwegian women, who were even offered financial and other forms of material aid to support them during the pregnancy and after giving birth.[15]

In his research on slavery and Afro-descendant families along the southern Pacific coast of Colombia, Mario Romero shows that belonging is defined by the maternal line and by being part of a web of relationships configured by both parents.[16] In the case of Afro-Colombian communities, identity is strongly rooted in transgenerational relations with their territory, in which the passing on of spiritual, cultural, agricultural, and other kinds of traditional knowledge as well as the land itself have been fundamental. Belonging, in that sense, is not something that is restricted to, for example, being able to identify who your relatives are. It is more about having access and contributing to those transgenerational webs of relations and knowledge. While the maternal line provides a reliable matrix through which the community expands, the responsibility for the child's socialization does not lay solely with the child's mother; it falls on an extended social network that includes uncles, aunts, cousins, and grandparents from both parents' sides of the family.

It is possible to trace these webs that signal belonging through people's surnames in San Miguel and the surrounding communities: Carabalí, Popo, Larrahondo, Mosquera, and Mina, among others. In Colombia, people are given and are registered with both of their parents' first surnames; the father's surname goes in first place and the mother's in second. Rosa, for instance, is Rosa Carabalí Mina, and her son is Angel Popo Carabalí, as he takes the first surname of his father, Popo. Because of the way in which family constellations expand, some people carry the same surname twice. For example, Rosa's mother's full name is Geraldina Mina Mina, as both of her parents' first surnames were Mina despite coming from different communities in the area and not being close relatives. Within these webs of belonging, it is relatively uncommon to find surnames that signal connections with other regions of the country. Over the last decade, increased mobility—for various reasons that include forced displacement driven by armed groups and people's search for better living conditions—has transformed this panorama to some extent. This includes transnational migration, which in the case of San Miguel, has mostly been to Ecuador and, more recently, to the south of Chile. However, more often than not, people who leave, especially those who do so for socioeconomic reasons, do not tend to come back and settle in the community.

Through tracing the surnames of San Miguel residents, I have come to realize that it is not uncommon for people to only have one surname—that of their mother. Unlike in other countries and other parts of Colombia where the father's surname signals the legitimacy of both the child and the mother, in San Miguel, having only one surname is not frowned upon, and even in those cases, it is not entirely unusual for the child to have some level of involvement with the biological father's network of relatives.[17] For children of single mothers, there is a range of different options. Some of them are registered only with their mother's first surname, others are given the surname of their mother's partner, and some are adopted by their mother's parents, in which case the children have the same surnames as their biological mother. I have observed this situation in cases where the mother was very young when she became pregnant. There seems to be some flexibility regarding the logic behind this, but the issue of legitimacy does not play a central role. "Whose surname do those children born of the abuse have?" I used to shyly ask people who mentioned these children to me, based on my own paradigm of a Catholic family. "Their mom's, of course!" they replied every time, speaking from the perspective of a moral order that refrains from shaming anyone on the basis of not having their father's surname or having two surnames despite not being recognized by their biological father.

As is the case with children of single mothers, for children born of conflict-related sexual violence, their maternal line ensures them a place within the community, and their surnames tell similar stories to the ones described earlier of children born to single mothers who were not conceived through paramilitary sexual violence. For instance, while Gloria's son carries the surname of Gloria's partner, Clemencia's son only carries her first surname despite her partner—the father of her other two sons—offering to give him his surname. Although the father's surname places the child within a web of relations and resources, it also gives the original holder of the surname power over the child, which was something Clemencia was not willing to countenance. At the same time, the surname also links the child to the surname holder's kin and resources. At first glance, this would appear to be convenient for both the child and the mother. However, some women, such as Clemencia, believe that it could also cause problems in the future; because the surname entitles the children to material resources such as inheriting land, the partner's relatives could resent having this addition to the family. "I'd rather die before opening the door for anyone to humiliate or hurt my son. What he gets, he will get from me and my work!" Clemencia declared.

In San Miguel, *knowing* who a child's biological father is bestows more power than *naming* the father. In the former case, the father contributes to this reproductive system of meaning by anchoring the child to a broader network of social ties, and knowing who the father is—even if the child has not been formally recognized—grants him or her access to social, cultural, and sometimes economic resources. For the reproduction of the community, "being from there" is regarded as an essential attribute. On many occasions, particularly in relation to people aspiring to positions of social and political power, I heard references to "not being from here" used in a negative way to describe a person—to signify unreliability and unpredictability. "Who were those men?" I asked one of the men involved in the negotiations about collective reparations, referring to the paramilitaries who confined the community for years.

"That's hard to say," he replied. "Those men were not from here; they came from other corners of the country. Some of them were bad, some of them were good people."

"What about the children who were born of their violence?" I continued the conversation.

"Those poor kids, with only a mother—you see them around causing trouble, not knowing where they came from or where they are going."

Clemencia has never regretted not leaving with her son's father when he offered, and yet throughout the years that I have known her, she herself has referred several times to the lack of a father for her son as a conflicting issue. "I've always been both mom and dad for him," is a sentence that you often hear in Colombia from single mothers like Rosa, and Clemencia is no exception; she often reiterates it proudly. Clemencia is not only proud of her son; she is also proud of herself. She knows that she has done as good a job as possible, considering how she herself was brought up and all the hardships she has endured in life. "I know things could have been different in my life if I had had a father to look after me as I was growing up, to give me advice, to protect me," Clemencia commented.

"What about your partner, the father of your other two sons?" I asked her.

She replied with the following:

I started living with him when my son was five. My son has always received love from his stepfather. From the very beginning, I told him [the partner]: "You do not scold my son. Before you scold my son, tell me, 'Your son did this,' and I am the only one allowed to talk to him." They have coexisted nicely, but sadly, there are boys who hate their stepfather. But in the case of my son, it is different because he has that emptiness [of not having a biological father]. At home, I've taught my son to do household chores. So now I tell him, "Make sure to have dinner ready for your dad when he comes back from work, bring him a fruit juice," and he does it! And it's not his dad but his stepdad! And when my son started drinking, partying, and talking to women, I went to my husband and told him: "Help me! He's not listening to me, but he'll listen to you!"

Women who are parenting children born of paramilitary sexual violence talk about at least three different father figures: the child's biological father, their foster father, and the father who never was. The first is the perpetrator of the horrors they've experienced, the one who is genetically part of their children's bodies, and whom they hope never manifests in any way and with whom they hope never to cross paths again. The second, often a partner or the father of their other children, is the one who lacks the legitimacy of the child's biological father, which makes it more difficult for him to guide or to get involved in their education. He faces the difficult task of gaining the woman's trust and a place in her child's life. Gloria's son grew up with his stepfather, who is also the father of his siblings. He is officially registered with both his surname and Gloria's surname, and yet, on the day Gloria shared with me that her son had been recruited by one of the illegal armed groups operating in the area, she did it largely because she needed to voice the deep sorrow she was feeling, and she did not know whom she could trust. "What does your husband say about the situation?" I remember asking her. "I haven't told him," she replied. "I don't want him or anyone to know. After all, he's not his father. I can't be sure if he'll support my son." The third figure women talk about is the father they hoped their children could have had. Very often, this is one they hoped that they themselves could have had growing up—a caring, supportive, responsible, and reliable father.

On one of the many afternoons that Clemencia, Gloria, and I spent talking about their expectations for their children's reparations, Gloria commented, "I think that reparations [for our sons and daughters] should start with psychosocial workshops. I think psychosocial workshops could play the role of the father. And what is a father to his children? He advises them, he is watchful, he gives them what they need. What does a father want for his children?" And Clemencia replied, "That nothing bad ever happens to them, that they do not go down a bad path." When women talk about the lack of a father in their children's lives, there is a longing for support, for a family network, and for a caring presence that could have made their lives, and those of their children, different. They talk about what the perpetrators took away from them, which in this case involves not only knowing who the father of their child is, and therefore his kinship, but also the possibility of maybe, against the odds, finding a man who could have stayed with them and who could have been a real, positive presence in their lives. Clemencia and the other women talk about the lack of a dad, but they do not mean specifically *that* dad.

ON THE PRESENCE OF THE MOTHER

I ran into Don German in the community-built bamboo kiosk that served as a bus stop. Located at the entrance to the dirt road that, for years, had been the main paramilitary checkpoint, this long, covered bench provided the shade that made the usually long wait for the bus under the hot mountain sun more bearable. While Don German waited for someone who was coming to visit him from Cali and I waited for my bus to take me back there, he told me the story of how, during the paramilitary occupation, he and his wife fled to Cali. They found a place in a shantytown that they tried to turn into a home. However, neither of them had a job, and it was very difficult to make a living in an unfamiliar urban place. He tried to get used to it for a year, but he could not bear the idea of their house in San Miguel being abandoned, along with their crops and animals, so he decided to return and try to withstand the presence of the paramilitaries. His wife stayed in Cali; she felt it was too risky to go back, and until the day when Don German and I were waiting for different buses together, she had not done so.

During that conversation, Don German expressed his curiosity about what I was doing in San Miguel; he had seen me working with the collective reparation process, and with the kids in the school, and with the women. I told him about my research and explained my interest in understanding women and children's experiences in war contexts—for example, "children who were born during *those* days"—to which he responded, "There are many of those [children fathered by paramilitaries] around here. But that comes as no surprise; they [paramilitaries] established their base in the school, so we had hundreds of men everywhere. They were single men—just normal that their presence attracted women! In those days, you could see women from different places coming here looking for them. Women from here were also after them. Just think about it; where there is a man, there is a woman."

"But there were abuses, weren't there?" I asked Don German.

"Those were violent times, and there was violence, but women fell in love. I don't want to say that there wasn't abuse, but in general, they fell in love," he said.

"What about the children who were born back then?" I risked asking, knowing that he would understand that I meant children fathered by paramilitaries.

"Imagine the problem—without a father!" he replied.[18] With the fading of the label of the father, narratives about people born of conflict-related sexual violence emerged in the tension between local frameworks for understanding gender, sexuality, and reproduction and frameworks for understanding violence against women, not only in the context of the armed conflict. While women's experiences of paramilitary violence during the lengthy period of occupation were normalized, the naturalization of patriarchal gender roles imposed on women the unquestionable duty of motherhood. Through that tension, their sons and daughters born of the abuse are presented as evidence of their mothers' faults—namely, having "succumbed" to paramilitaries and not raising their children "properly."

Intertwined notions of gender, biology, and ethnicity can be found in the perpetrators' legitimation of conflict-related sexual violence, in outsiders' discourses about sexual violence in war contexts, and in the women's community's understanding of their children conceived and born of this violence and their role in the child's identity and upbringing.[19] Although in San Miguel, there is a recognition that the paramilitaries raped women and girls, local notions of gender, sexuality, and reproduction—outside the context of war—have played a part in denying women's experiences of violence and survival during the paramilitary confinement and its aftermath. To accurately reflect on the embodied experiences of women in San Miguel, however, requires an understanding of their Afro-Colombian bodies as sites of historical, cultural, and political struggles.

Afro-Colombian women in Colombia have frequently been represented as an embodiment of multiple and contradictory stereotypes produced in opposition to feminine white, urban, and Catholic ideals.[20] The body of the Afro-Colombian woman has been understood both as merchandise and as a source of profit in its productive and reproductive capacity—an object of men's domination and pleasure constrained by the legal system, Christian morality, and the economic system of slavery. During colonial times, Afro-Colombian women's sexuality was regulated according to fluctuations in the economic system that understood their bodies as commodities that existed to serve the white and mestizo order. For instance, reproduction was incentivized during the sixteenth and seventeenth centuries, when the demand for enslaved people was high. Throughout the centuries of oppression endured by the Afro-Colombian people, political and cultural processes have objectified the bodies of Afro-Colombian women in association with men's desire and pleasure.[21] In the intersection between the oppressive systems of class, capitalism, and patriarchy that exclude and subordinate on the basis of ethnicity, an imaginary, subordinated, homogenous Afro-Colombian woman has been produced whose identity is assumed to be fixed as a maid, matriarch, or sexualized body.[22] The stereotype of these women as sexualized bodies, in combination with racist and classist logics that deem rurality and

Afro-Colombian culture as inferior, informs the policies and practices of sexual violence in the context of the armed conflict.[23]

The language that surrounds conflict-related sexual violence contains the discursive reproduction of gendered notions of identity, sexuality, and ethnicity.[24] While in San Miguel, I have often heard mention—mainly from men—of women "falling in love" and "being attracted to paramilitaries." In the stories told by women, their language reveals the objectification of their Afro-Colombian identities as sexualized and subordinated bodies. The conversation in which Rosa told me about the day she was raped is illustrative of many other conversations I have had with women. Rape was regarded not only as a physical violation of their bodies but also as a discursive production of domination over their identities and sexuality. Rosa recalled how, on the day she was raped and every day after that, paramilitaries would yell things like "This *negrita* is very good at making love!" and "I've heard this *negrita* likes making love; I should try her sometime!" at her. "I felt so much shame and fear!" Rosa was keen to emphasize. Shame was a constant reference in these conversations with women.

In the case of San Miguel, it is possible to see the way in which local notions of gender, sexuality, and reproduction played a part in the normalization of the different forms of violence perpetrated against women during the paramilitary occupation. As women were expected to cook, do household chores, and fulfill men's "sexual needs," among other tasks, the imposition of those activities by combatants was interpreted within that patriarchal framework as "natural" and expected. This normalization was reinforced through the consolidation of the paramilitary social order that, for several years, ruled the community. After more than four years of occupation, what was previously understood as abnormal—including all forms of sexual violence such as forced nudity, forced partnership, or rape—had permeated people's lives and imaginations and become part of the norms of social control. This is to suggest not that people agreed with those norms imposed by the paramilitaries but that people became accustomed to them as a part of their everyday lives. In the normalization of violence against women and girls, the reproduction of patriarchal notions of gender disregarded the context of war and projected their gendered expectations onto women. Within the frameworks of those logics, women's experiences of pregnancy and their children born of the paramilitary abuse were understood as part of women's gendered, expected duties.

At both the international and domestic levels, attention to gendered experiences of war has tended to focus on conflict-related sexual violence, which, after decades of struggles from the women's and feminist movements, is no longer understood as collateral or inevitable in war contexts. Becoming pregnant, giving birth, and raising a child are not inevitable either—nor can they be understood as collateral issues. Unwanted and forced motherhood is reproductive violence, and yet it tends to be unintelligible when seeking to address gendered victimhood. Among the different forms of conflict-related reproductive violence such as forced contraception and forced sterilization, forced motherhood remains one of the most neglected, as it is often unseen behind assumptions of motherhood as women's "natural labor." This should not be interpreted as a denial of the perpetration of sexual violence, but it does mean that people's understanding of the scope of victimhood tends to end with the experience of sexual violence. Forced motherhood, however, encompasses at least three forms of violence. First, women experience conflict-related sexual violence, with severe, long-term consequences for their integral health and social status. Second, they face unwanted pregnancies that are a reminder of the violence they have experienced while exacerbating their already precarious socioeconomic conditions. Third, when these women give birth, in some cases due to a lack of access to safe and free abortion, the unwanted pregnancy becomes forced motherhood. Despite the suffering they have endured through their experiences of violence, women are still expected to fulfill their gender roles as nurturers. Motherhood, in this context, is understood as part of women's expected labor.

Interdisciplinary scholarship on forced motherhood has addressed the ambivalence with which women are treated after giving birth. The relevant literature has mostly explored the cases of Rwanda and northern Uganda, showing that when conflict-related sexual violence is connected to ethnic cleansing or broadening the perpetrator's group, women tend to be marginalized and stigmatized for raising a child of "the enemy."[25] In the northern Ugandan case, the literature explores the experiences of women abducted by the LRA during captivity and its aftermath. During the period of captivity, children limited women's chances of survival, and in its aftermath, children increased the discrimination that women experienced.[26] Despite this, women have also reclaimed motherhood and worked on addressing intergenerational trauma with their children.[27] For mothers of children born of rape committed during the Rwandan genocide, some of the coping strategies they have used include leaving their communities and marrying a man from elsewhere in order to transform their social status as rape victims. Through marriage, however, women often found themselves in abusive relationships where they were forced to abandon their children born of war.[28]

In Colombia, unlike in the contexts just mentioned, forced pregnancies have not been perpetrated with the intention of genocide or enlarging the perpetrator's group. People born of war-related sexual violence are not associated with "otherness" and are not discriminated against based on the logic of identity transmission. They do, however, endure other forms of violence that, together with experiences of forced motherhood, remain to be fully seen, named, studied, and addressed. Despite its unintelligibility, information about forced motherhood exists in the margins of testimonies about other forms of gendered violence, particularly sexual violence. Marxist feminists have shown us capitalism's coercion of women's reproductive functions and the ways in which it thrives on the reproductive work of racialized women and other feminized bodies.[29] The sexual division of labor that was installed through the capitalist system naturalized reproductive work as women's labor, confining women to procreation and motherhood.[30] Procreation, argues Silvia Federici, was put to the service of capitalist accumulation, and reproduction became the space in which women's exploitation and resistance took place. In Colombia, the normalization of women's role as mothers has rendered accounts of forced motherhood invisible. Despite women mentioning their children born of the paramilitary abuse in their testimonies, those references are often interpreted in reports, legal documents, and the media as reinforcing women's representation as passive victims of conflict-related sexual violence or women's "natural resilience" through motherhood.[31]

The normalization of the labor of motherhood has also obscured the intergenerational impacts of war. When Clemencia's sister gave birth to her son conceived of paramilitary abuse, for example, she was unable to breastfeed or look after him. It was their mom, aunties, cousins, and Clemencia herself (until she went into a coma) who looked after both the newborn baby and her sister, who spent most of her days crying. In the face of women's physical, emotional, and psychological struggles caused by their experiences of war, extended networks of relatives—often women who have endured war—assume the responsibilities relating to the child's care.[32] In the case of impoverished racialized communities, this has the effect of exacerbating the precarity of their situation. The perpetrators, for their part, have benefited from the naturalization of the labor of motherhood. Founded on patriarchal notions of family, the existence of offspring has contributed to impunity, as in some cases, victims and communities are less likely to identify experiences of conflict-related sexual violence as actual violence when there are children born as a result—for example, in cases like Clemencia's, where women realized that being associated with one combatant could prevent them from being raped by other members of the armed group. On the other hand, women's organizations have identified that in some cases, the existence of offspring makes it less likely that women will seek justice, whether because they feel a certain level of loyalty associated with biological kinship or because they are afraid that doing so could endanger their sons or daughters.[33]

The symbolic weight of women's role as mothers overpowers their experiences of violence to the extent that in my conversations with people in San Miguel and the surrounding communities, I frequently encountered the assumption that children fathered by paramilitaries were the result of consensual relationships. Among women's experiences of the paramilitary occupation, stories like Clemencia's, which could be interpreted as consensual, need to be read within the dynamics of war, survival, and women's resistance. Throughout the long years of paramilitary occupation, some women in San Miguel may have assumed the role of partners of paramilitaries. Different types of strategic decisions are involved in those arrangements. In a context where access to food and medicine was restricted, some women traded themselves in exchange for protection and meeting the basic needs of their families. Faced with the constant threat of sexual violence, some women preferred to be associated with the one paramilitary who had already raped them or who at least appeared to present himself in a friendly manner. In a reality in which paramilitaries represented absolute power and the imaginary future was completely constrained by that social order, some women fell in love.

In conversation with Theidon's conceptualization of strategic pregnancies in Peru as ways in which women reclaimed some control over their bodies by deciding to get pregnant by someone from their community instead of risking pregnancy by a soldier through gang rape, some women in San Miguel also sought to, as Theidon describes it, ensure the name of the father.[34] Unlike in the Peruvian case, however, ensuring the name of *that* father, a paramilitary, represented for women their association—and their children's—with the reality in which paramilitaries ruled. Returning to local biologies as systems of meaning, the question of transmission can also be viewed in terms of status. In their research on teenagers born in the context of the abductions and rapes that their mothers suffered in northern Uganda by members of the LRA, and whose formative years were spent in the bush witnessing and enduring profound violence and hardship, Myriam Denov and Atim Angela Lakor show that for these teenagers, "war was better than peace."[35] At least during captivity, they grew up with a sense of belonging, with a protective father, and with the social power and status that their father's rank within the LRA conferred. In San Miguel, the story of the teenager who wielded a machete at his little brother and who had been told by his mother to stand up for himself because he is the son of a *paraco* reminds us that status, regardless of whether it is driven by fear, can also be transmitted from parents to children. During the period of the occupation, some women in San Miguel may have recognized the potential contribution that the father could make to their children's identity in terms of positionality.

Although she was unaware of it, Clemencia had developed preeclampsia during her pregnancy. She recalls that one afternoon, she was in bed looking after her sister's newborn baby (also conceived by the paramilitary abuse she had endured, as mentioned earlier) when she started feeling dizzy and disorientated. The last thing she remembers is calling her sister because she thought that she was dying. When she regained consciousness in a hospital in Cali, she discovered that she had already given birth and was, in fact, waking up from a month of being in a coma that no one really expected her to recover from. During that month and in the weeks that followed, Clemencia's mom was by her side. Despite their difficult relationship, she stayed with Clemencia and looked after her daughter and her newborn baby in any way that she could, even begging for money in the streets so that she could buy food and medicine and pay other hospital expenses. Clemencia recalled that when she woke up, she was confused and weak, and it was not until the nurse brought the baby to her and she was able to start breastfeeding him that she felt that she was coming back to life. "Ever since then," Clemencia asserted, "I've devoted my life to him. Even more than to my other two children. Because I know that I am the only thing he has." Clemencia knows that she could have stopped the pregnancy when she had the chance; friends offered to help her, but she insists it wasn't what she wanted. Regardless of the difficulties she faced, she wanted to be a mother, and she has done her best to raise her son:

> I have not allowed anyone in my family to interfere in the upbringing of my son. I've done everything in my power, and I've used everything that I have. I've yelled, I've used my fists, I've brought down the wrath of God on people, but I have not allowed anyone to humiliate him. I don't want anyone else to come and give him orders—no, I have not allowed that. But then there he is, with only what I have been able to teach him, which is the same thing I have been taught myself, to work like an animal. That's all.

For women in contexts of war, agency is often restricted to choosing between the lesser of two evils. The same gendered notions of identity, sexuality, and reproduction that underpin practices of war-related gender-based violence, including sexual violence, also operate to blame and judge women for having endured the violence that they have experienced. In the intersection between the normalization of sexual violence during the paramilitary occupation and the naturalization of the labor of motherhood, women carry the blame imposed on them: for having "succumbed" to the paramilitaries sexually and emotionally, for having denied their children the knowledge of who their father was, and for not having been able to raise the child in accordance with the norms of the community.

CONCLUSIONS

At first glance, people born of paramilitary sexual violence are no different from other children and teenagers in San Miguel. Time and again, people in the community would tell stories about this generation of young people and children who were babies or had not been born during the paramilitary occupation—their violent behavior, their lack of values, their inability to pay attention at school, and their lack of interest in working on the land. Yet among the many grievances associated with the younger generations, some are particularly salient, as they refer to people who embody a clear trace of the long years of paramilitary confinement and the violence the community endured. To outsiders, particularly those working on gender issues within the human rights and transitional justice fields, the presence of children born of conflict-related sexual violence was revealed through the label of their biological father. The label was treated as a mark of stigma that signaled an unbreakable connection between the paramilitary and the child's identity, which doomed those children to ostracism and the perpetuation of their biological fathers' violence and deprived women of power over their sons' and daughters' identities. Over time, and with the transformation in the dynamics of war, the use and power of the label inside the community faded, and with it, the visibility of the gendered victimhood that those children embodied. However, the receding of the label does not mean that all traces of the biological fathers disappeared. Instead, it created space to see the gendered politics of reproduction that have contributed to the unintelligibility of children born of conflict-related sexual violence and to the normalization of their mother's experiences of reproductive violence.

Unlike other children born of conflict-related sexual violence around the world, in Colombia, those children are not understood as "other," as identity is transmitted by both mothers and fathers. In the context of San Miguel, the question surrounding children born of conflict-related sexual violence is not one of belonging, as in this system of transmission, the mother ensures the child's place within the community. Nonetheless, the lack of a biological father is presented as *the* issue associated with those people born of paramilitary sexual violence. Although biological fathers in the community tend to have an unreliable presence in the lives of women and children, the lack of a father is presented as both an explanation for behaviors that the community understands as unacceptable and an exoneration of their faults. Absence in relation to the biological father who was a perpetrator of all forms of violence, including sexual violence, does not necessarily refer to the paramilitary member's noninvolvement in the child's life. Although the child's belonging to the community is ensured through the maternal line, the fact that they do not have an identifiable biological father deprives people born of the paramilitary abuses of access to his web of kinship and, therefore, to the passing down of transgenerational knowledge and various types of resources. For these people, traces of the biological father do not linger in the presence and power of the label. Rather, they exist in the implications of having an absent father.

The vanishing of the label of the father freed these children from the direct and cruel associations that it implied, removing the target from their chests and the burden from their shoulders. However, it also created an illusion—the illusion that they are like any other person of the same age and that they are like any of their siblings. This illusion is very often conjured through the imposition on women to perform the labor of motherhood regardless of their own life trajectories and regardless of the dreams they had for themselves before they experienced conflict-related sexual violence and before they became forcibly pregnant and gave birth to an unwanted child, sometimes under circumstances where abortion was not an option. Women are expected to be loving and caring and to provide for their sons and daughters, often in militarized contexts of economic hardship and scarcity, while dealing with the numerous wounds that their children's biological fathers have left on their bodies and souls. Women are expected to do the reproductive work of raising their children, and no matter what difficulties they face, they will still be judged for their experiences of conflict-related sexual violence—for having endured them and for the ways they have found to cope with their outcomes. For women, the traces of their child's biological father exist in the multiple consequences that the sexual violence perpetrated by them left on their lives, including their sons and daughters who might physically resemble them and for whom they are doing the best they can despite their own life histories.

4 · MEMORIES OF ABSENCE
Collective Reparations and Impossible Witnesses

On a Sunday afternoon in July 2000, Astrid left her mom's house with the intention of going to visit a friend who was sick. The journey from Astrid's mom's house to her friend's was similar to all the other journeys people made on foot in San Miguel every day. It involved traversing dirt roads snaking across the green landscapes nestled in red-soil mountains; a scattering of rural houses with chickens, pigs, and dogs in their yards; community-constructed bamboo bridges crossing creeks; and unmarked paths weaving up and down hills through cassava, plantains, mango trees, and coffee plantations. That particular day, when Astrid started walking along these familiar paths, the forest started moving with her, as if it was slowly coming alive. She was not aware of it at first, but she could feel the trees waking up around her with her every move. It was her first encounter with the many hundreds of paramilitaries from the United Self-Defense Forces of Colombia (AUC), Calima Bloc, who, attired in green camouflage, were moving across mountains and forests, slowly making their way to the small community school to set up their base camp in San Miguel, from where they would operate to the north of Cauca for the next four years. That day, Astrid left her house and fell down a rabbit hole, only to discover that everyone she knew was falling down it with her.

For Astrid, that memory of the forest coming to life, surrounding her and marching along with her, marks the beginning of her recollections of what she experienced during the paramilitary occupation endured by the residents of San Miguel for over four years. During that time, the paramilitaries of the Calima Bloc imposed their own social order and took control over people's lives. Through the use of weapons and fear, they effected a transformation of everyday life—of the ways in which people moved around, worked on, and enjoyed their

FIGURE 4. Path by the creek, San Miguel, 2022

landscapes. People saw their neighbors and loved ones being killed, disappeared, or thrown into the Cauca River. They were tortured; dispossessed of their houses, crops, and animals; and deprived of their autonomy and joy. Children were recruited, taken out of school, and divested of their childhood games. Women were forced to cook and do laundry for the paramilitaries. They were also raped and forced into sexual encounters in exchange for food and protection from other paramilitaries. They were stripped of their independence and experienced the loss of contentment and sense of safety that they had previously enjoyed within their own houses, while walking the dirt roads they had known their whole lives, and while taking baths in the creek as they had always done, just like their mothers and grandmothers before them. The imposition of curfews, the restrictions on movement within the community and beyond its borders, and food shortages were accompanied by a transformation of the traditional practices that had been passed down from generation to generation—of familiar bodies, relationships, and landscapes. People felt enraged, lost, scared, saddened, guilty, ashamed, and helpless as a result.

This chapter addresses the struggles surrounding memories of the past and the invisible presence of people born of conflict-related sexual violence within those collective memories. It interrogates the logic and methodologies that the architecture of transitional justice has prioritized in the recollection and acknowledgment of experiences of violence and questions what happens within those negotiations when the mark of victimhood—in this case, the label *paraquitos*—has vanished. In this chapter, I argue that narratives about people born of conflict-related sexual violence inhabit the space of absence that lies in between silence, with its power to conceal, and unintelligibility, with its inability to see. Their invisible presence needs to be understood as part of the gendered system of power relations that has rendered their bodies unintelligible and, as discussed in chapter 3, normalized women's labor of motherhood. This chapter conceptualizes people born of conflict-related sexual violence as impossible witnesses: They emerged from the violent past but did not inhabit it. They cannot reconstruct, firsthand, the saga of the violence experienced by their communities or the distinct form of violence by which they became, according to the current legal framework, officially recognized as victims.

In the aftermath of the years of confinement, the inhabitants of San Miguel, both as individuals and as a community, gradually started to recover what they had lost. They drew on all the economic, spiritual, emotional, and social resources available to them to reconstruct their lives, to keep going, and to bring the community back together. As joy and hope regained their place in people's lives, grief also emerged as a new companion: grief for those aspects of life that had changed forever, for the loved ones who were never coming back, and for the dreams and futures that had been taken away from them. As explained in chapter 2, with the passage of the 2011 Victims and Land Restitution Law (hereafter Victims' Law), Colombia developed the legal framework through which to deliver integral reparations both for the individual harms people had suffered and for the collective harms that had affected entire communities. This legislation presented the inhabitants of San Miguel with the promise of symbolic and material redress for the damage they had suffered during the occupation. For San Miguel, the possibility of receiving collective reparations that could contribute to the reconstruction of the different layers of the community life that had been destroyed by the paramilitary confinement also came with expectations about what those reparations could achieve in terms of creating a better future for the community—one that was not defined by the interconnected systems of oppression that had historically marginalized them as Afro-Colombian peasants and that made the paramilitary occupation possible.

The construction of collective memories of the past through narratives about people's experiences of the period of paramilitary occupation and their memories, not only of those experiences but of how they transformed the community, were central to the heavily bureaucratized process of collective reparations. Those narratives entailed questions not only about past events that had transformed the community but also about what the community had been like before those events occurred and what kind of future people from San Miguel wanted to build. Like all narratives that invoke the past, they are constituted of both presences and absences: what is said, what is not said but can nonetheless be perceived, and what is neither said nor perceived. Thanks to the multisituated work of the diverse feminist movement in Colombia as discussed in chapter 1, women's experiences of the armed conflict have slowly gained a place in the collective memories of war in the country and the collective struggles that they represent. Women's experiences of reproductive violence, however, are yet to find a clearly defined place within those memories and struggles. Among those, attention to the motherhood that resulted from conflict-related sexual violence and the presence of people born of the abuse is yet to emerge.

COLLECTIVE REPARATIONS AND GENDER JUSTICE

The 2011 Victims' Law, which established the normative framework for the domestic reparations program, recognizes that the Colombian armed conflict has affected people at both an individual and collective level, as elucidated in chapter 2. The aim of collective reparations is to offer material, political, and symbolic reparations to collectivities for the harms that the armed conflict, according to human rights and international humanitarian law, has caused to attributes that are essential for the social and physical group's survival.[1] In that regard, in addition to establishing an integral form of redress for individuals, the law also instituted reparations for collective harms that include measures of restitution, compensation, rehabilitation, satisfaction, and guarantees of non-repetition. As is the case with individual reparations, the Unit for the Assistance and Integral Reparations of Victims (hereafter Victims' Unit or the Unit) oversees the different stages involved in the implementation of all the measures that together comprise collective reparations, starting with assessing the collectivity's testimony and ending when the implementation is complete. On the Victims' Unit website, the Collective Reparations Route is defined as "the path to heal the wounds and rebuild a productive and harmonious community life, hand in hand with the victims and with a State that can be trusted."[2]

According to the Victims' Law, this type of reparations must address harms resulting from violations of collective rights, mass violations of the individual rights of those who belong to the group, and the joint impact of the violation of individual rights. The law identifies different types of subjects of collective reparations that, due to the harms they have suffered, underwent deep transformations of the attributes that characterized them as communities, groups, or organizations.[3] The types of subjects recognized by the law are peasant communities, neighborhood communities, communities of ethnic peoples, and political and social organizations that existed before the victimizing events. The Victims' Unit also takes into account the following attributes when assessing the transformations that they have undergone: practices related to their shared life and identity, forms and means of organization and interactions both within and between the group and its environment, collective projects that have taken place across time, self-identification and recognition by others, and sociospatial relationships with a particular territory.

As is the case with individual victims, the Victims' Unit must grant collectivities victim status and include them in the Unified Registry of Victims before they can embark on the process of seeking collective reparations. There are two ways this process can be started. The first involves the state approaching the collectivity and directly offering them recognition of their victimhood. For the "inclusion by invitation," the Victims' Unit cross-referenced its mapping of victimizing events and marginalized groups across the country with armed conflict databases, reports, and academic research. The second and most common method is similar to the process that individuals follow when they request inclusion as victims in the registry, as explained in chapter 2. In this case, representatives of the collectivity must give their testimonies at the attorney general's office, the ombudsman's office, the municipal *personerías*, and when abroad, the consulates. For the purpose of testimony taking, the Victims' Unit created a standardized form, the Unified Form for Testimonies for Collective Subjects, on which the statement is recorded and then analyzed at the Unit's national level.

Once the collectivity is recognized as a victim and included in the Unified Registry of Victims, there is a five-stage process that must be followed in order to access the collective reparations.[4] The first stage, "Identification," entails the creation of baseline information about the collectivity: its main characteristics, hypotheses about the victimization, an initial assessment of the harms caused to the collectivity's attributes, and a map of relevant actors within the collectivity. During this stage, the Victims' Unit also identifies what planning tools are available to the collectivity, if any. The second stage of the process, "Preparation," follows two paths. One takes place with the collectivity and involves various meetings at which the Victims' Unit explains the process of collective reparations and answers any questions that the collectivity might have. The second path involves the Victims' Unit informing relevant public and private institutions about the early stages of the process of collective reparations. For communities of Afro-Colombian and Indigenous peoples, this stage includes initiating a prior consultation with the community and its highest governing bodies to define and delineate the subsequent stages of the collective reparations process. The third stage, "Assessment and Characterization of Harms," entails identifying in detail the harms caused to the attributes of the collectivity. During the fourth stage, "Formulation of the Comprehensive Plan for Collective Reparations (PIRC)," the Victims' Unit and representatives of the collectivity define the specific actions to be taken for each of the measures of reparation that are going to be implemented and set out a schedule for them. The fifth and last stage, "PIRC Implementation," refers to the execution of the actions agreed upon within three years after the approval of the PIRC.

The community of San Miguel embarked on the process of collective reparations by invitation. "The story of San Miguel started in August 2012," recalled Liliana, who was then a social worker for the Victims' Unit and led the process of implementing collective reparations with the community in the first few years. By the time I interviewed her in 2016, Liliana had left the Victims' Unit but remained as a referent for people in San Miguel who spoke of her with deep gratitude for her commitment to the community and the process. She explained how the work with the community began. When the Victims' Unit's regional office opened in the department of Cauca in June 2012 and the process of identifying potential cases for collective reparations started, the municipality of Buenos Aries, where San Miguel is located, was quickly put on the agenda because there had been a previous attempt at conducting a process of collective reparation there by the National Commission of Reparation and Reconciliation (CNRR).

The CNRR, which was a body created under the 2005 legal framework for the demobilization of paramilitaries, among its many and varied functions, sought to guarantee victims' participation in the transitional justice mechanisms that were available at the time, produce truth narratives about the armed conflict, and oversee the demobilization process. When the 2011 Victims' Law replaced the CNRR with other agencies, including the Victims' Unit and the National Center of Historic Memory, the CNRR had already conducted seven pilot processes of collective reparations across the country. Among those, the municipality of Buenos Aires was the only one to take place in the department of Cauca and had been unsuccessful. As Liliana explained, "The CNRR tried to do the collective reparations process with the whole municipality, which is not only massive but . . . also extremely diverse in terms of ethnic populations, types of victimizations, and landscapes. That was a very long process that didn't have a happy ending because it was too ambitious."

Having learned from the experience of the CNRR, the Victims' Unit in Cauca approached the municipality with the intention of focalizing its actions. Through the mapping process of the dynamics and impacts of the armed conflict, they identified that the whole municipality had been affected, and accounts of forced displacement, selective killings, disappearances, and torture were widespread. However, in terms of more defined collectivities, there were two that had what could be described as clearer boundaries. The first refers to the massacre perpetrated by paramilitaries in 2001 in the region known as Alto Naya, which has gained a place in the country's collective reconstructions of the armed conflict, including some visibility outside the region via national journalistic and academic reports. On April 10–13, 2001, during Easter week, a group of five hundred paramilitaries from the Calima Bloc marched to the Naya region from Timba, burning down houses; torturing and killing over 100 people, mainly Afro-Colombians and Nasa Indigenous people; and displacing around 3,500 people.[5] The second involves the area of La Balsa, one of the seven administrative divisions of the municipality of Buenos Aires. When the Victims' Unit started mapping the armed conflict's dynamics in Buenos Aires, they discovered that the area of La Balsa had endured the strongest sustained presence of paramilitaries between the late 1990s and the demobilization of the Calima Bloc in December 2004. However, Liliana explained that although the area of La Balsa implied certain delimitations—as it was, for example, mostly inhabited by Afro-Colombians—it was still too geographically large to be treated as one unit, being composed of five different rural communities scattered along the Cauca River valley and up the mountainside.

The strategy pursued by the Victims' Unit was to keep mapping within the region of La Balsa. In alliance with women's organizations from Buenos Aires, in August 2012, the Victims' Unit organized an in situ event whereby people from all five communities could come and talk about their experiences. "The idea was not to take new testimonies but to understand in more detail what kind of victimizing events had occurred in La Balsa and where exactly those people were," explained Liliana. It was at that event that the team from the Victims' Unit first began to hear about women's experiences of sexual violence. Talking to women and checking the individual cases within the Unified Registry of Victims, Liliana and the other people working in the Victims' Unit's collective reparations team realized that a lot of women who were already registered as victims of forced displacement were also victims of war-related sexual violence and that many of them came from San Miguel. "Talking to people that day," Liliana recalled, "we realized that there was a high rate of women who were victims of sexual violence in the area. And when we kept asking, we realized that many of those cases came from San Miguel. So we said, 'We have to go to San Miguel.' It was because of the women that we arrived in San Miguel."

Subsequently, in December 2012, the two-person team from the Victims' Unit—Liliana as the leader and a psychologist—that would be in charge of the process of collective reparations with the community organized a three-day visit to San Miguel. The idea was to form a clearer picture of the specific experience of the community during the years of confinement and, of utmost importance, to start building trust with people, especially given that the main state presence they were historically familiar with manifested as inadequate infrastructure and a lack of health centers, schools, drinking water, and electricity. The three-day visit was informal in nature: the duo from the Victims' Unit sat outside Clemencia's house, as she was very active and outspoken in the interactions that led to the process of obtaining collective reparations, wearing their institutional vests and speaking to everyone who wanted to talk. Liliana explained, "There is no other way of building trust with people but to be *there*, listening with genuine interest and respect. And for people, it was the first time they could relate to the state in that way. Also, [with] my own ethnic identity, as a Black woman myself, people knew they could trust me. You trust people from your own community."

In this way, by talking to person after person, Liliana and her psychologist colleague started to gain a better understanding of what had happened in the community during the years of paramilitary confinement. They realized that in San Miguel, there was a huge underreporting of individual victimizing events within the Unified Registry of Victims, as the people who were already in the registry were included under the categories of forced displacement or the killing of a loved one. This initial flurry of activity culminated in a two-day event in February 2013, when the ombudsman's office visited the community to take individual testimonies in response to people's requests to be included as victims. Liliana recalled with pride,

> That's how everything started. By gaining their trust. People saw that in a very short time, something had happened; we arrived in August 2012, and in February 2013, we had made the testimony-taking event possible, and we, as the state, went there, to their own community. We also gained their trust because we believed them, because we said, "What happened to you as individuals and as a community should never have happened." That was essential for women who suffered sexual violence, many of whom had given birth to children and didn't know that they had the right to reparations, to receive psychosocial care.

During the early stages of the collective reparations process, things moved swiftly, and women from San Miguel and La Balsa and the Victims' Unit itself became driving forces. This was the case until it ceased to be. The Victims' Unit invited the inhabitants of San Miguel to start the process of collective reparations in August 2012, an invitation that was accepted by the community on the seventeenth of that same month, represented by San Miguel's *junta de acción comunal* (community action board). In Colombia, community action boards are legally recognized forms of nonprofit organizations based on solidarity and democratic participation and organized by social groups, such as small communities and neighborhoods, for the purpose of internal management. After the invitation had been accepted, on October 14, 2013, Astrid, then spokeswoman for San Miguel as president of the community action board, delivered the testimony that was necessary for them to be included in the Unified Registry of Victims. San Miguel was officially included in the registry on February 25, 2014, which is when the Victims' Unit issued the legal resolution that recognized San

Miguel's victimhood status and marked the formal beginning of the collective reparations process. On August 27, 2014, however, the statement was required to be updated, and Astrid had to testify again, this time in Bogotá and in the midst of increasing tensions within the community.

During those first few years of interactions, advocacy, and negotiations that preceded the process of collective reparations, the Victims' Unit worked closely with the community action board to gain trust and move the process forward, thanks in no small part to women like Astrid and Clemencia. As a result of many months of hard, unpaid labor, San Miguel managed the process of working toward its inclusion in the Unified Registry of Victims as a peasant community. With regard to the collective reparations process, its inclusion as such meant that there was no need for a prior consultation, because this is only required when the collectivity makes a request to be included as an *ethnic* subject of collective reparations. The other significant difference is that in the case of ethnic subjects of collective reparations, negotiations between the collectivity and the Victims' Unit must take place directly with the highest legitimate and legal authority, according to each ethnic group's self-governance systems. In the case of Afro-Colombian communities, the relevant bodies are *consejos comunitarios* (community councils), created under Law 70 of 1993, which is the legal framework that recognizes the rights of Afro-Colombian communities as peoples and sees that their cultural identity is rooted in the collective ownership of the land they have historically inhabited based on traditional sociocultural practices.

Each council comprises several Afro-Colombian communities that have traditionally shared the same territories. Among their functions, community councils must preserve Afro-Colombian cultural identity and oversee the coordination, economic management, and internal administration of their collective lands according to their self-governance system. Together with six other communities, San Miguel belongs to the Community Council of the Cauca River Basin and Micro-basin of the Teta and Mazamorrero Rivers. However, in the case of San Miguel, the community council had little, if any, real presence in the community; during the initial negotiations that formed part of the collective reparations process, no one in San Miguel seemed to be aware that they were part of a community council. Historically, San Miguel had used the organizational form of a community action board. This means not that San Miguel did not identify itself as an Afro-Colombian community, because it did, but simply that it did not regard itself as belonging to the community council.

Both Law 70 of 1993 and the establishment of community councils are the results of Afro-Colombian people's historical struggles against the colonial violence and state discrimination that have systematically denied them their rights, collective identity, and self-governance systems. However, after decades of armed conflict and state violence, many Afro-Colombian self-governance and collective systems across the country had become fragmented. The case of San Miguel and its membership of the Community Council of the Cauca River Basin and Micro-basin of the Teta and Mazamorrero Rivers reflects this situation. During the early years of negotiations with the Victims' Unit, this community council, as a legitimate authority within the Afro-Colombian community's self-governance system, was still taking shape, discovering where its own boundaries lay, and understanding its potential and its political power, but it was also asserting itself with the communities that were members of the council. The new resolution that included San Miguel in the Unified Registry of Victims as an ethnic subject of collective reparation was issued on March 3, 2015. In the meantime, the collective reparations process had been put on hold, and the community found itself torn between two different local authorities who were disputing leadership of the aforementioned reparations process, and the Victims' Unit had to negotiate with both of them.

"Where were they [the leadership of the community council] when we were going through hell [during the paramilitary confinement], when we women were quietly enduring everything they [the paramilitaries] imposed on us? But now they [the leadership of the community council] come here and want to impose their terms and dictate the course of the reparations!" a woman from the community action board remarked to me, the deep frustration evident in her voice, after a meeting with the Victims' Unit in San Miguel. When I arrived in San Miguel in early 2016, everyone in the community was talking excitedly about the resumption of the collective reparations process. After the initial momentum of the early years, during which time women's experiences and their leadership were significant forces, the process was adjourned for more than a year. "Why was the collective reparations process stopped after all that hard work people talk about?" I asked Liliana.

"I'll tell you why," she replied with a sly smile. She then continued,

When we arrived in San Miguel, we knew that they were a Black community, but nobody knew that they belonged to a community council. Time went by, and in a meeting of the departmental Victims' Committee, someone complained to us that we were carrying out a collective reparations process without consulting the relevant ethnic authority. In that meeting with the Victims' Committee, I met Hector [the representative of the community council], who was also new because the community council had been inactive. We were more active than they were! And people took a long time to recognize them as their authority. And then, when we started to work with Hector, we found out that this community council also included Lomitas Norte and Sur, which were going through their own processes of collective reparations, but unlike San Miguel, everything had moved slowly there. And the community council wanted to stop the San

Miguel process in order to be able to combine all these processes together. We had to stop everything and start from the beginning!

During the time that the collective reparations process was suspended, some changes occurred. When the process resumed, the highest authority that represented the community was the community council, and all the negotiations regarding the collective reparations had to go through this body. The community action board, however, had managed to assert some level of power over the process, mostly based on its legitimacy within the community. For example, as previously mentioned, it was Astrid, then the president of the board, who delivered the statement updating the community's status from that of subject of collective reparation to ethnic subject of collective reparation in the Unified Registry of Victims. The day that the community's testimony was updated is often described—mostly by people who had actively participated in the initial stages of the process with the Victims' Unit and who belonged to the community action board—in epic terms: "The day in Bogotá when Astrid and Clemencia fought Hector and stood up for the community!" In 2016, however, Astrid lost her position as president of the community action board, and the community elected Gabriel, a man who was a member of the community council and more closely aligned with the new power dynamics. Liliana was no longer working at the Victims' Unit, and the process was now the responsibility of Carmen, a mestiza who had lots of experience working with peasant communities and Indigenous peoples but was not familiar with this part of Cauca. She had to legitimize herself in the eyes of the council and the action board in order to be able to negotiate with both and learn about the community's experience of occupation and regain its trust after the initial momentum had been lost.

The women in San Miguel who actively participated in the early years of work with the Victims' Unit did not belong to local, national, or international women's organizations and did not self-identify with feminist agendas. However, almost unknowingly, they were advancing issues of gender justice. Through her research on high-risk feminism in Colombia, Julia Zulver shows that when women mobilize and raise their voices to make the different forms of violence they experience visible, when they reject and denounce impunity in contexts of war and political transition, and when they demand truth, justice, and redress, they are blamed and targeted with violence for committing a double transgression: speaking out against violence (regardless of whether that violence is perpetrated by armed groups or not) and challenging patriarchal gender roles.[6]

After the tensions developed between the community council and the community action board, Astrid, Clemencia, and some of the other women who had been active and outspoken were slowly pushed aside, ostracized, and excluded from the process of implementing collective reparations. They grew tired of fighting and of being called "difficult" and "rude." However, during the initial years of working with the Victims' Unit, these women advanced issues of gender justice; they attempted to organize actions and employ strategies designed to render visible what they, as women, had lived through during the years of the paramilitary confinement and to lift the veil of normalization that had been imposed on many of those experiences—in particular, the various forms of sexual violence they had endured, as explored in chapter 3. They worked not only to ensure that those experiences were included in the process of collective reparations but also to use collective reparations as a platform from which to subvert the power relations that had historically oppressed San Miguel as an Afro-Colombian peasant community.

The conditions in San Miguel during both the paramilitary occupation and its aftermath were not conducive to women's collective mobilization. Speaking about her research, Zulver identifies some of these conditions as the presence of a charismatic leader, knowing that not acting won't guarantee safety but that acting might bring about transformation, and the production of a sense of belonging—a collective identity that extends beyond coming from the same place—based on solidarity and agency.[7] Throughout the period during which I visited and worked with the community, I have heard women—and not only those who were leading forces during the early years of the quest for collective reparations—talking about how difficult it is for women to organize within the community: "There is a lot of mistrust among us. There is a lot of gossip," some of them claim. Rosa, one of the women I have known for a long time, once told me with some regret, "Back then [during the paramilitary confinement], we were scared, and we felt ashamed of what we were going through. I see now that we pointed at one another. Maybe because we felt that if we pointed at someone else, people wouldn't know we were going through the same? Silly us, because everyone knew anyway. I feel that we should be able to trust one another because we are going through the same thing, but sometimes it seems to be the opposite. I don't know why. I wish we could work together."

The gender justice work of women like Astrid and Clemencia also needs to be understood historically. They may not have been able to create a collective and sustained form of mobilization during the paramilitary occupation or to challenge the new power dynamics brought about by the community council, but they contributed to making visible the different forms of gender-based violence that they, as women, have experienced not only at the hands of armed groups but also at the hands of their neighbors and relatives. They also opened cracks in patriarchal power relations to allow younger generations of women and girls to play active roles in the political life of the community, work they continue to undertake despite the obstacles and adversity they face. As I have observed the spaces in which the decision-making surrounding the process of implementing collective reparations takes place, it has become apparent that although those spaces remain masculine in terms of their leadership, young women and girls have progressively gained ground there—not just by signing attendance sheets but by raising issues of gender-based violence and rewriting agendas.

I have also observed that nowadays, young women and girls tend to be more active than young men in other political scenarios beyond the process of collective reparations. For example, they are becoming involved in municipal youth networks and committees, and they actively participate in training workshops and art-based projects within the community and with other communities. In these contexts, they actively position themselves as young, rural, Afro-Colombian women raising concerns relating to San Miguel and its future as a peasant Afro-Colombian community living in a militarized context and questioning the neoliberal policies that threaten their traditional agricultural practices and continue to cause ecological devastation. Although this is not something I have researched in depth, my perception is that young women and girls are more willing to work together, to trust one another, and to talk and act in solidarity.

COLLECTIVE MEMORIES

When I arrived in San Miguel in early 2016, the collective reparations process was progressing to its third stage: "Assessment and Characterization of Harms." Although the situation had become more settled with regard to the community action board and the community council, some tension between them remained, and the council was still trying to legitimize itself within the community. Carmen, as the newly appointed leader of the process from within the Victims' Unit, was negotiating with both bodies to establish the prior consultation that would allow them to carry out the "Assessment and Characterization of Harms" before moving on to the fourth stage, formulating the PIRC. Through conversations with Astrid, who was president of the community action board at that time; Carmen; and the Collective Reparations Support Group, a volunteer group of people from the community whose job was to support and monitor the development of the collective reparations process, it was agreed that I would draft a document that, eventually, could contribute to the characterization of harms. It was envisaged that after approving the document, the community would present it to the Victims' Unit. Although the document was not part of the official process, which could not proceed until prior consultation had been established and had to be led by the Victims' Unit with the community's full participation, they thought it could help trigger conversations within San Miguel about what the inhabitants had lived through and how the years of paramilitary confinement had affected them—in other words, to start working toward the construction of collective memories of the paramilitary confinement that San Miguel had endured.

With Astrid and members of the support group, it was agreed that I would base the document on four types of sources: secondary literature about the history of San Miguel and the dynamics of the armed conflict in that part of the country, individual interviews with people from the community, social cartography sessions held with groups of men and women separately, and the 2015 resolution issued by the Victims' Unit that recognized San Miguel as an ethnic subject of collective reparation. The resolution, for its part, translated Astrid's testimony into the legal terminology of the Victims' Law. It stated that at the individual level, people had experienced slavery, extrajudicial killings, raids, threats, crimes against personal freedom and integrity (sexual violence), forced displacement, personal injuries, discrimination, torture, recruitment, and arbitrary detention. As a means of creating a context in which to locate Astrid's testimony within a broader network, the resolution drew on academic and journalistic research to reconstruct the dynamics of the armed conflict in Buenos Aires. However, the purpose of that exercise was to validate the testimony and the recognition of San Miguel's victimhood status. The process through which the community had to collectively produce narratives of its past and, based on those, negotiate measures of reparation with the Victims' Unit that could transform their future was yet to take place.

Elizabeth Jelin conceptualizes collective memories as subjective processes that are the constant objects of interpretation and struggle.[8] It is people, in this context, who imbue the past with meaning, but that meaning cannot be understood outside of the power relations in which people's actions take place in the present. Memories, Jelin claims, must be examined historically, in the sense that meanings of the past change according to broader social and political scenarios, and because the place allocated to specific memories or narratives of memories is constantly being negotiated through sociocultural and ideological elements. According to Maurice Halbwachs, individual memories are always socially reconstructed within specific networks of social relations and cannot be understood outside of these.[9] People's recollections and silences are shaped by the social frameworks to which they belong—including family, religion, rurality, ethnicity, and social class—and it is precisely within those frameworks that memories become the objects of labor and are suffused with meaning.

Collective memories of the past are anchored in people's experiences and in material markers. In the case of San Miguel, some of them recall specific events, while others refer to patterns of violence that reshaped the everyday lives of its inhabitants during the period of paramilitary occupation.[10] When talking about this time, people frequently refer to the story of the young man who was killed because when he was asked to play a song at a party, he did not do so fast enough, or the day of *la balacera* (the shooting) when a group of guerrillas tried to ambush a paramilitary unit that was patrolling the area, resulting in a confrontation between the two groups positioned on opposite hills, which, in what people describe as a miracle, did not kill anyone from the community in the cross fire. "That day, my aunt tried to hide under her bed, but she didn't fit," recalled the youngest of the eight men who participated in one of the social cartography sessions Astrid and I had organized. At this revelation, everyone present laughed nervously. Within the almost four years of paramilitary occupation, those events—which occurred during the early stages of the paramilitary presence—occupy a distinctive place in people's active recollections.

There are other markers that are not characterized by the same type of discernible boundaries yet have nonetheless gained a place in people's memories because they did not simply disrupt the everyday life of the community but became the norm. Curfews, checkpoints, the destruction of crops, difficulties obtaining food and medicines, and having to leave the doors of their houses open for paramilitaries to come in and help themselves to everything and everyone inside are commonly referred to when people talk about that aspect of the past. "We were prisoners—prisoners in our own land," people would often remark. The school, one of the primary meeting places for this scattered, rural community, was transformed into a military storage and training center. From the first day of confinement, the paramilitaries assumed control of the school, daubing the acronym *AUC* for Autodefensas Unidas de Colombia on the walls, storing their weapons and supplies in the three classrooms, sleeping in the corridors, performing military exercises on the premises, loitering around armed with their weapons, and forcing teachers and children to become part of the social order they imposed. A disproportionately large tiger sitting outside the school: that was how a group of women represented the paramilitary occupation of the school during one of the social cartography sessions.

Within that world, time and timelines had their own rules and pace; recollections of the moment when the paramilitaries arrived are easily defined, and like Astrid's account of the forest coming to life, everyone has their own stories of their first interactions with the paramilitaries who were heading toward the rural school in San Miguel. However, the same is not true of the moment when the occupation ended. This is partly because the paramilitaries did not all retreat at the same time but maintained a constant—although much less dominant—presence in the area even after their demobilization in December 2004. Some narratives even mention their return in 2010 to collect weapons and money that they had hidden, and there are always whispers of people having seen *them*—described as an anonymous collective presence—in nearby towns. The perception of time and the blurriness that characterizes people's memories of the paramilitary occupation and the events that took place after demobilization, however, are also shaped by the different ways in which that lived reality of the past, through traces that remain in the social and material landscape, inhabits the present. During one of the social cartography sessions we held with the women, Doña Miriam declared, "It really was like a nightmare." While briefly averting her gaze, she added, "Sometimes it feels like we are still living in it."

"What happened after they [the paramilitaries] arrived?" I asked the eight men in the social cartography session.

"El terror, muchacha. La incógnita," said Don Efraín. The terror, the unknown. The constitution of the everyday reality of violence that people experienced for approximately four years, with its accompanying events that disrupted the ordinary; its new dynamics that did not have a place within people's universe of meaning; and the state violence manifested in the intentional negligence of a government that was supposed to protect them and yet was conveniently absent, appeared—suddenly and unexpectedly—as a different world from the one they grew up in. The contradiction between living in their familiar landscapes and yet not being able to fully apprehend them created a world whose boundaries were blurred and perceived as surreal—yet with very real consequences. As such, the occupation is often described as a bad dream, one that lasted for years. "It was like having a nightmare," Don Efraín continued, "but instead of waking up, we were living in it."

THE GENDERED POLITICS OF MEMORY

"We are going to need more paper, colors, and markers," Astrid observed as we were planning the social cartography sessions with the women of the community. She expected the women to be more receptive to our invitation and felt that the men might be reluctant to join the conversation we were proposing. Astrid's understanding of the social dynamics of the community was, as always, confirmed by people's responses to the invitation, and while in the women's case, we were able to work on four different maps, with the men, we worked on just one. Consistent with the literature on the gendered dynamics of testimony, this was not, however, the only difference we encountered in the social negotiations that people engage in when bringing their experiences of the past into the present.[11] Producing those maps reflected the gendered politics of testimony and the labor of memories through which narratives of people's experiences intrude upon the present in the shape of both words and the absence of them.

Questions about the purpose of remembering were repeatedly raised among the women as a reminder of the blurred relationship between the past, present, and future. "Why do we want to remember that?" Doña Teresa asked the other women in her group rhetorically. "We could have drawn something else. What's the point of going back over the past?" None of the five women replied to Doña

Teresa. Briefly, they directed their gaze toward the social cartography map with the drawings that Doña Rosa had been using, a moment ago, to narrate the story of her pregnant daughter and how she had killed herself by drinking a bottle of aguardiente—a strong, sugarcane-based alcoholic drink—and swallowing pills after the paramilitaries had killed her partner. "We didn't make it to the hospital; she died on my lap," Doña Rosa had just told us when Doña Teresa pointed out the blurred relationship between past and present. One of the younger women in the group then turned to me and whispered, "There is a lot of fear among us. Here, we don't speak; we don't know if those people are coming back."

In the women's negotiations about what to include in the narratives they were weaving together and how to do so, what mattered to them was the experience of San Miguel as a community. That is not to say they did not share personal stories, but those personal stories were always framed within the context of broader common experiences. Women, for instance, often started conversations with questions about the collective time frame they wanted to represent, such as "When did they [the paramilitaries] arrive at the school?" "When did *our* nightmare start?" "When did it end?" and "Has it ended?" At the center of their maps, often occupying a significant area of the piece of paper, the school was presented as the heart of their narratives, like the dark heart of the regime of terror they endured, which had disrupted everything and imposed a new social order. In all of the maps that the women produced in the cartography sessions, they drew a frame of little men, one after the other, very close to the edge of the paper, as if they were hoping that these men would fall off the page and somehow disappear from their memories, from their bodies, and from their nightmares.

The men, for their part, briefly addressed the question of why they should remember the past at the beginning of the session but then did not return to it.

"Why do we want to remember? Even if it's painful?" Don Gabriel asked the other men in the group.

"So that we can receive reparations for all the detriment that we experienced during the time those people stayed here," answered Don Efraín, and they all nodded in agreement. The men's conversations included the language of transitional justice: harms, accountability, redress, and state obligations. Although there were several pieces of paper available for the eight men who participated to use, they all sat together with one sheet of paper. First, they used a ruler to divide the paper into eight sections—four along each side with a gap down the middle between them. Each of the men drew a separate representation of their own personal story. Jorge, the youngest man in the group, just a kid back then, whose dog was stabbed and left to die, recalled, "The day after [paramilitaries stabbed the dog], my dad found it; it was still alive. My dad brought some medicines and healed the wounds. The dog survived eighteen stab wounds."

FIGURE 5. Detail from men's social cartography, San Miguel, 2016

"This is real; this is all real," Jorge noted as he pointed to the different parts of his drawing: his bleeding dog, a dead body left close to the family home, and paramilitaries watching TV in their living room.

In the construction of the social cartography produced by the men, they placed their personal experiences at the center, and it was through the narratives of their individual stories that they found common ground regarding the years when people had to stop growing their crops on the paramilitaries' orders, endured hunger, and checkpoints became part of the everyday militarized landscape as sites of torture. During that time, paramilitary and state violence were essentially one and the same. Don Efraín remembered, "One day I asked a cop in Santander [de Quilichao] what could one do, as a civilian, in an area where there were *paracos* [slang for paramilitaries]. 'Treat them nicely,' he advised. We were prisoners, and it was a very difficult prison because no visitors were allowed, not even if they were your children who lived outside San Miguel. Not even for funerals."

The women who accepted our invitation to explore the cartography of their collective stories embodied different experiences of the paramilitary occupation and what had happened since then. They all, however, experienced the constant threat posed by the omnipotent presence of paramilitaries and their gendered logic of social control. Carmen, who was a teenager during that time and one of the many students who were forced to drop out of school and stay at home with her parents—who were attempting to keep her as safe as possible from the repertoires of paramilitary violence—pointed at the drawing of one of the houses and explained the following while the other women nodded in agreement: "We had to live together with the fear and with them [paramilitaries]. They made you leave the door of your house open so that they could sleep inside. There was nothing we could tell them. How could we have dared to tell them otherwise? We had to cook for them and wash their clothes. They were among our crops, in the forest, in the creek where we fished and took baths, on the paths and roads around every corner. According to the will of Lord Jesus Christ, whatever they said was what happened."

Among all the experiences of gender-based violence, different forms of sexual violence—and the constant threat of them—became part of everyday life for women, as explained in chapter 3. In the context of the social cartography sessions, however, the women decided not to map those experiences. By contrast, stories about their experiences of sexual violence had become part of other people's narratives of San Miguel, and they played a part in negotiating the community's process of seeking collective reparations. By the time the social cartography sessions were held, most of the women from the community had already given their testimonies—many of them more than once—and had been included in the Unified Registry of Victims. Those who endured sexual violence had been asked to talk about their specific experiences in front of statement takers, psychologists, social workers, lawyers, and even perpetrators during a hearing on sexual violence that formed part of the Justice and Peace Law paramilitary hearings. On the one hand, informed by this context, the years following the implementation of the Victims' Law prioritized actions toward women and what was understood to be the particular harm they had suffered: sexual violence. Thus, many women in San Miguel, as was the case for numerous women across the country, had their compensation expedited. However, this also implied that women were being dragged into the victimhood system, characterized by its overbearing bureaucracy, endless form filling, and power to fragment people's identities. But women were not the only ones who were talking about those fragments of their stories. In the case of San Miguel, women's stories of sexual violence became central to the process of collective reparations and the negotiations with the Victims' Unit; this also meant that other people, such as members of the community council, assumed some form of ownership over the women's stories and experiences.

Transitional justice frameworks often view silence as an obstacle to redressing experiences of mass violence, and it is assumed that there is a moral and political responsibility on the part of institutions and people working in armed conflict–related fields to "break" that silence.[12] However, silence, understood as a historical and cultural artifact with its own boundaries and content, serves to unveil the different forms that memories may assume in the present and under particular circumstances.[13] As there is no universal form of silence, its content reveals the social negotiations that take place within people's universe of meanings. In this sense, for instance, Lawrence Langer argues that silence can emerge in the absence of words to express that which is senseless, as some forms of violence are unrepresentable through language.[14] Veena Das argues that silence can also represent agency via an active attempt to deny certain experiences an existence through words.[15] In women's accounts of their experiences during regimes of violence and oppression, Fiona Ross notes, silence is in itself a form of language that does not necessarily need to be translated into words but has meaning within its own historical, cultural, and political context.[16] The women of San Miguel who participated in the social cartography sessions did not narrate stories of sexual violence. This does not mean, however, that they concealed their specific gendered experiences of violence as women, as they did in fact share stories in which it was precisely the reproduction of patriarchal gender roles that made brutality toward them by the paramilitaries possible and, as discussed in chapter 3, often not understood as violence.

Following Ross's research on the South African Truth and Reconciliation Commission, the active search by transitional justice mechanisms for women's testimonies about sexual violence has disregarded other dynamics of gender-based violence that are also present in these testimonies.[17] In the case of South Africa, Ross argues that women testified about how the apartheid system imposed violence upon domestic life and families, intergenerational relations, and gender roles. Building on this point in her research about the Peruvian Truth and Reconciliation Commission, Kimberly Theidon argues that by pursuing stories of sexual violence, the commission produced other forms of silence that disregarded the gendered dimension of war. "There is a bit of irony," Theidon notes, in that "commissions are tasked with investigating the truth, and yet the broader truths that women narrated were too frequently reduced to the sexual harm they had experienced."[18] The types of logic and techniques that sought to address women's experiences of war obscured the nonsexual forms of violence that women endured as well as women's narratives about their struggles to survive and resist. At the same time, those systems of extraction created other forms of violence by focusing on "breaking the silences" that could reveal specific stories of sexual violence. In her work, Theidon invites us to ask, Why is there an expectation that women will come forward and narrate their stories of sexual violence even when they have chosen not to? Why does the right to reparations impose an obligation to speak?[19]

The presence of silence questions the forms of logic and techniques that have predominantly been used within the academic and policy-oriented fields that seek to address mass violence, trauma, and suffering in war contexts. Although "giving voice" to survivors of those experiences and rendering their testimonies visible have been presented as attempts to challenge the power structures that oppressed victims, the institutionalized use of this kind of testimonies has also placed the burden of bringing the past into the present on those who survived while at the same time tending to ignore the unnameable layers of the experiences of violence.[20] In San Miguel, among the women who participated in the social cartography sessions were mothers and other relatives of children and young women and men born of paramilitary sexual violence. The women knew about my academic research that sought to understand the production of narratives about their children and also that I was writing a document that could potentially contribute to the collective reparations as well as to measures that would help their sons and daughters. And yet during the first few months of 2016 in which we held the social cartography sessions, conducted interviews, and shared long walks, they never once mentioned to me their children as being born of their experiences of sexual violence. Silence has its own meaning and is part of the labor of memories and the agency of women who are constantly negotiating their experiences of the past in relation to their present and future.

I can only conjecture about why, in that moment, they did not share with me that aspect of their experiences. Fear, self-protection through silence, and a lack of trust in me, in the process of collective reparations, and in the state's promises that had repeatedly failed them are, of course, all plausible explanations. It is also possible that the categories through which my research and the 2011 Victims' Law have sought to understand the experiences of these women and their children born of conflict-related sexual violence do not fully represent them. When women's agency has been restricted to choosing between the lesser of two evils, as explained in chapter 3, I suggest that their agency over their bodies, their sexuality, and their reproductive lives can also take the guise of refusing to name their experiences as sexual and reproductive violence or their children as victims.

As discussed in chapters 2 and 3, women have been assigned the responsibility of including their sons and daughters in the Unified Registry of Victims. Through their own testimonies of war-related sexual violence, women must explicitly express the wish for their sons and daughters born of the abuse to be recognized as victims too. Doing so involves overcoming the various physical, emotional, and mental scars that sexual violence has left on their lives, piecing together the requisite information that they need to understand to advance their children's access to reparations, and navigating the convoluted and often revictimizing bureaucracies of redress. It also entails the enormous emotional burden of negotiating with themselves in relation to what information they want their children to have about their own stories of sexual violence and who the child's biological father is, what information they themselves actually have and remember, and what they feel they can share with their children. Women's silence and issues of disclosure have been at the heart of the Victims' Unit's discussions about how to guarantee the right to reparations to children born of conflict-related sexual violence for a considerable time. In a 2016 interview with Diana Tamayo, then head of the Victims' Unit team for Gender and Differential Approaches in the Directorate of Reparations, she referred to this situation when talking about the issues faced by the Victims' Unit regarding the inclusion of children born of conflict-related sexual violence in the Unified Registry of Victims, discussed in chapter 2:

> We asked ourselves why, up to 2015, there haven't been any cases of children and young women and men born of wartime sexual violence being discussed in the Directorate of Reparations? What we realized later is that there were some cases, but those few cases had been stored in a separate database, and the area in charge of gathering the information did not know what to do with those. Because in their testimonies women say, "My son or my daughter was born of what happened to me, but they are never going to find out. I do not want them to find out." What do we do? Do we include that child or not? Because his or her mom explicitly says that she doesn't want the child to find out. And if I include the child, how do I do it without going against the will of the mother?[21]

"Can I ask how you told your sons?" I asked Clemencia and Gloria one afternoon in September 2021, after I had known them for several years, had witnessed their struggles to obtain reparations for their sons, and had even been introduced by them to their sons as someone who cared about them receiving the reparations to which they were entitled.

"Ha! I haven't," replied Clemencia, widening her eyes.

"Me neither. It's too hard!" exclaimed Gloria, knocking on the table, which is something we Colombians do to avoid bad luck or to conjure good luck.

"I'm curious now. What do your sons think their reparations are related to?" I asked.

"To be honest," replied Clemencia, "I have no idea! I've never talked about that part with him. All I've said is that he has the right to reparations."

"So what do they know?" I asked.

"That's what I'd like to know!" said Gloria.

"I've thought about that question for a long time, and I'm certain that they know," noted Clemencia, emphasizing the word *know*. She elaborated further:

They know what people have told them. I've always been scared of telling him because I don't know how he will react. I'm not afraid of losing him because I've been both mom and dad to him and we're close. But I don't know how he'll deal with that story. I don't know what kind of person he'll become after that conversation. I don't feel that I can tell him what I've lived. But he knows—because of what people have told him and because he has a *vacío*, an emptiness. As a mother, I don't know what knowledge he has, what he thinks. But I know that he *knows*.

In San Miguel and the surrounding communities, women have taken different paths with regard to disclosing their experiences of conflict-related sexual violence to their children conceived by the paramilitary abuse. Some women chose to share their stories with their children early on in their lives. One woman told me that she had found the strength she needed to tell her daughter in the arms of Jesus Christ: "The Lord gave me the strength I needed. My daughter knows; I told her when she was a child. Sometimes she even says that she'd like to meet him [her biological father]. I told her because it was too heavy a burden to carry, and I already carry a lot." Some women, like Clemencia and Gloria, have not told their sons and daughters because they want to protect them—from themselves, from the information, but also from the potential danger posed by the child's biological father. One woman told me, "I've never lived with him [her son]. I sent him to live with my mom, because what if he [the perpetrator] comes back looking for us? I don't want him to find my son. When my son asks about his dad, all I tell him is that he doesn't have a dad. And then my son *understands*; he sees that that question affects me deeply. I cry and the *sentimiento me agarra* [the feeling grabs me], and he stops asking. I wish I could do something else for him [her son]." Many of those women who haven't talked to their children about their fathers seem to have in common the belief that their sons and daughters already *know* and that they wish they had the necessary support and tools available to lift that burden from their shoulders, both for themselves and for their children.

Dipali Anumol and Samuel Munderere talk about the devastating effects of forced disclosure based on Munderere's work at Survivor's Fund with survivors of sexual violence perpetrated during the Rwandan genocide and their sons and daughters born as a consequence of what they lived through. In Rwanda, in order for children to be registered and obtain not only a national ID but access to other rights such as education, they are required to know and disclose the name of their father. For single mothers and their children, this is problematic and results in a series of cultural and political harms as they have to navigate the implications of often being unable to provide a name. In the case of women who are victims of rape perpetrated during the genocide, the implications are even worse, as in addition to all the physical, mental, emotional, and social consequences of what they have endured, they are also pushed into a situation that compels them to talk to their children about the reasons behind them not having a father. Often without any kind of psychosocial and emotional preparation and support for women or their children available, this forced disclosure adds more layers of distress to the mother and her child and may jeopardize or damage the relationship between them. In contrast, if disclosure takes place whenever the mother feels she is ready, usually after working through her own experiences and in the context of emotionally safe spaces with sustained support and counseling available for both the mother and her child, the initial pain that the information causes can turn not only into relief for the mothers but also into a reassuring sense of identity and belonging for their sons and daughters.[22]

In chapter 2, I addressed the ongoing construction of the bureaucracies of redress for people born of conflict-related sexual violence, the unintelligibility of the category itself, and the role that has been assigned to the mothers in this process. Since the implementation of the Victims' Law in 2011, there have been some efforts within the Victims' Unit to guarantee their access to reparations. However, those efforts have not kept pace with the actual needs and stages in the lives of these young women and men. Despite their right to integral reparations, which should include measures of rehabilitation, satisfaction, compensation, and guarantees of non-repetition, the main concerns both for women and within the Victims' Unit have revolved around their financial compensation. This comes as no surprise, considering the economic hardships that many of the women and their children have had to endure. After prolonged discussions between those working with war-affected children and women in war contexts, the Victims' Unit chose to respect women's decisions regarding the inclusion of their children in the Unified Registry of Victims. In doing so, the Unit was attempting to acknowledge women's agency and allow them to determine their own processes by not forcing disclosure.

However, there are at least two aspects of this situation that are troubling. On the one hand, in contexts of militarized colonial, state, and economic violence, women are once again forced to choose between two evils. As Kimberly Theidon expresses it, "Being forced to choose reparations for one's child and concerns about what this information might do to them, is a moral dilemma that in itself may constitute a gendered harm."[23] On the other hand, while it makes sense to respect women's silences and allow them to choose their own paths, this must also be accompanied by a strategy to offer timely, specialized, and sustained integral psychosocial, emotional, and even spiritual support to both women and their children. Otherwise, the burden and responsibility will continue to be placed on women, adding another layer of institutional violence to the labor of motherhood discussed in chapter 3. As Clemencia previously described, just because women have chosen not to have *the* conversation with their children does not mean that their children do not know; rather, the women and their sons and daughters have had to deal with the information and its consequences using whatever resources they have to hand, often at great cost to everyone involved.

At the collective level, the situation has taken on a whole new dimension of complexity, as including people born of conflict-related sexual violence in processes of collective reparations entails having open conversations about them, which is precisely what many of the mothers do not wish to do—and even if they did, they often do not have the necessary emotional and psychosocial support available. This also involves significant risks and could cause harm to both the women and their children. In the case of San Miguel, the PIRC includes thirty-five measures of reparation. These are some of them:

- Supply of materials for the construction of a greenhouse and delivery of seeds for reforestation.
- Supply of logistics for the development of intergenerational encounters with the purpose of opening spaces for dialogue between older people, adults, young people, children and women of the community, and to strengthen traditional knowledge about Afro-Colombian crafts and gastronomy.
- Delivery of building materials for the reconstruction and adaptation of the community center. Provision of infrastructure for the community to develop cultural, social and educational activities.
- Supply of logistics for the celebration of traditional festivities.
- Delivery of the economic resources corresponding to the payment of the collective compensation. The resources of the compensation measure will be used to leverage the production projects for commercial purposes.[24]

In my 2016 interview with Liliana, when she was no longer part of the Victims' Unit and the process of collective reparations had resumed under Carmen's leadership, I asked Liliana if she thought there would be a place for those children born of conflict-related sexual violence in San Miguel's collective reparations, to which she replied, "I'm not optimistic. It was through our interactions with women that we heard that people were calling those children *paraquitos* . . . and although I personally tried to call attention to their situation, we started working in San Miguel because of what happened to the women, and they were our priority." Several years later, when the community was involved in the planning stage of the PIRC, I asked Carmen the same question. She responded, "It will depend on what women manage to negotiate [with the community council, the community action board, and the Collective Reparations Support Group], but to be honest, I don't see it very clearly. I've tried to suggest it, but with *that* topic, there is so much at stake that I don't even know what a measure that involves them [children born of conflict-related sexual violence] would look like."

"Is there something about children born of conflict-related sexual violence in the Comprehensive Plan for Collective Reparations?" I asked the two people who, after Carmen left, had taken over leadership of the implementation stage in 2019.

"There isn't. Maybe it never really came out in the 'Characterization of Harms' stage. I haven't heard about that," one of them replied.

I have also asked the women themselves, including Clemencia and Gloria, if there is anything about their children in the PIRC. They have said, "After all that work at the beginning and throughout the years, there is nothing!" However, among the thirty-five measures listed in the Victims' Unit Excel spreadsheet, there are two that are concerned with gender-based violence and women who are victims of sexual violence and their children. Under the category "Guarantees of Non-repetition," the following is listed: "Conducting training on the prevention of gender-based violence and discrimination based on sexual diversity." Under the heading "Rehabilitation Measures," this line is provided: "Assistance and logistical support for the development of psychosocial workshops for mothers and children affected by sexual violence." During the implementation stage, these measures have translated into workshops and activities being held with members of the community. Frequently, the people who participate in them are the same ones who belong to the Collective Reparations Support Group, and more often than not, the sessions are entertaining but quite vague in terms of their purpose. I have attended some of the sessions held in response to the measure concerned with the prevention of gender-based violence and discrimination based on sexual diversity. Activities have been carried out involving people talking about their past, achievements they feel proud of, and things that they associate with being a man or a woman. However, the only reason I was aware that those workshops constituted part of that measure of collective reparations is because it said so on the photograph that the Victims' Unit employees who conduct the sessions are expected to take as part of the evidence that they need to provide the Victims' Unit with.

As for the measure relating to "women and children affected by sexual violence," there is not much I can say other than that the people who should be directly involved in it, women like Clemencia and Gloria and their sons and daughters, have no idea it even exists. As I recall Carmen's words when I asked her if she thought there would be a place for children born of conflict-related sexual violence in the PIRC—"I don't even know what a measure that involves them would look like"—I am not surprised that the two Victims' Unit employees who are leading the implementation stage do not connect this measure to the young women and men who were born of paramilitary sexual violence. After everything the women have been through—their experiences of war and the years of institutional violence they have endured engaging with the bureaucracies of victimhood and seeing other people assume ownership of their stories—I am also not surprised that after the early stages of the process of collective reparations, they preferred to keep their children away from the collective labor of memories.

In September 2021, a couple of years after the initial tensions between the community action board and the community council, and well into the implementation stage of the collective reparations process, I was chatting with a group of women from San Miguel who had all survived paramilitary sexual violence. We were talking about the possibility of holding a meeting whereby they could discuss reparations for their sons and daughters born of the sexual abuse they endured with a representative from the Victims' Unit at the national level. One of the women commented,

> I think it's great that we're talking about this because it's long overdue. But before we move forward, I have a demand to make, and I'm sure I speak on behalf of everyone present here. That all, and I mean all, the communication that concerns us women and our children happens directly with us. Not with the community council, not with the community action board. With us. They don't care about us, about what's best for us women and for our children. They say that all the projects, that everything that happens here must first go through them, but I don't agree. They didn't live through what we did; they weren't pregnant and didn't breastfeed our children. I don't want to find out later that they used our names and what we lived through to get things, projects. Because when that happens, we are the last ones to find out. We don't even get any of the benefits from those projects!

IMPOSSIBLE WITNESSES

Oral and written testimony, as a methodology, has gained a privileged place within the architecture of transitional justice in an attempt to understand the past and address the consequences of mass violence. In the legal, psychosocial, and academic systems of knowledge that claim expertise in the understanding of mass violence, suffering, and trauma, making the narratives of the experiences of those subjects who are labeled as victims visible has been naturalized as the privileged strategy used by societies to designate roles, responsibilities, and harms—what has been referred to as coming to terms with the past—and for survivors to engage in what is expected to be a cathartic process of healing.[25]

This strategy relies on the emotional, social, and physical willingness, ability, and capacity of people to communicate their experiences, and it also depends on the social, cultural, political, and economic contexts in which that communication could take place. Giorgio Agamben notes that in Latin, there are two words for witness: *Testis*, from which the word *testimony* originates, describes a person who represents a third party and, in the case of a trial or lawsuit, can remain unbiased, with no allegiance to any of the parties involved. The second word, *superstes*, describes someone who has lived through something, who has experienced an event and can bear witness to it. The testimony of the survivor, warns Agamben, is not neutral and does not pretend to be. This testimony surpasses the legal boundaries of the definitions of harm, but it is often edited and filtered in the name of achieving the ultimate goal of producing a legal judgment. The testimony of the survivor of violence and atrocity is a reminder that the ultimate aim of law is the production of judgments but not necessarily the establishment of justice and truth. This is to say not that a judgment is not desired, for that is a political and ethical responsibility, as well as a state obligation, but that when seeking to understand and address contexts of violence and oppression, the law is not exhaustive.[26]

The stories from San Miguel that I have reconstructed throughout my many years of visiting the community have at their core accounts of witnesses and survivors who, in the context of my research but also in that of collective reparations, have brought the past into the present. Some come from stories about themselves, neighbors, and loved ones that people decided to share with me in interviews and social cartography sessions or while taking photographs, waiting for the bus, walking together, or seeking shade under a mango tree. Others come from women's legal statements and my own observations, which have revealed much about their engagement with the bureaucracies of transitional justice in order to gain access to their right to redress. Primo Levi talks about the role of the witness in giving testimony, and he refers to the witness-as-participant and the witness-as-observer.[27] Reflecting on his own experience in Auschwitz, Levi describes the witness-as-participant—the *Musselmann* in the jargon of the camp—as "the true witness," the one who lost their humanity and life within the architecture of atrocities. The impossibility of the testimony of the true witness, argues Jelin, is that, by definition, they cannot bear witness, and therefore, their experiences cannot be reconstructed through their own testimonial narratives.[28] Agamben points out that no one has returned from the gas chambers of Auschwitz, while Jelin complements this remark by observing, "As no one has returned from the death flights in Argentina."[29]

The witnesses-as-observers, those who survived, can bear a double testimony; they can narrate how they saw others reach the point of no return, painfully losing their humanity, and they can also describe their own experience of violence.[30] However, Agamben argues that this testimony contains a lacuna that can be located at the intersection between two impossibilities: The first has been described previously and is concerned with narrating the experience of someone who cannot bear witness.[31] The second refers to the language of testimony and conveying through words experiences that cannot be known and represented in a common language.[32] This type of testimony, "in order to bear witness, needs to present through language what is, in essence, senseless."[33]

Within what the anthropologist Alejandro Castillejo Cuéllar calls the development of an industry of extraction of testimonies, there are groups of intermediaries whose job is to collect narratives of traumatic events and suffering and turn them into products with a life of their own: news articles, documentaries, academic papers, reports, and legal documents.[34] In the case of Buenos Aires, and particularly San Miguel, this extractive industry has been led by the Victims' Unit and fueled by the promise of redress—both collective and individual. In order for the architecture of transitional justice that was put in place to operate effectively, however, people needed to come forward, offer their narratives, and request their recognition as victims. Within the political economy of victimhood, testimonies became an essential part of the transaction between promises and expectations. In the historical contexts of economic extraction, Castillejo Cuéllar argues, such an industry of testimony reproduces other forms of violence by demanding that people put their experiences of suffering into words in exchange for symbolic and material benefits.

If *Musselmann* are Levi's true witnesses who are unable to narrate their own stories, people born of conflict-related sexual violence can be construed as *impossible witnesses*. They have emerged from the past but they do not belong to it. They cannot offer their testimonies, firsthand, of their community's experiences of paramilitary violence or of the many abuses their mothers endured and in relation to which they are, according to the Victims' Law, officially recognized as victims. They were conceived as a result of conflict-related sexual violence, but the task of reconstructing testimonies about the violence through which they were conceived falls upon other people. This does not mean, however, that they do not have testimonies to share, because in different ways, their identities, life stories, and opportunities are intertwined with the experiences of violence their mothers endured. Their testimonies, however, are not the same as those of their mothers; they are their mothers' children, but they are not only that.

Consequently, their testimonies encompass traces of their mothers' experiences and how they have overcome them (or what they sense in relation to this), their own experiences while growing up, and how they imagine their futures within their specific sociocultural and economic contexts. In some cases, those contexts are still shaped by militarization and war, as is true for Gloria's son, who had been recruited by various armed groups. Their testimonies are not narrated in the past tense and do not necessarily correspond to a language that is legible within the system of victimhood. Although these young women and men have claims, dreams, and hopes, they do not fit into the paradigm of addressing past harms. Rather, their focus is on justice—being able to enjoy life with their families and communities without armed groups, extractive industries, neoliberal policies, environmental devastation, and the constant threat of dispossession and hunger hanging over them.

CONCLUSIONS

The 2011 Victims' Law created the legal framework for individual and collective victims of the Colombian armed conflict to obtain access to their right to integral reparations. In the case of collective reparations, the negotiation and construction of collective memories of the past occupy a central place in the bureaucracies of victimhood and redress, as those narratives are the foundations for understanding how the armed conflict affected entire collectivities, causing harms that transformed what was essential for their existence as a social group and their reproduction. Those collective memories, like all narratives of the past, weaved together presences and absences, silences and concealment—aspects people work to remember and aspects they try to forget. The negotiations that are part of the labor of memories entail power relations that define both the gaze through which the past may be brought into the present and expectations about how the outcome of those negotiations will become part of the future people want to inhabit.

For women, creating space for and gaining recognition of their experiences within collective memories of periods of armed and political violence has been a long, hard, and fierce fight. After years of political organizing, advocacy, and systematic recollection of testimonies, as discussed in chapter 1, women's experiences of war-related sexual violence have now gained a more clearly defined place among collective memories of war and, therefore, within struggles for truth, justice, and redress, including guarantees of non-repetition. Although this is a significant achievement for victims across the world and women's and feminist movements, the ways in which conflict-related sexual violence was assumed by transitional justice frameworks to be the dominant experience of women in war contexts created further issues. While the aforementioned focus rendered invisible the other experiences of war that women endured and were part of, the techniques and methodologies that transitional justice mechanisms have prioritized imposed on women the duty to "break the silence" about their stories of sexual violence and to repeatedly tell those stories in terms that are legible within transitional justice frameworks.

People born of conflict-related sexual violence are yet to gain a place in collective memories of the past and the struggle for a better future that they represent. In relation to the victimhood system and its bureaucracies of redress, women have been assigned responsibility for the inclusion of their children born of war-related sexual violence in the system. While this decision was informed by the commitment to respect women's own processes and experiences, the fact that it was not accompanied by timely, specialized, and sustained psychosocial, emotional, and spiritual support for women and their children has meant that women have been forced to negotiate with themselves regarding the emotional burden of disclosure and concealment. It also implies that the responsibility for the right of people born of war-related sexual violence to access integral reparations has fallen on women, constituting a form of institutional violence related to the naturalization of women's labor of motherhood. Women want a better present and future for their children regardless of whether it is achieved through individual or collective reparations or through any other path that guarantees their right to education, housing, and health. Women want justice for their sons and daughters; they want them to have opportunities, to be joyful, and to enjoy their lives. Women want to talk about them, but they do not want to talk about them on other people's terms.

For the young women and men born of war-related sexual violence, this situation has brought loneliness and uncertainty about their identity, their sense of belonging, their lives, and their relationship with their mothers, families, and communities. They are impossible witnesses of the experiences that, under legal terms, entitled them to integral reparations; their testimonies tend to be illegible within the system of victimhood, with its past-oriented logic and language of harms. Their testimonies, however, should act as a reminder that when justice is primarily conceived of through the lens of the past—and in particular, legal definitions of harms—there is a lot that is not accounted for.

CONCLUSION
Toward Futures of Reproductive Justice

The first time I heard about the poultry farm was in 2016. It was around the time that the process of collective reparations was resuming, and I was working on the document that could potentially contribute to the "Assessment and Characterization of Harms" stage. As people were sharing their stories of the period of paramilitary occupation with me and I was becoming more familiar with the geography of San Miguel—its hills, dirt roads, and creeks; the presence and movement of sounds, fog, and light; and the colors and smells that changed throughout the day—references to the poultry farm started to become apparent, uninvited but undeniable. The story went that a woman from a different part of the country had been buying land from local residents in the community. People speculated that most likely, news about the collective reparations was out, and this woman was buying land while it was still cheap in anticipation of a promising future return on her investment. People said that they did not blame their neighbors for selling. A lot of them did not want to stay there after everything they had been through. Some did not have it in them to keep fighting against the advancement of the sugarcane monocrops that were encroaching from the valley and the economic policies that squeezed small farmers; others were getting old and did not have the resources and family support of the new generations, who were now moving to the cities and taking jobs in the sugarcane industry or in the gold mines in the area now under the management of multinationals. According to rumors, the woman was going to open a poultry farm with sheds massive enough to raise over five thousand chickens.

People in the community were worried. As we talked, they expressed their concerns about the air and water pollution that would undoubtedly result from such a large enterprise. Although there was a faint sense of hope regarding the jobs that the poultry farm could offer to people in the community, their concern grew when they thought about the unwanted attention the project could bring to San Miguel. After all they had suffered during the paramilitary confinement, people in the community felt uncomfortable with the idea of itinerant strangers coming to work on the farm and dreaded the prospect of the farm attracting other types of businesses that were against the best interests of the community—for example, illegal armed groups bribing the farm for security or running brothels. A huge concern was the impact that such a large enterprise could have on what was essential for the community. The farm had not even started operating yet, but people could already see that the creek had been diverted, with devastating effects on fishing and other everyday activities such as doing laundry, swimming, and gathering together in the afternoons. With the community's hopes pinned on the collective reparations process, into which they had poured huge efforts, and expectations of the positive transformations it could entail for San Miguel, people were also afraid that the poultry farm could attract unwelcome attention from outsiders who might seek to profit from and exploit the collective reparations process.

I discussed this situation in the document I was writing: outsiders buying large plots of land, the community losing access to essential sources of water and communal footpaths, and the implications this could have for the life and future of San Miguel. I wrote about people's concerns and fears. After all, as people pointed out several times, measures of reparation did not exist in a vacuum. Their design required an understanding of both the harms that San Miguel had experienced due to the paramilitary occupation and the conditions under which the community currently lived. This involved economic dynamics, the presence and activities of legal and illegal armed groups, and the various transformations that had taken place within the ecosystem, among others. Although there was not a direct link between the paramilitary confinement and the poultry farm, for many people in San Miguel, there was a clear connection among people's willingness to sell the land that had traditionally been in their families for generations, the lingering memories of the period of paramilitary rule, and the possibility that it could happen again. For some, there was also a clear association between an outsider's interest in making a large investment while land was still cheap and the potential profit and benefits she could reap from doing so now that the collective reparations process could attract all sorts of resources to the area.

After the community action board had approved the document, we handed it to Carmen, who was the Unit for the Assistance and Integral Reparations of Victims (hereafter Victims' Unit or the Unit) representative responsible for the collective reparations process in San Miguel at that time. Carmen told me later that the document did indeed serve as input for the "Assessment and Characterization of Harms" stage and was used as a first draft for the official document that the Victims' Unit produced after the prior consultation with the community.

Conclusion

FIGURE 6. Poultry farm viewed from the community cemetery, San Miguel, 2022

The only section that the Unit did not take into consideration, Carmen told me, was the part about the poultry farm, as "it had no connection with the paramilitary occupation and the various harms caused to the community." Over a period of several years, and after many visits to San Miguel, I have observed the poultry farm thrive, as is evident not only from its ever-growing size but also from the clouds of flies and lingering stench of filth, feces, and ammonia that often extend the boundaries of the farm across dirt roads, creeks, and into people's houses and farms. "It's like they are trying to expel us from our own community, you know?" a thirteen-year-old girl I was walking with once told me as she waved her arms in front of her face to shoo away the flies.

She was part of a group of girls from the community with whom we worked, for over two years, to create fictionalized and nonfictionalized narratives about San Miguel. The latest of the stories they created was called *El misterio de La Chorrera* (The mystery of La Chorrera). This story, which we produced and printed as a fanzine, was about the adventures of Maria, a twelve-year-old girl from the community, and her dog Toby and their quest to solve the most pressing mystery the community had ever faced: One of the main wells from the river, La Chorrera, had changed. Instead of producing the clear waters that people drank from, cooked with, and took baths in, La Chorrera was now brown, thick, and sludgy and smelled like rotten chickens. People were growing increasingly thirsty and hungry, and those who dared to cook with the water from it or who had no choice but to drink it—children and adults alike—were becoming very sick. As no one could understand what was happening, Maria and Toby embarked on a journey to La Chorrera's source to try to find answers.

When they finally arrived, they realized that workers from the poultry farm, which adjoined the river, were using large amounts of chicken manure to fertilize the grounds, including those by the river basin. The manure was draining into the water, polluting the river that had been an essential part of San Miguel for generations. In the story, the community works collectively to earn enough money to buy the land back from the poultry farm's owners; they organize a fair at which people sell produce from their crops and small farm animals they have raised, cook traditional dishes, invite outsiders to taste some of their ancestral drinks, dance, and play some of the games that had often been talked about by the older generations. In the story, after the community buys the land and the poultry farm is consigned to the past, everyone goes to the river well—now replete with clear, fresh water—to celebrate and welcome back the turtles, butterflies, fish, and worms that had been forced to flee their home. Happiness. That is how Maria describes the way the community feels in the knowledge that the river will still be there, as an intrinsic part of San Miguel, to be visited by them and the new generations who are yet to come.

Unlike the fictional account of Maria and Toby's adventure, it looks unlikely that the poultry farm will be leaving San Miguel any time soon. If anything, it aggregates some of the different forms of violence that, historically, the community has endured and that, time and again, have threatened the reproduction of biological and social life. Not only it is built on legalized practices of land dispossession and its very existence constitutes a form of ecological destruction, but it also shows the subtle and not-so-subtle ways in which armed groups operate beyond military operations. During the paramilitary occupation, the commanders chose as their residence the rural house that today oversees and is effectively the headquarters of the poultry farm. Stories about the house are rarely heard, as people would rather avoid them. However, at some point in our conversations, a couple of women mentioned the house to me in passing. One of them, Sofia, was in her thirties during the paramilitary confinement. She recalls that one afternoon she was at home when she heard a man calling her name. When she came outside, the man, who was a paramilitary she had not seen before, told her that one of the commanders had sent word that, that evening, she was to wear something nice and meet him at the house. That was just the first of countless times that Sofia was forced to go to the house and perform the tasks they imposed on her and other women and girls from the community. In that house, women were raped, sometimes locked up for days, and forced to cook dinner, do laundry, serve guests at parties, and participate in drinking games.

Conclusion 145

The context in which Sofia shared this story with me was one that revealed much about the political economy of the armed conflict and its ever-changing dynamics. Around the time of the 2022 presidential elections, the situation was quite tense in different parts of the country. Various illegal armed groups, like the one that recruited Gloria's son, were strengthening their military presence in parts of the country that were strategic for businesses such as the cocaine production chain, engaging in armed confrontations with other legal and illegal armed groups, terrorizing communities, committing massacres, and imposing curfews and other restrictions on mobility. In Buenos Aires, the municipality in which San Miguel is located, an order for everyone to drive with the windows down had been put in place so that *they* could see who was in the car. After noticing writing on a wall proclaiming "Windows down or bullet," I asked the person who was driving me around exactly what that meant. "Exactly what it says. You didn't think we always drive with the windows down because of COVID, did you?" he jokingly replied. At that time, some of those armed groups were also threatening entire communities and warning them not to vote for the presidential ticket that would later become the first left-wing party to be elected in the country, composed of Gustavo Petro as president and Francia Márquez, an Afro-Colombian woman from the same part of the country as San Miguel and an environmental activist and lawyer, as vice president.

Sofia had been updating me on the current situation in San Miguel. Armed men in camouflage uniforms had been seen driving motorcycles around the community. They had even called a meeting, which they held in the community kiosk built with resources from the collective reparations, to announce their presence to the community and to "invite" everyone to collaborate with them and their enterprises; it was in everyone's interest to do so, they said. They had also "suggested" that people should not leave the community after sunset. "It gets dangerous out there," they said, and then continued, "We would not like anything to happen to the dear people of this community." Shortly after those announcements, Gloria told me, "It broke my heart to know that that man speaking in front of everyone as if he was all innocent had taken my child away from me. That he knew where my child was, and I didn't." As the elections drew closer, Sofia told me that things were getting even worse: armed men wearing balaclavas were now roaming freely around the community; they did not talk to anyone, but they certainly made their presence felt.

"Where are they staying?" I asked worriedly.

"Where do you think? In the poultry farm house! I'm sure they'll always be welcome there." Sofia also told me there was a rumor that the woman who owned the land was the sister of one of the paramilitary commanders who led the occupation.

The question of why people born of conflict-related sexual violence remain unseen in Colombia—despite the existence of the legal category that entitles them to redress, despite having been singled out by their communities through the label that associated them with their biological fathers, and despite their presence in the lives of their mothers—needs to be asked together with questions about their contexts. The contexts in which they grow up, in which they are expected to imagine their possible options and futures, and in which they get lost among the many challenges that their mothers, their communities, and they themselves have to negotiate and overcome just to survive their everyday lives. In the Afro-Colombian rural community of San Miguel, the poultry farm tells a story of reproductive violence that exists in the overlapping landscapes of colonial legacies of exclusion, the extractive economies, and the armed conflict, threatening the biological and social reproduction of the community and its future generations. Despite this, the ways in which the poultry farm has developed and even thrived by pulling together so many different threads, as well as its ability to belong to different times simultaneously and to continue to exist in the background while slowly becoming central to so many aspects of the everyday life of San Miguel, has made it invisible to the process of collective reparations. While this process attempts to address the legally defined harms of the past, the present and future of the community are at risk from the threat of old and new foes that have become adept at collaborating.

Feminist peace-building agendas in Colombia have underscored the defense of life and territories, exposing the connections among militarization, extractive economies, environmental devastation, and the different forms that intersectional violence takes, including sexual violence.[1] Feminism has also underscored the urgent need to creatively organize in order to advance the interconnected struggles of reproductive autonomy, gendered justice, and peace building and assign a differentiated place to reproductive violence.[2] The transformation of the frameworks through which the feminist movement approaches these matters has entailed a shift from understanding them on an individual basis to understanding them as interconnected social justice issues that must be anti-capitalist, anti-racist, anti-militarist, anti-patriarchal, and trans-inclusive.[3] Seeking to understand the plight of people born of conflict-related sexual violence as only of importance to reproductive autonomy, gendered justice, or peace building has contributed to both their unintelligibility as individual subjects and the imposition on their mothers to unquestioningly perform their patriarchal role as nurturers, despite their own experiences of violence and healing and in contexts of scarcity, environmental pollution, militarization, and economic impoverishment.[4] Adopting a reproductive justice framework within human rights and transitional justice endeavors can contribute to *seeing* people born of conflict-related sexual violence in a way that goes beyond merely presenting them as

Conclusion   147

numbers within the population of victims and understanding their experiences in their own right, beyond their mothers' experiences of violence.

As women like Clemencia and Gloria have firmly declared, when it comes to their children, they are the ones who must set the terms of the conversations. Respecting women's own processes and guaranteeing support in their disclosure negotiations and in their relationships with their sons and daughters must be a priority in order to avoid revictimizing women and causing harm to their children. However, this cannot be achieved without integral strategies to guarantee timely, sustained, and specialized psychosocial, emotional, and spiritual support for both women and children along the way.[5] But it is not only about disclosure and the different forms that it can take throughout the lives of people born of conflict-related sexual violence. For women like Clemencia and Gloria, it also needs to be accompanied by tangible policies and strategies to guarantee access not only to integral reproductive health services, including abortion, but also to fertility treatments in cases when, for example, the physical and mental consequences of sexual violence, pregnancy, or giving birth lead to difficulties in having children in the future. They need comprehensive maternal support, including integral maternal health and access to community-based and government social and financial resources, so they can look after their children without worrying about whether there will be clean water to drink and food to eat or whether there will come a day when their children will be recruited by one of the old or new armed groups.

Respecting women's rights to decide their own terms in relation to their children cannot keep being used as an excuse for the lack of accountability and redress in relation to forced motherhood. To advance conceptual and policy agendas, addressing the invisibility of accounts of forced motherhood within gendered narratives of war will in turn contribute to promoting debates about reproduction within peace and security agendas. Within the field of transitional justice, more comprehensive meanings of justice and redress are required, and with regard to guarantees of non-repetition, this must include actions such as the total decriminalization of abortion and the demilitarization of society. It also entails questioning the frameworks through which we have been taught not to see the naturalization of reproductive labor while thinking in a way that moves beyond legal categories and past-oriented temporalities of harm and crimes. In terms of peace building, addressing the issue of forced motherhood invites us to reimagine gender roles and care outside of capitalism's monopoly over our subjectivities. Emancipatory peace projects can no longer reproduce the idea that women's role as caregivers is natural or that women contribute to peace through their "nurturing essence."[6] For this to happen, we need to question ideas about women as inherent peacemakers based on a reductionist association of the feminine with nature, procreation, and nurture.

As for people born of conflict-related sexual violence, a reproductive justice framework could allow us to think in more interconnected ways about what justice could mean for them. Recognizing that reparations do not mean the same for them as for their mothers opens paths to perceiving them through a paradigm of justice that is not guided by questions about how to remedy the harms of the past.[7] It needs to be acknowledged that advancing justice for them involves understanding not only how they were conceived and the implications this has had for their lives but also that justice is not restricted to addressing the violence their mothers have endured. We are still to understand what their own "poultry farms" are and work together in a way that ensures they can grow up and grow old and dream of futures that belong to them. They may be their mother's children, but they are much more than that.

UNVEILING THE UNINTELLIGIBLE

"How many children born of conflict-related sexual violence are there in San Miguel?" I have been asked time and again by people who, with a policy-oriented, legal, academic, or general interest, are trying to produce a map of the gendered geographies of war and victimhood in Colombia. The magazine article in which I first read about Buenos Aires cites a figure of thirty, while a footnote in a report from the ombudsman's office notes the presence of seventeen.[8] People in San Miguel would say *muchos* (a lot). As previously mentioned, because of my commitment to maintaining their anonymity and not singling them out, I do not disclose the precise number I have evidenced throughout the many years of visiting the community and working with their mothers. I do believe, however, that questions about revealing *the number* provide insights into the tensions that underlie the ways in which they are visible and yet remain unseen; their unintelligibility persists despite the existence of the category within the Victims' and Land Restitution Law (hereafter Victims' Law), despite harmful labels that have sought to connect them with the violence perpetrated by their biological fathers, and despite their physical presence in their communities and, of course, in their mother's lives and struggles.

The past few years have witnessed a historic moment of unprecedented international attention to the situation of people born of conflict-related sexual violence. Since the 1990s, a growing international interdisciplinary group of scholars and human rights advocates has raised awareness about the plight of children born of conflict-related sexual violence across the world. In particular, they have drawn attention to three interconnected aspects: first, the various forms of discrimination these people have endured, which can even endanger their lives and well-being as they grow older; second, the lack of public policies and normative frameworks to guarantee their rights and development in safe

Conclusion   149

and loving contexts; and third, the knowledge gap about them that has been part of the debates about how best to proceed in order to protect them and guarantee their fundamental rights. This gap entails methodological questions about how to approach them and epistemological questions about the forms of violence they have experienced, the risk of potential harm that working with them could cause, how to work with them and their mothers when it comes to the disclosure of women's experiences of violence, and what kinds of resources, institutions, and frameworks would be most suited to addressing their needs and supporting them and their mothers as they grow older.

In a globally groundbreaking decision, the 2011 Victims' Law recognized children born of conflict-related sexual violence as direct victims of the armed conflict in Colombia, and as such, they are entitled to integral reparations. Their inclusion within this normative framework, however, has not translated into specific policies, strategies, or programs designed to guarantee their rights. This situation is not so much connected to institutional and social denials of their existence or the difficult, even life-threatening circumstances that many of them face throughout their lives. I show that the lack of attention they have received, including from institutions and actors who work with conflict-affected children and conflict-related gender-based violence, is largely attributable to the lack of frameworks to *see* them as independent subjects.

Rather than a story of denial, this is a tale of *unintelligibility*. In Colombia, the inclusion of children born of conflict-related sexual violence in the Victims' Law was the result not of advocacy by the networks working with war-affected children, whose resources were primarily focused on child recruitment, but of efforts by the feminist and women's social movements and their fight to achieve justice, truth, and redress regarding conflict-related sexual violence. Despite the visibility that their inclusion in the Victims' Law bestowed on them, people born of conflict-related sexual violence have remained largely unseen by the actors and institutions in charge of implementing the law and by society at large. Beyond the scope of legal discussions, the context in which we, as a society, have *seen-them-without-really-seeing-them* is closely linked with the lenses through which we have approached them. Their existence was rendered visible through either the framework for understanding conflict-related sexual violence or women's reproductive autonomy and the right to abortion in particular. When viewed through the former, children born of conflict-related sexual violence have served as an adjective for their mothers' victimization, while the latter has presented them as unwanted lives.

At the same time that this situation has contributed to their unintelligibility as independent subjects who are entangled with war in ways specifically associated with their mothers' experiences of violence but who are more than those experiences, it has also prevented broader social conversations about the reproductive violence forced upon their mothers. In recent years, however, the feminist and women's movements have undergone a shift in their understanding of women's reproductive autonomy. The contemporary Latin American feminist movement has changed its strategy from focusing on individual campaigns, such as the decriminalization of abortion, to developing platforms for the coordination of political forces, struggles, and campaigns across borders to fight for interconnected social justice issues.

In the fields that are involved with armed and political violence, transitional justice, and peace building, the transformation of the frameworks to think about women's reproductive lives is now translating into a more nuanced understanding of reproductive violence and gendered victimhood. For women and their children born of conflict-related sexual violence, this can contribute to unveiling the ways in which women have been expected to fulfill their patriarchal gender roles as nurturers in militarized contexts, amid environmental devastation and economic hardship, and with constant fear and uncertainty about what kind of future their children, their communities, and they themselves will have. Similarly, such a transformation has created space for conversations in which people born of conflict-related sexual violence have a place, not only as their mothers' children, but as individual subjects in their own right.

Over the last ten years, the Victims' Unit has attempted to fill the category of children born of conflict-related sexual violence with meaning while seeking to create a bureaucratic system of reparations in which this category could exist. However, the Unit had no specific previous knowledge to draw on to complete these tasks. The challenge of addressing this knowledge gap regarding what working with people born of conflict-related sexual violence entailed was made even more complex by the mass scale of the ongoing war in Colombia and the need to create a system for the domestic reparations program as a whole. Conceptual and methodological debates about the inclusion of children born of conflict-related sexual violence within this system were fueled by developments that have taken place in the fields involving work with conflict-related gendered-based violence—in particular, women's experiences of conflict-related sexual violence—and war-affected children. Seeking to avoid revictimizing women and respecting their right to follow their own process regarding concealment and disclosure, the category of children born of conflict-related sexual violence became nested within the system established to redress the consequences of sexual violence. Despite attempts made by individuals within the Victims' Unit to render the category of children born of conflict-related sexual violence visible and legible within the victimhood system, it remains blurred and, along the way, has become hidden within the sexual violence reparations system.

After more than a decade since the implementation of the Victims' Law, for people born of conflict-related sexual violence, efforts to make the category

Conclusion 151

legible without causing harms to the mothers have not translated into effective access to their right to reparations and, therefore, fostering the transformative processes that redress could have on their present and future. Developments regarding access to reparations have so far amounted to, on the one hand, an exercise in quantifying the existence of children born of conflict-related sexual violence within the overall population of victims and, on the other hand, delivering measures of compensation to an appallingly small number of people. In this case, the numbers serve the purpose of showing accountability, giving the Victims' Unit something to include in its reports, while concealing the lack of real progress in relation to what integral measures of reparations could look like for these people and the transformative impact they could have on their lives and those of their mothers.

Within the architectures of transitional justice, creating and measuring the categories of victimhood is part of an exercise in which a certain reality is produced and governed; it offers a sense of intelligibility, meaning, and stability to a world that has been shaken and reshaped by armed conflict. It serves a purpose in contributing to breaking the silence around impunity, injustice, and oblivion. And yet, in the search for that sense of order, deeper questions can easily get lost. *Muchos* (a lot) is the word that people in San Miguel would use to refer to what people understand to be a large number of boys, girls, teenagers, and young adults born of paramilitary sexual violence. It is through this category, which might seem blurred in the context of sociolegal and policy discourses, that people describe what we, as outsiders, tend not to perceive.

Attempts to fill the knowledge gap and produce bureaucracies of reparations for children born of conflict-related sexual violence have followed the harm-centered logics that have guided the bureaucracies of redress created to deliver measures of integral reparations for victims of war-related sexual violence. This constitutes one of the layers that contribute to their unintelligibility. While their sheer number serves to confirm their existence within the realm of victimhood, questions about their legibility have not been accompanied by debates about what kind of reparations they need and, in broader terms, what justice should look like and how to achieve it. Redress, in the case of these children and young people, needs to go beyond the paradigm of justice that addresses the victimizing events of the past. For people born of conflict-related sexual violence, who often live in militarized contexts of colonial and economic violence, redress must be grounded in a paradigm of justice that allows them to dream of a future that belongs to them.

In San Miguel, the consolidation of the paramilitary social order that became established in the early 2000s redefined the meaning of agency for women and men. People were not locked up, and yet they lost their freedom and autonomy. Although they were living in familiar landscapes and sleeping in their own houses, the ways in which they had traditionally interacted with their neighbors, grown their crops, tended their animals, enjoyed the river, and gathered together in the afternoons after a long, hard day working in the fields were destroyed and replaced by the categories and rules imposed by the paramilitaries. For women and men, that implied living in a constant state of fear and the threat of being labeled as a guerrilla sympathizer—of being killed, disappeared, or tortured. It implied the existence of everyday checkpoints, curfews, and limited access to food and medicine. For everyone, it implied hunger, sleeping with the doors of their houses open, and seeing paramilitaries take possession of their animals, crops, and lands. During that period, men were forced to participate in the maintenance of that order in the public domain that their gender role, within a patriarchal structure, assigned to them—namely, running errands such as going to neighboring towns to buy credit for mobile phones belonging to the paramilitaries, taking messages from one place to another, and raising and butchering livestock to feed the hundreds of men who were always around.

Women, for their part, were forced to fulfill the patriarchal roles befitting of their gender, according to which they were expected to cook for the paramilitaries and do their laundry. As part of this, the soldiers also objectified women in order to "release men's sexual needs," and as the self-appointed governing authority, they not only assumed ownership of women's bodies but robbed them of their peace of mind, their dreams, and their freedoms. During the occupation, many women and girls from the community had to endure rape, forced nudity, and coerced partnerships, and all of them had to live their lives in constant fear, with the threat of sexual violence hanging over them every day. As a result, many had to drop out of school and, in some cases, were never able to finish their education. Many of them carry the consequences of both the abuse they endured and the lack of specialized and timely physical, emotional, and mental health support to address the harm caused by the perpetrators of sexual violence. And many years after those events, women are still dealing with the effects of, for example, sexually transmitted diseases, damage to their reproductive systems, or scars on different parts of their bodies. Many were burdened with constant feelings of fear, guilt, and mistrust and could never feel safe and secure while walking alone in the forest, taking a bath in the creek, or just lying in bed in the dark before falling asleep. They were also deprived of the joy and pleasure that came with dancing and laughing, meeting someone they liked, or embarking on a new relationship.

For some women, forced pregnancies were part of their experiences of sexual violence and many of them gave birth to children born of the abuse they endured. Several years after the demobilization of the paramilitary bloc that confined San Miguel, those children were singled out by people in the

Conclusion   153

community with the label that linked them to their fathers: *paraquitos*. The label soon became a whisper that traveled beyond the community and rendered the existence of those children visible to outsiders, especially those working on gender issues within the human rights and transitional justice fields. It was taken as a mark of stigmatization that doomed these children to live permanently with their biological fathers' legacy of violence, condemning them to be their fathers' emissaries to both their mothers and their communities forever. Over time, the use of the label within the community faded and so did its power. With it, the mark of gendered victimhood that those children embodied and that had gained some level of attention among outsiders also vanished. By the time I started visiting San Miguel, those teenagers appeared at first glance to be no different from other people of the same age. However, in Colombia, unlike other war contexts in which there are children born of conflict-related sexual violence, they are not understood as "other" because identity is transmitted by both mothers and fathers.

The fading of the label *paraquito* removed the mark that created the direct connection between the biological fathers and the children. However, it also created the illusion that those children were like any other person of the same age, and this impression has been conjured through the naturalization of women's labor of motherhood. Regardless of their life trajectories, their experiences of conflict-related sexual violence, and the consequences that those have left for their lives, women are expected to perform the reproductive work associated with their patriarchal gender roles: to be caring, to nurture their sons and daughters, to provide for them, and to raise them to be good members of the community. The fading of the label, nevertheless, does not mean that all traces of these children's biological fathers disappeared. For the children, those traces remain in the cultural implications of not having an identifiable father, a situation for which women are not uncommonly blamed and that is presented by the community both as an explanation and exoneration for what people regard as unacceptable behavior. For the women, the traces of their sons' and daughters' biological fathers can also be found in the consequences that the sexual violence has had on their lives. This includes their children, for whom they are doing the best they can, despite the testing conditions in which they are raising them.

At the collective level, the negotiation and production of memories about the past occupy a central place in the bureaucracies of victimhood and redress, for they are the foundation upon which to understand and identify the harms that the armed conflict has caused to entire groups, transforming the very fabric of what was essential for their existence as social groups. In addition to creating the legal framework for individual victims to access their right to reparations, in Colombia, the Victims' Law included collective victims within its domestic reparations program. San Miguel, as a collectivity, joined this victimhood system in 2012, when it embarked upon the process of accessing reparations due to the various harms caused by the years of paramilitary confinement. In San Miguel, women, both from the community and the Victims' Unit, were driving forces in the early stages of the collective reparations process. Through their work, and often at great cost to their peace of mind and safety, they advanced issues of gender justice. On the one hand, they managed to render visible to transitional justice mechanisms and the community what they, as women, had lived through during the years of the paramilitary occupation—in particular, the various forms of sexual violence that the paramilitaries perpetrated against them and the multiple consequences that it had for their bodies and their lives more generally. On the other hand, they opened up spaces for the younger generation of girls and young women to play an active part in the political life of San Miguel, even beyond the past-oriented process of seeking collective reparations.

As is the case with international and other domestic contexts in Colombia, for women in San Miguel, gaining recognition of their experiences of sexual violence has come at a cost. While it is a significant achievement that sexual violence is no longer understood as a collateral damage of war and is now part of the quest for truth, justice, and redress, including guarantees of non-repetition, the focus, methodologies, and techniques assumed by the transitional justice paradigm for understanding gendered victimhood have proved problematic. Not only have women seen their conflict-related gendered experiences that are not connected with sexual violence largely disregarded, but they have also been burdened with the duty of "breaking the silence" about their stories of sexual violence and, over a period of several years, have had to repeatedly tell those stories in terms that are legible within transitional justice frameworks.

During the early stages of my work in San Miguel, and while I was writing the document that could serve to advance the process of obtaining collective reparations, women shared their own stories with me and those of other women in their families. Stories of grief and mourning, of longing for times when they felt safe bathing in the creek or walking in the dark through the mountains, of pining for times when they could dream about what they would become as adults, of times when the community would gather together for several days in their traditional parties. Women told me about experiences of sexual harassment in their houses, on the dirt roads, in the creek, and in the fields; of forced nudity at the ubiquitous checkpoints spread throughout their community; and of rape. Over a period of several months, we shared moments, walks, and conversations about the past, the present, and the future of San Miguel. I knew that some of them had children who were born of the paramilitary abuse they had endured, and although they knew about my research, the commitment I had made to the community action board and the Victims' Unit, and the potential implications that the document I was writing could have in terms of collective reparations, they never talked about their children as being born of conflict-related sexual violence.

"Women do not want to talk about their children" is something that I have repeatedly heard when I have asked about the lack of progress that has been made regarding obtaining reparations for people born of conflict-related sexual violence by the Victims' Unit at the national level or about their absence from the collective reparations process in San Miguel. Although this might be true in a lot of cases, I have also observed that in the context of their resolute quests to achieve a better future for their children, women do talk about them. However, they may not do so loudly, and not to everyone, and not in terms that are legible for transitional justice frameworks, which tend to concentrate on victimizing events and legal harms as well as being focused on the past. Sometimes I wonder if women really did not mention their children to me while I was writing the document or if the harm-centered "lenses" through which I was having those conversations with them did not allow me to understand what they were saying. In addition to this, women's experiences of navigating the victimhood system in pursuit of their own cases have revealed to them the institutional violence that has become intrinsic to the bureaucracies of reparations, with their painfully slow pace and fragmented processes. In another dimension of the gendered politics of testimony, women may want to talk about their children, and especially how to achieve a better future for them, but not on other people's terms or in ways that could expose them to the violence of transitional justice, legal and illegal armed groups, or their own communities.

Women have been assigned responsibility for the inclusion of their sons and daughters born of conflict-related sexual violence in the victimhood system. From the Victims' Unit's perspective, this decision constituted part of their commitment to avoid revictimizing women and interfering in their relationships with their children. However, this decision was not accompanied by concrete strategies to support women throughout the disclosure process and while the children were growing up. While women have had to avail themselves of whatever resources they have access to in order to deal with the various issues involved in the tension between disclosure and concealment, the responsibility for securing their children's right to reparation has fallen upon them. Although not intended to create further violence, the bureaucracies of victimhood and the accompanying gendered politics of testimony have created a form of institutional violence related to women's labor of motherhood.

Within this victimhood system, people born of conflict-related sexual violence are *impossible witnesses*. They cannot bear testimony to the experiences of violence on the basis of which they are legally recognized as victims entitled to redress; they have their own testimonies to share. However, those testimonies are not the same as those of their mothers. As long as the system of victimhood continues to be informed by past-oriented logics and the language of harm, the testimony of people born of conflict-related sexual violence will remain illegible within the system that seeks to achieve truth, accountability, and redress.

ACKNOWLEDGMENTS

I started working on this book by the River Colne and in the brutalist library at the University of Essex. Page after page, its words have taken different shapes as I traveled the red-soil mountains of the north of Cauca in Colombia and became familiar with the changing colors of the landscape along the Cauca River and across the valleys that lead up to the mountains from Cali. This book is also grounded in the Bluegrass region of Kentucky and in the rainy and yet open blue skies of Bogotá, where sunsets reflected in the mountains evoke a sense of belonging. I have added, changed, and deleted words and thoughts in airports, coffee shops, libraries, university offices, and my mum's living room. I have found inspiration and energy to keep writing among the various blues of the Caribbean Sea and the deep grays of the Pacific Ocean. I wrote its last words during the windy winter days in Edinburgh, with the sunrise starting to flirt its way toward longer days with brighter lights. Throughout the years of working on this book, there were moments when I felt that I had lost my roots, only to understand that those roots were expanding as I learned to name and feel the many places I now call home. This book is the result of a journey of love, longing, solidarity, and curiosity, and I can only be grateful for the joy of knowing that it is my own.

A las mujeres de Buenos Aires, en el norte del Cauca. A ustedes, mi más profunda admiración y mi más sentido agradecimiento por haberme abierto las puertas de sus vidas, y seguirme recibiendo a lo largo de los años. Este libro sólo ha sido posible gracias a ustedes, a su inmensa generosidad, sentido del humor y fortaleza para vivir la vida y seguir encontrando nuevos caminos. Tan solo espero que estas páginas le puedan hacer un mínimo de justicia a los momentos que hemos compartido y a las historias que ustedes me han confiado.

To Colin Samson, I am greatly indebted for his mentorship, generosity, and friendship and for being a constant source of critical thinking and inspiration over the years. I am thankful to Carlos Gigoux, Renos Papadopoulos, Nigel South, Yasemin Soysal, Ewa Morawska, Pam Gadsby, Clara Sandoval, Ingvill Mochmann, Kimberly Theidon, Erin Baines, and Diana Ojeda, who offered their generous feedback, insight, and encouragement at different stages of researching and writing this book. At the Instituto de Estudios Sociales Culturales Pensar of the Pontificia Universidad Javeriana, I had the luck of working with colleagues who continue to be a source of inspiration, joy, and support: Juliana Flórez Flórez, María Fernanda Sañudo, Martha Lucía Márquez Restrepo,

158   Acknowledgments

Óscar Hernández Salgar, Carlos Arturo López, Camila Esguerra Muelle, Claudia Pineda Chaves, and Lilia Coca. To Lisa McKee, whose thorough work proofreading this book was priceless, and to the two anonymous reviewers who offered generous and critical comments and suggestions that helped me take the manuscript to the next level. At Rutgers University Press, I extend my gratitude to Kimberly Guinta for having believed in my project and to Peggy Solic for her ongoing encouragement, enthusiasm, and support. Additionally, my thanks go out to the dedicated production team who transformed the manuscript into a book that my mum can proudly display on her shelves.

This book was possible thanks to the funding offered at different stages by the Departamento Administrativo de Ciencia, Tecnología e Innovación en Colombia (Colciencias), the Newton Caldas Fund, the Gilchrist Foundation, the Society of Latin American Studies (SLAS), the Feminist and Women's Studies Association (United Kingdom and Ireland), the Sociological Review Foundation, the University of Essex, and the Pontificia Universidad Javeriana in Bogotá.

Research for this book has taken place in different moments over the years, and I am indebted to the many people who have shared their time, work, and experiences with me. I am lucky enough that many of them became part of my life and allowed me to become part of theirs. The ombudsman's office in Popayán opened its archive to my research. In particular, I am grateful to Catalina Balcazar and Pilar Correa. The Unit for the Assistance and Integral Reparations of Victims in Bogotá and Popayán also opened their doors to my research. I am especially grateful to Jimena Yasnó and Eva Valencia for their willingness to share their expertise and commitment with me and for their patience in walking me through the intricacies of the world of reparations. I am also thankful to Alejandra Coll for generously sharing her time, critical thinking, and networks with me and my project.

To Paula Forero, Nicole Chavarro, and Sandra Suárez, who worked with me during pandemic times and helped me find ways of continuing to be in San Miguel despite the distance and isolation. To Sara Cano, whose work transcribing hours and hours of interviews has been invaluable. A Mildred Mosquera de la vereda de San Miguel, quien como representante del proceso de reparación colectiva y presidenta de la junta de acción comunal en el 2016, confió en mí y me invitó a irme quedando. A Cecilia Herrera de la Asociación de Mujeres Afrodescendientes del Norte del Cauca, un agradecimiento infinito por compartir conmigo su generosidad de conocimiento y espírito. I had the fortune of finding inspiration to finish this book in Edinburgh while I was getting ready to start a new chapter in my life. Although I have many people to thank for this, I would like to mention the support of Julia Zulver, Roxani Krystalli and Claire Duncanson.

In Cali, I am deeply grateful to la familia Puerto Tobón. Liliana Tobón's support and sharp sense of humor during the first stage of fieldwork were invaluable.

Over the years of conducting the research that led to this book, Cali became a second home to me in Colombia. For this, I am hugely indebted to Estefanía Renjifo and Martín Lievano, who welcomed me into their family with open arms and are an endless source of kindness and generosity.

A lo largo de estos años, mi mamá ha sido una fuente infinita de apoyo y amor. Todo lo que hago y todo lo que soy se lo debo a ella. Cada paso que doy en la vida, está inspirado en su amor y fortaleza. A Andrea Parra Triana y María Isabel Acevedo Parra, quienes junto con mi mamá son mis raíces. A mi papá, cuyo interés en mi trabajo me ha brindado una fuente enorme de apoyo. To Cia White and Anne Huntington, their curiosity and sense of adventure are an endless source of inspiration.

Friendship and love have been essential fuel behind every single page of this book. Along the way, I have been extremely lucky to have found laughter, feasts, walks, and unconditional support when the frustration came, without which this book would not have been possible. I have no words to express my deepest gratitude to these people, who very often have believed in me more than I could ever believe in myself: Carlos Vallejo, Paloma Carretero García, Andrea del Pilar Gonzalez, Claire Kyle, Itzel Toledo, David Murrieta, Miriam Lizcano, Yira Catalina Martínez, Tilotama Pradhan, Sergio Lo Iacono, Aiko Ikemura Amaral, Can Zuo, Karina Fernández, Rodrigo Caimanque, Sandino Caimanque Fernández, Mónica Díaz, Yamil Nares, Farah and Nabil Nares Díaz, and Hannah Meszaros Martin. To Alejandra Díaz de León and Luis Palerm Torres, who changed my meaning of friendship. To Sanne Weber, Natalia Niño Machado, Oscar Pedraza Vargas, Adriana Rudling, Teresa Fernández Paredes, and Juliana Laguna Trujillo, who have offered invaluable insights that have helped me shape the ideas that made it into this book.

All my love and gratitude to Bill McClanahan, my life partner and accomplice. Te amo. And I love our life together. Con todo mi corazón, gracias.

NOTES

INTRODUCTION

1. *Semana*, "'Los paraquitos'"; Defensoría del Pueblo, "Nota de Seguimiento N⁰ 029-09."
2. Unidad para las Víctimas, "Registro Único de Víctimas (RUV)."
3. Lee, "Unintended Consequences"; Mookherjee, *Spectral Wound*.
4. Arthur, "How 'Transitions' Reshaped."
5. De Greiff, "Theorizing Transitional Justice."
6. Bueno-Hansen, *Feminist and Human Rights Struggles*.
7. Schaap, "Forgiveness, Reconciliation"; Santamaría et al., "Decolonial Sketches"; Bueno-Hansen, *Feminist and Human Rights Struggles*, 18.
8. For feminist studies, see Bell and O'Rourke, "Does Feminism Need a Theory?" For decolonial studies, see Brown and Ní Aoláin, "Through the Looking Glass"; Lemaitre Ripoll, "Transitional Justice"; Bueno-Hansen, *Feminist and Human Rights Struggles*; Santamaría et al., "Decolonial Sketches"; Pastor and Santamaría, "Experiences of Spiritual Advocacy"; and Gonzáles Villamizar and Bueno-Hansen, "Promise and Perils." For queer studies, see Bueno-Hansen, "Emerging LGBTI Rights Challenge"; Schulz and Touquet, "Queering Explanatory Frameworks"; Fobear and Baines, "Pushing the Conversation Forward"; and Fobear, "Queering Truth Commissions." See also Rubio-Marín and de Greiff, "Women and Reparations."
9. Sandoval Villalba et al., *Study on the Situation*.
10. Laverty and de Vos, "Reproductive Violence"; Justicia Transicional, *Una radiografía*.
11. Brown and Ní Aoláin, "Through the Looking Glass"; Kirby, "Ending Sexual Violence in Conflict."
12. Skjelsbaek, "Sexual Violence and War"; Kirby, "Ending Sexual Violence in Conflict."
13. Theidon, "Gender in Transition."
14. Baaz and Stern, *Sexual Violence as a Weapon?*
15. Baaz and Stern, "Curious Erasures."
16. For the experiences of war-related sexual violence of cisgender men, see Eichert, "'Homosexualization' Revisited"; and Schulz, *Male Survivors*. For those of people with diverse gender identities, expressions, and sexual orientations, see Bueno-Hansen, "Emerging LGBTI Rights Challenge."
17. Baaz and Stern, *Sexual Violence as a Weapon?*
18. Schulz and Touquet, "Queering Explanatory Frameworks"; Theidon, "Reconstructing Masculinities"; Bueno-Hansen, "Emerging LGBTI Rights Challenge."
19. Schulz and Touquet, "Queering Explanatory Frameworks."
20. Drumond, Mesok, and Zalewski, "Sexual Violence."
21. Schulz, "Towards Inclusive Gender."
22. Laverty and de Vos, "Reproductive Violence."
23. Chaparro-Buitrago, "Debilitated Lifeworlds"; Justicia Transicional, *Una radiografía*.
24. Grey, "ICC's First 'Forced Pregnancy' Case."
25. Chaparro-Buitrago, "Debilitated Lifeworlds"; Theidon, *Legacies of War*; Weitsman, "Children Born of War."

162   Notes

26. Gutiérrez and Salazar, "Reproducción comunitaria de la vida"; Fraser, *Cannibal Capitalism*; Esguerra Muelle, Ojeda, and Fleischer, "Forced Displacement."
27. Federici, *Caliban and the Witch*.
28. Weitsman, "Children Born of War"; Carpenter, *Forgetting Children Born of War*; Denov and Lakor, "When War Is Better."
29. Weitsman, "Children Born of War"; Markovic, "Vessels of Reproduction."
30. Grieg, *War Children of the World*; Mochmann and Larsen, "'Children Born of War'"; Carpenter et al., *Protecting Children*; Lee, *Children Born of War*.
31. Carpenter, *Born of War*; Theidon, Mazurana, and Anumol, *Challenging Conceptions*.
32. Apio, "Uganda's Forgotten Children"; Theidon, "Hidden in Plain Sight"; Goodhart, "Children Born of War"; DeLaet, "Theorizing Justice."
33. Carpenter, *Born of War*.
34. Carpenter et al., *Protecting Children*.
35. Carpenter et al. discuss this knowledge gap. See also Neenan, *Closing the Protection Gap*.
36. Mertus, "Key Ethical Inquires."
37. Ross and Solinger, *Reproductive Justice*, 9.
38. Ross, "Reproductive Justice."
39. Enloe, "Feminist Thinking"; Cockburn, "Militarism and War."
40. Gago, *Feminist International*; Flórez Flórez, *Lecturas emergentes*.
41. Sandoval Villalba et al., *Study on the Situation*.
42. Unidad para las Víctimas, "Registro Único de Víctimas (RUV)."
43. Unidad para las Víctimas.
44. CEV, *Informe final*.
45. CEV, *Hay futuro si hay verdad*.
46. Humanas-CIASE, *Vivencias, aportes y reconocimiento*.
47. Unidad para las Víctimas, "Sistema Nacional."
48. Sandoval Villalba et al., *Study on the Situation*.
49. Sandoval Villalba et al.; Global Survivors Fund, *Global Reparation Study*.
50. Municipio de Buenos Aires, "Nuestro municipio."
51. Ng'Weno, *Turf Wars*.
52. Muñoz, "Procesos de desterritorialización."
53. Guzmán and Rodríguez, "Social Order Reconfiguration."
54. Indepaz, "Masacres en Colombia"; CEV, *Hay futuro si hay verdad*.
55. Centro Nacional de Memoria Histórica, "¡Basta ya!"
56. Centro Nacional de Memoria Histórica.
57. Muñoz, "Procesos de desterritorialización."
58. Verdad Abierta, "El recorrido sangriento."
59. Verdad Abierta, "La larga y cruel lucha."
60. Taussig, *Defacement*.
61. Goldstein, *Qualitative Research*; Das, *Violence and Subjectivity*; Das, "Language and Body."
62. Castillejo Cuéllar, "Las texturas del silencio."
63. Das, *Life and Words*; Das, "Citizen as Sexed."
64. Mookherjee, *Spectral Wound*.
65. Ross, "Speech and Silence."
66. Neenan, *Closing the Protection Gap*.
67. Enloe, "III 'Gender' Is Not Enough," 97.
68. Viveros Vigoya, "La interseccionalidad"; Viveros Vigoya and Gregorio Gil, "Sexualidades e interseccionalidad."

Notes   163

69. Caicedo, "Introducción"; Gómez and Ojeda, "Feminismo y antropología en Colombia"; Enloe, "III 'Gender' Is Not Enough."
70. Viveros Vigoya and Gregorio Gil, "Sexualidades e interseccionalidad."
71. Butler, *Frames of War.*
72. Uribe, "Dismembering and Expelling"; Castillejo Cuéllar, *La ilusión de la justicia.*
73. Indepaz, "Masacres en Colombia"; Indepaz, "Lideres sociales."
74. Theidon, *Legacies of War;* Anumol and Munderere, "Moving Beyond."
75. Mertus, "Key Ethical Inquires."
76. Theidon, *Legacies of War,* 8.
77. Van Dijk, "Free the Victim."
78. Krystalli, "Narrating Victimhood."
79. Vera Lugo, "Humanitarian State."

CHAPTER 1   BETWEEN POLITICAL STRUGGLES

1. Boezio, "Opening Remarks."
2. United Nations Security Council Resolution 2467 (2019), 7.
3. Grieg, *War Children of the World;* Carpenter et al., *Protecting Children;* Denov, "Children Born of Wartime Rape."
4. Mochmann and Larsen, "'Children Born of War'"; Mochmann and Lee, "Human Rights of Children."
5. Carpenter, *Born of War.*
6. Carpenter, "Setting the Advocacy Agenda."
7. Unidad para las Víctimas, "Registro Único de Víctimas."
8. Unidad para las Víctimas, "Ocultos a plena luz."
9. Butler, *Bodies That Matter.*
10. MADRE, "Charo Mina-Rojas Speaks."
11. UN News, "Eradicating Sexual Violence."
12. Theidon, "Hidden in Plain Sight."
13. Rocío Mojica, interview with the author, Bogotá, March 7, 2016.
14. Esther Ruíz, interview with the author, Bogotá, March 7, 2016.
15. Vera Lugo, "Humanitarian State"; Krystalli, "Narrating Victimhood."
16. Dávila Sáenz, "Land of Lawyers"; Vallejo, "Pricing Suffering"; Vera Lugo, "Humanitarian State."
17. María Eugenia Morales, interview with the author, Bogotá, June 10, 2016.
18. Carpenter, "Setting the Advocacy Agenda"; Lee, *Children Born of War.*
19. Weitsman, "Children Born of War"; DeLaet, "Theorizing Justice."
20. Grieg, *War Children of the World.*
21. Enloe, "III 'Gender' Is Not Enough."
22. Mazurana and McKay, "Child Soldiers."
23. Baines, "Complex Political Perpetrators."
24. Weber, "From Gender-Blind."
25. CEV, *Hay futuro si hay verdad.*
26. CEV, *No es un mal menor.*
27. Jaramillo Gomez, Ocampo Talero, and Osorio Perez, "¿Qué jóvenes rurales?"
28. CEV, *No es un mal menor.*
29. CEV.
30. Alejandra Coll, Zoom interview with the author, November 24, 2021.

Notes

31. Carpenter, "Setting the Advocacy Agenda."
32. Carpenter, *Forgetting Children Born of War*, 52.
33. Mertus, "Key Ethical Inquires."
34. Carpenter, "Setting the Advocacy Agenda."
35. Denov and Lakor, "When War Is Better"; Mertus, "Key Ethical Inquires."
36. Carpenter, *Forgetting Children Born of War*.
37. Julissa Mantilla, Skype interview with the author, February 19, 2016.
38. Theidon, "Hidden in Plain Sight."
39. Mantilla, interview with the author.
40. Weitsman, "Children Born of War."
41. Carpenter, *Forgetting Children Born of War*.
42. Centro Nacional de Memoria Histórica, "¡Basta ya!"
43. Sanchez Parra and Lo Iacono, "(Re)Productive Discourses."
44. Sanchez Parra and Lo Iacono, 31.
45. Sanchez Parra and Lo Iacono.
46. Skjelsbaek, "Sexual Violence and War."
47. Baaz and Stern, *Sexual Violence as a Weapon?*
48. Céspedes-Báez, "Creole Radical Feminist Transitional Justice."
49. Baaz and Stern, *Sexual Violence as a Weapon?*
50. Sandvik and Lemaitre, "Beyond Sexual Violence"; Schulz, *Male Survivors*; Weber, "From Gender-Blind"; Zulver, *High-Risk Feminism in Colombia*; Bueno-Hansen, "Emerging LGBTI Rights Challenge."
51. Theidon, "Gender in Transition"; Schulz, "Towards Inclusive Gender."
52. Cerosetenta, "Marea verde."
53. Fried, *From Abortion to Reproductive Freedom*.
54. Davis, "Racism, Birth Control."
55. Davis.
56. Olufemi, *Feminism, Interrupted*.
57. Davis, "Racism, Birth Control," 119.
58. Price, "What Is Reproductive Justice?"; Roberts, "Reproductive Justice."
59. Ross and Solinger, *Reproductive Justice*, 9.
60. Ross and Solinger, 9.
61. Ross, "Reproductive Justice."
62. Lozano and Restrepo, "Libres en la clandestinidad."
63. Esquivel and Vargas, "Una potencia feminista."
64. Stepan, *"Hour of Eugenics."*
65. Ojeda, Sasser, and Lunstrum, "Malthus's Specter and the Anthropocene."
66. Sanchez-Rivera, "From Preventive Eugenics"; Chaparro-Buitrago, "Debilitated Lifeworlds."
67. Sánchez Gómez, "Cuarta tertulia."
68. Wills, *Inclusión sin representación*.
69. Meertens and Zambrano, "Citizenship Deferred."
70. Céspedes-Báez, "Creole Radical Feminist Transitional Justice."
71. CEV, *Informe final*; Cruzat and Zúñiga, "Aborto en América Latina."
72. Cruzat and Zúñiga, "Aborto en América Latina."
73. Prada et al., "Unintended Pregnancy."
74. Gonzalez Velez and Melo Arevalo, *Causa justa*, 53–55.
75. Gonzalez Velez and Melo Arevalo, 46.
76. Médicos sin Fronteras, "Acceder a la salud."

Notes 165

77. Gonzalez Velez and Melo Arevalo, *Causa justa*, 79.
78. Dalen et al., *El ejercicio de la interrupción*.
79. Gerstein and Ward, "Supreme Court Has Voted"; Casas Isaza and Martinez, "How Latin America Could Inspire."
80. Osborn, "What the United States."
81. Bergallo, Sierra, and Vaggione, *El aborto en América Latina*.
82. Casas Isaza and Martinez, "How Latin America Could Inspire."
83. Flórez Flórez, *Lecturas emergentes*.
84. Gago, *Feminist International*.
85. Mantilla, interview with the author.
86. Congreso Nacional de Colombia, "Gaceta 692."
87. Congreso Nacional de Colombia, "Gaceta 63."
88. Mantilla, interview with the author.
89. Mantilla, interview with the author.
90. *El Espectador*, "Conservadores exigen."
91. From the author's field notes.

CHAPTER 2   THE BUREAUCRACIES OF VICTIMHOOD IN THE MAKING

1. Uprimny-Yepes and Guzmán-Rodríguez, "En búsqueda."
2. Unidad para las Víctimas, "Indemnización."
3. Corte Constitucional de Colombia, "Auto 206 del 2017."
4. Unidad para las Víctimas, "Resolución 1049," 2.
5. Unidad para las Víctimas, 3.
6. Unidad para las Víctimas, "Indemnización."
7. Unidad para las Víctimas, "El estado expresó voluntad."
8. Unidad para las Víctimas.
9. Comisión de Seguimiento y Monitoreo, "Octavo Informe de Seguimiento," 440.
10. Sánchez León and Sandoval Villalba, "Go Big or Go Home?"
11. Sandoval Villalba et al., *Study on the Situation*.
12. Jaramillo-Sierra and Buchely-Ibarra, "La etnografía burocrática"; Rivera Cusicanqui, *Violencia (re)encubiertas en Bolivia*.
13. Sandoval Villalba et al., *Study on the Situation*.
14. Recalde Castañeda and Abadía Cubillos, "Un día en la casa."
15. Recalde Castañeda, "'En lo que esté a mi alcance.'"
16. Offices of the Victims' Unit, interview with the author, Bogotá, August 17, 2022.
17. Personal conversation with the author, Bogotá, August 29, 2022.
18. Merry, *Seductions of Quantification*.
19. Neenan, *Closing the Protection Gap*.
20. Unidad para las Víctimas, "Registro Único de Víctimas (RUV)."
21. Offices of the Victims' Unit, interview with the author.
22. Offices of the Victims' Unit, interview with the author.
23. Offices of the Victims' Unit, interview with the author.
24. Unidad para las Víctimas, "Resolución 00171."
25. Unidad para las Víctimas, "Registro Único de Víctimas (RUV)."
26. María Eugenia Morales, interview with the author, Bogotá, June 10, 2016.
27. Unidad para las Víctimas, "Ocultos a plena luz."
28. Comisión de Seguimiento y Monitoreo, "Octavo Informe de Seguimiento," 424.

29. Although it was not until the passing of the Victims' Law that Colombia officially acknowledged the existence of the armed conflict, by then the country had already created various legal frameworks and information systems for addressing issues such as the mass forced displacements and individual and collective demobilization of combatants. Thus, when the Unified Registry of Victims was created in 2011, the system migrated the existing database of victims, most of whom had suffered forced displacement, which even at that stage had already surpassed three million Colombians.

30. Recalde Castañeda, "'En lo que esté a mi alcance.'"
31. Departamento Administrativo de la Función Pública, "Decreto 48 de 2011," art. 29.
32. Pellegrino, "Cifras de papel."
33. Sandoval Villalba et al., *Study on the Situation*, 54.
34. Sanchez Parra, "What's Killing Them."
35. Arthur, "How 'Transitions' Reshaped."
36. Rubio-Marín and de Greiff, "Women and Reparations."
37. De Greiff, "Theorizing Transitional Justice."
38. Pellegrino, "El papel de la respuesta."
39. Lemaitre Ripoll, "El estado siempre llega tarde."
40. Baines and Oliveira, "Securing the Future," 358.

CHAPTER 3   CONTESTED IDENTITIES

1. Goffman, *Stigma*.
2. Link and Phelan, "Conceptualizing Stigma."
3. Mukangendo, "Caring for Children"; Apio, "Uganda's Forgotten Children."
4. Theidon, "Hidden in Plain Sight."
5. Carpenter, *Forgetting Children Born of War*; Carpenter et al., *Protecting Children*; Mochmann and Lee, "Human Rights of Children."
6. Theidon, *Legacies of War*.
7. Theidon, "Hidden in Plain Sight."
8. Das, "Citizen as Sexed."
9. Theidon, *Legacies of War*, 40.
10. Lock, "Tempering of Medical Anthropology."
11. Theidon, "Hidden in Plain Sight."
12. Toogood, "Bad Blood."
13. Toogood.
14. Mochmann and Larsen, "'Children Born of War.'"
15. Weitsman, "Children Born of War"; Mochmann and Lee, "Human Rights of Children."
16. Romero, "Familia afrocolombiana."
17. Theidon, *Legacies of War*.
18. Don German, interview with the author, San Miguel, April 18, 2016.
19. Weitsman, "Children Born of War."
20. Camacho Segura, "Silencios elocuentes."
21. Mina-Rojas, *Derrotar la invisibilidad*.
22. Lozano Lerma, "El feminismo no puede ser"; Lozano Lerma, "Mujeres negras."
23. Viveros Vigoya, "Dionisios negros"; Arocha, "La inclusión de los afrocolombianos"; CEV, *Informe final*.
24. Weitsman, "Children Born of War."

Notes 167

25. Woolner, Denov, and Kahn, "'I Asked Myself'"; Akello, "Experiences of Forced Mothers."
26. Denov et al., "Mothering in the Aftermath."
27. Oliveira and Baines, "'It's like Giving Birth.'"
28. Denov and Piolanti, "Mothers of Children."
29. Gutiérrez and Salazar, "Reproducción comunitaria de la vida"; Fraser, *Cannibal Capitalism*; Esguerra Muelle, Ojeda, and Fleischer, "Forced Displacement."
30. Federici, *Caliban and the Witch*.
31. Sanchez Parra and Lo Iacono, "(Re)Productive Discourses."
32. Corporación Humanas, *Violencia sexual contra mujeres*.
33. Corporación Humanas, *La violencia sexual*.
34. Theidon, "Hidden in Plain Sight"; Theidon, *Legacies of War*.
35. Denov and Lakor, "When War Is Better."

CHAPTER 4   MEMORIES OF ABSENCE

1. Unidad para las Víctimas, "Reparación colectiva."
2. Unidad para las Víctimas, "Ruta de atención y reparación."
3. Unidad para las Víctimas.
4. Unidad para las Víctimas.
5. Some people in San Miguel claim that although it is believed that paramilitaries marched from the town of Timba to perpetuate the Naya massacre, they actually did it from San Miguel. See also Jimeno, Castillo, and Varela, "A los siete años."
6. Zulver, *High-Risk Feminism in Colombia*.
7. Zulver.
8. Jelin, *Los trabajos de la memoria*.
9. Halbwachs, *On Collective Memory*.
10. Jelin, *Los trabajos de la memoria*.
11. Ross, "Speech and Silence"; Theidon, "Gender in Transition"; Baines and Stewart, "'I Cannot Accept'"; Jackson, "Speech, Gender and Power."
12. Theidon, "Gender in Transition."
13. Castillejo Cuéllar, "Las texturas del silencio."
14. Langer, *Holocaust Testimonies*.
15. Das, "Language and Body."
16. Ross, "Speech and Silence."
17. Ross.
18. Theidon, "Gender in Transition," 474.
19. Theidon.
20. Castillejo Cuéllar, "Las texturas del silencio."
21. Tamayo, *Coordinadora Equipo Enfoque Diferencia*.
22. Anumol and Munderere, "Moving Beyond."
23. Theidon, *Legacies of War*, 33.
24. From the author's field notes.
25. Obradović-Wochnik, "'Silent Dilemma.'"
26. Agamben, *Remnants of Auschwitz*.
27. Levi, *Drowned and the Saved*.
28. Jelin, *Los trabajos de la memoria*.
29. Agamben, *Remnants of Auschwitz*; Jelin, *Los trabajos de la memoria*.

168   Notes

30. Levi, *Drowned and the Saved*.
31. Agamben, *Remnants of Auschwitz*.
32. Langer, *Holocaust Testimonies*.
33. Agamben, *Remnants of Auschwitz*, 39.
34. Castillejo Cuéllar, "Las texturas del silencio."

CONCLUSION

1. Paarlberg-Kvam, "What's to Come"; Gonzáles Villamizar and Bueno-Hansen, "Promise and Perils."
2. Paarlberg-Kvam, "What's to Come"; Laverty and de Vos, "Reproductive Violence."
3. Gago, *Feminist International*.
4. Berman-Arévalo and Ojeda, "Ordinary Geographies."
5. Theidon, *Legacies of War*.
6. Forcey, "Women as Peacemakers"; Sylvester, *War as Experience*.
7. Baines and Oliveira, "Securing the Future."
8. *Semana*, "Los paraquitos"; Defensoría del Pueblo, "Nota de Seguimiento Nº 029-09."

BIBLIOGRAPHY

Agamben, Giorgio. *Remnants of Auschwitz: The Witness and the Archive.* New York: Zone Books, 1999.

Akello, Grace. "Experiences of Forced Mothers in Northern Uganda: The Legacy of War." *Intervention* 11, no. 2 (2013): 149–156.

Anumol, Dipali, and Samuel Munderere. "Moving beyond Rwanda's 'Children of Bad Memory': A Conversation on Working with Mothers and Children Born of Wartime Rape." In Theidon, Mazurana, and Anumol, *Challenging Conceptions,* 256–264.

Apio, Eunice. "Uganda's Forgotten Children of War." In Carpenter, *Born of War,* 94–109.

Arocha, Jaime. "La inclusión de los afrocolombianos: Meta inalcanzable." In *Los afrocolombianos,* edited by Adriana Maya, 6:333–395. Geografía Humana de Colombia. Bogotá: Instituto Colombiano de Cultura Hispánica, 1998.

Arthur, Paige. "How 'Transitions' Reshaped Human Rights: A Conceptual History of Transitional Justice." *Human Rights Quarterly* 31, no. 2 (2009): 321–367.

Baaz, Maria Eriksson, and Maria Stern. "Curious Erasures: The Sexual in Wartime Sexual Violence." *International Feminist Journal of Politics* 20, no. 3 (July 3, 2018): 295–314. https://doi.org/10.1080/14616742.2018.1459197.

———. *Sexual Violence as a Weapon of War? Perceptions, Prescriptions, Problems in the Congo and Beyond.* Africa Now. London: Zed Books, 2013.

Baines, Erin K. "Complex Political Perpetrators: Reflections on Dominic Ongwen." *Journal of Modern African Studies* 47, no. 2 (June 2009): 163–191. https://doi.org/10.1017/S0022278X09003796.

Baines, Erin, and Beth Stewart. "'I Cannot Accept What I Have Not Done': Storytelling, Gender and Transitional Justice." *Journal of Human Rights Practice* 3, no. 3 (2011): 245–263.

Baines, Erin, and Camile Oliveira. "Securing the Future: Transformative Justice and Children 'Born of War.'" *Social & Legal Studies* 30, no. 3 (June 1, 2021): 341–361. https://doi.org/10.1177/0964663920946430.

Bell, Christine, and Catherine O'Rourke. "Does Feminism Need a Theory of Transitional Justice? An Introductory Essay." *International Journal of Transitional Justice* 1, no. 1 (March 1, 2007): 23–44. https://doi.org/10.1093/ijtj/ijm002.

Bergallo, Paola, Isabel Cristina Jaramillo-Sierra, and Juan Marco Vaggione. *El aborto en América Latina: Estrategias jurídicas para luchar por su legalización y enfrentar las resistencias conservadoras.* Bogotá: Siglo XXI Editores, 2019.

Berman-Arévalo, Eloísa, and Diana Ojeda. "Ordinary Geographies: Care, Violence, and Agrarian Extractivism in 'Post-conflict' Colombia." *Antipode* 52, no. 6 (2020): 1583–1602. https://doi.org/10.1111/anti.12667.

Boezio, Geraldine. "Opening Remarks of SRSG Patten at the Global Survivors Fund Event: Reparations for Survivors of Conflict-Related Sexual Violence; Status and Prospects, 27 September 2021." Office of the Special Representative of the Secretary-General on Sexual Violence in Conflict, September 27, 2021. https://www.un.org/sexualviolenceinconflict/statement/opening-remarks-of-srsg-patten-at-the-global-survivors-fund-event

Bibliography

-reparations-for-survivors-of-conflict-related-sexual-violence-status-and-prospects-27-september-2021/.

Brown, Kris, and Fionnuala Ní Aoláin. "Through the Looking Glass: Transitional Justice Futures through the Lens of Nationalism, Feminism and Transformative Change." *International Journal of Transitional Justice* 9, no. 1 (March 1, 2015): 127–149. https://doi.org/10.1093/ijtj/iju027.

Bueno-Hansen, Pascha. "The Emerging LGBTI Rights Challenge to Transitional Justice in Latin America." *International Journal of Transitional Justice* 12, no. 1 (March 1, 2018): 126–145. https://doi.org/10.1093/ijtj/ijx031.

———. *Feminist and Human Rights Struggles in Peru: Decolonizing Transitional Justice.* Champaign: University of Illinois Press, 2015.

Butler, Judith. *Bodies That Matter: On the Discursive Limits of "Sex."* New York: Routledge, 1993.

———. *Frames of War: When Is Life Grievable?* London: Verso, 2009.

Caicedo, Alhena. "Introducción: Antropología y feminismo; Confluencias y tensiones." In Caicedo, *Feminismo y antropología*, 9–14.

———, ed. *Feminismo y antropología.* Bogotá: Asociación Colombiana de Antropología, 2019.

Camacho Segura, Juana. "Silencios elocuentes, voces emergentes: Reseña bibliográfica de los estudios sobre la mujer afrocolombiana." In *Panorámica afrocolombiana: Estudios sociales en el pacífico*, edited by Mauricio Pardo Rojas, Claudia Mosquera, and María Clemencia Ramírez, 167–212. Bogotá: Instituto Colombiano de Antropología e Historia Universidad Nacional de Colombia, 2004.

Carpenter, Charli, ed. *Born of War: Protecting Children of Sexual Violence Survivors in Conflict Zones.* Bloomfield, Conn.: Kumarian, 2007.

———. *Forgetting Children Born of War: Setting the Human Rights Agenda in Bosnia and Beyond.* New York: Columbia University Press, 2010.

———. "Setting the Advocacy Agenda: Theorizing Issue Emergence and Nonemergence in Transnational Advocacy Networks." *International Studies Quarterly* 51, no. 1 (2007): 99–120. https://doi.org/10.1111/j.1468-2478.2007.00441.x.

Carpenter, Charli, Kai Grieg, K. Sharkey, and Giulia Baldi. *Protecting Children Born of Sexual Violence and Exploitation in Conflict Zones: Existing Practice and Knowledge Gaps.* National Science Foundation; University of Pittsburgh Graduate School of Public and International Affairs; Ford Institute for Human Security, December 2004. https://www.files.ethz.ch/isn/15144/Protecting_Children_Report.pdf.

Casas Isaza, Ximena, and Catalina Martinez. "How Latin America Could Inspire and Inform the US Fight for Reproductive Justice." Just Security, August 2022. https://www.justsecurity.org/82632/how-latin-america-could-inspire-and-inform-the-us-fight-for-reproductive-justice/.

Castillejo Cuéllar, Alejandro. *La ilusión de la justicia transicional: Perspectivas críticas desde el sur global.* Bogotá: Universidad de los Andes, 2017.

———. "Las texturas del silencio: Violencia, memoria, y los límites del quehacer antropológico." *Empiria: Revista de metodología de ciencias sociales*, no. 9 (2005): 39–60. https://doi.org/10.5944/empiria.9.2005.1003.

Centro Nacional de Memoria Histórica. "¡Basta ya! Colombia: Memorias de guerra y dignidad." July 2013. http://www.centrodememoriahistorica.gov.co/micrositios/informeGeneral/.

Cerosetenta. "Marea verde: Un paisaje sonoro sobre la despenalización del aborto." February 25, 2022. https://cerosetenta.uniandes.edu.co/marea-verde-un-paisaje-sonoro-sobre-la-despenalizacion-del-aborto/.

Céspedes-Báez, Lina M. "Creole Radical Feminist Transitional Justice: An Exploration of Colombian Feminism in the Context of Armed Conflict." In *Truth, Justice and Reconciliation in Colombia: Transitioning from Violence*, edited by Fabio Andres Diaz Pabon, 102–118. London: Routledge, 2018. https://www.taylorfrancis.com/chapters/edit/10.4324/9781315148373-7/creole-radical-feminist-transitional-justice-1-lina-c%C3%A9spedes-b%C3%A1ez.

Chaparro-Buitrago, Julieta. "Debilitated Lifeworlds: Women's Narratives of Forced Sterilization as Delinking from Reproductive Rights." *Medical Anthropology Quarterly* 36, no. 3 (2022): 295–311. https://doi.org/10.1111/maq.12700.

Cockburn, Cynthia. "Militarism and War." In *Gender Matters in Global Politics: A Feminist Introduction to International Relations*, edited by Laura J. Shepherd, 105–114. London: Routledge, 2010. https://www.taylorfrancis.com/chapters/edit/10.4324/9780203864944-18/militarism-war-cynthia-cockburn.

Comisión de Seguimiento y Monitoreo a la Implementación de la Ley 1448 de 2011. "Octavo Informe de Seguimiento al Congreso de la República (2020–2021)." Ministerio de Justicia, August 18, 2021. https://www.minjusticia.gov.co/ojtc/Documents/Politica%20de%20Justicia%20Transicional/Informes_de_seguimiento_ley_victimas/8.%20COMPILADO%20OCTAVO%20INFORME%20CSMLV%20(2)%20conAMMG.pdf.

Comisión para el Esclarecimiento de la Verdad, la Convivencia y la No Repetición (CEV). *Hay futuro si hay verdad: Hallazgos y recomendaciones.* Bogotá: Comisión de la Verdad, 2022.

———. *Informe final: Mi cuerpo es la verdad.* Bogotá: Comisión de la Verdad, 2022.

———. *No es un mal menor: Niñas, niños y adolescentes en el conflicto armado.* Bogotá: Comisión de la Verdad, 2022.

Congreso Nacional de Colombia. "Gaceta 63." Senado de La Republica Colombia, March 2011. http://leyes.senado.gov.co/proyectos/images/documentos/Textos%20Radicados/Ponencias/2011/gaceta_63.pdf.

———. "Gaceta 692." Ministerio de Justicia, September 2010. https://www.minjusticia.gov.co/ojtc/Documents/Victimas/Documentos/gaceta_692.pdf.

Corporación Humanas. *La violencia sexual, una estrategia paramilitar en Colombia: Argumentos para imputarle responsabilidad penal a Salvatore Mancuso, Hernán Giraldo y Rodrigo Tovar.* Bogotá: Ediciones Ántropos, 2013.

———. *Violencia sexual contra mujeres en Tumaco: Documentación y reflexión sobre los daños en mujeres racializadas.* Bogotá: Ediciones Ántropos, 2018. https://www.humanas.org.co/violencia-sexual-contra-mujeres-de-tumaco-documentacion-y-reflexion-sobre-los-danos-en-mujeres-racializadas/.

Corte Constitucional de Colombia. "Auto 206 del 2017." April 28, 2017. https://www.corteconstitucional.gov.co/T-025-04/AUTOS%202016/Auto%20206%20del%2028%20de%20abril%20de%202017%20Suspenci%C3%B3n.pdf.

Cruzat, Daniela, and Mariana Zúñiga. "Aborto en América Latina: La hora de Colombia." Produced by Daniela Cruzat and Mariana Zúñiga. *El Hilo*, February 25, 2022. Podcast. https://elhilo.audio/podcast/aborto-colombia/.

Dalen, Annika, Diana Esther Guzmán-Rodríguez, Margarita Martínez Osorio, and Nina Chaparro González. *El ejercicio de la interrupción voluntaria del embarazo en el marco del conflicto armado.* Dejusticia, January 26, 2016. https://www.dejusticia.org/publication/el-ejercicio-de-la-interrupcion-voluntaria-del-embarazo-en-el-marco-del-conflicto-armado/.

172 Bibliography

Das, Veena. "The Citizen as Sexed: Women, Violence, and Reproduction." In *Women and the Contested State: Religion, Violence, and Agency in South and Southeast Asia*, edited by Monique Skidmore and Patricia Lawrence, 29–50. Kroc Institute Series on Religion, Conflict, and Peacebuilding. Notre Dame: University of Notre Dame Press, 2007. http://site.ebrary.com/lib/universityofessex/Doc?id=10423302.

———. "Language and Body: Transactions in the Construction of Pain." *Daedalus* 125, no. 1 (January 1, 1996): 67–91.

———. *Life and Words: Violence and the Descent into the Ordinary*. Berkeley: University of California Press, 2007.

———. *Violence and Subjectivity*. Berkeley: University of California Press, 2000.

Dávila Sáenz, Juana. "A Land of Lawyers, Experts, and 'Men without Land': The Politics of Land Restitution and the Techno-legal Production of 'Dispossessed People' in Colombia." PhD diss., Harvard University, 2017. https://dash.harvard.edu/handle/1/41128811.

Davis, Angela. "Racism, Birth Control and Reproductive Rights." In *Women, Race, and Class*, 202–220. New York: Random House, 1981.

Defensoría del Pueblo. "Nota de Seguimiento Nº 029-09: Segunda Nota al Informe de Riesgo Nº 034-06; Emitido el 16 de agosto de 2006." Copy in the author's possession. Accessed November 24, 2009.

de Greiff, Pablo. "Theorizing Transitional Justice." *Nomos* 51 (2012): 31–77.

DeLaet, Debra. "Theorizing Justice for Children Born of War." In Carpenter, *Born of War*, 128–148.

Denov, Myriam. "Children Born of Wartime Rape: The Intergenerational Realities of Sexual Violence and Abuse." *Ethics, Medicine and Public Health* 1, no. 1 (2015): 61–68.

Denov, Myriam, Amber Green, Atim Angela Akor, and Janet Arach. "Mothering in the Aftermath of Forced Marriage and Wartime Rape: The Complexities of Motherhood in Postwar Northern Uganda." *Journal of the Motherhood Initiative for Research and Community Involvement* 9, no. 1 (2018): 158–176.

Denov, Myriam, and Atim Angela Lakor. "When War Is Better Than Peace: The Post-conflict Realities of Children Born of Wartime Rape in Northern Uganda." *Child Abuse & Neglect* 65 (March 1, 2017): 255–265. https://doi.org/10.1016/j.chiabu.2017.02.014.

Denov, Myriam, and Antonio Piolanti. "Mothers of Children Born of Genocidal Rape in Rwanda: Implications for Mental Health, Well-Being and Psycho-social Support Interventions." *Health Care for Women International* 40, nos. 7–9 (2019): 813–828.

Departamento Administrativo de la Función Pública. "Decreto 48 de 2011." Función Pública, December 20, 2011. https://www.funcionpublica.gov.co/eva/gestornormativo/norma_pdf.php?i=45063.

Drumond, Paula, Elizabeth Mesok, and Marysia Zalewski. "Sexual Violence in the Wrong(ed) Bodies: Moving beyond the Gender Binary in International Relations." *International Affairs* 96, no. 5 (September 1, 2020): 1145–1149. https://doi.org/10.1093/ia/iiaa144.

Eichert, David. "'Homosexualization' Revisited: An Audience-Focused Theorization of Wartime Male Sexual Violence." *International Feminist Journal of Politics* 21, no. 3 (2019): 409–433.

El Espectador. "Conservadores exigen priorizar discusión de penalización del aborto." September 21, 2011. https://www.elespectador.com/politica/conservadores-exigen-priorizar-discusion-de-penalizacion-del-aborto-article-300915/.

Enloe, Cynthia. "'III Gender' Is Not Enough: The Need for a Feminist Consciousness." *International Affairs* 80, no. 1 (January 1, 2004): 95–97. https://doi.org/10.1111/j.1468-2346.2004.00370.x.

Enloe, Cynthia. "Feminist Thinking about War, Militarism, and Peace." In *Analyzing Gender: A Handbook of Social Science Research*, edited by B. Hess and M. Ferree, 526–547. London: SAGE, 1987.

Esguerra Muelle, Camila, Diana Ojeda, and Friederike Fleischer. "Forced Displacement, Migration, and (Trans)National Care Networks." In *A Feminist Urban Theory for Our Time: Rethinking Social Reproduction and the Urban*, edited by Linda Peake, Elsa Koleth, Gökbörü Sarp Tanyildiz, and Rajyashree N. Reddy, 215–235. New York: John Wiley & Sons, 2021. https://doi.org/10.1002/9781119789161.ch9.

Esquivel, Gloria Susana, and Lina Vargas. "Una potencia feminista." Produced by Gloria Susana Esquivel and Lina Vargas. *Womansplaining*, March 30, 2022. Podcast. https://cerosetenta.uniandes.edu.co/womansplaining-una-potencia-feminista/.

Federici, Silvia. *Caliban and the Witch*. New York: Autonomedia, 2004.

Flórez Flórez, Juliana. *Lecturas emergentes*. Vol. 2, *Subjetividad, poder y deseo en los movimientos sociales*. Bogotá: Editorial Pontificia Universidad Javeriana, 2014.

Fobear, Katherine. "Queering Truth Commissions." *Journal of Human Rights Practice* 6, no. 1 (March 1, 2014): 51–68. https://doi.org/10.1093/jhuman/hut004.

Fobear, Katherine, and Erin Baines. "Pushing the Conversation Forward: The Intersections of Sexuality and Gender Identity in Transitional Justice." *International Journal of Human Rights* 24, no. 4 (April 20, 2020): 307–312. https://doi.org/10.1080/13642987.2019.1673980.

Forcey, Linda Rennie. "Women as Peacemakers." *Peace & Change* 16, no. 4 (1991): 331–354. https://doi.org/10.1111/j.1468-0130.1991.tb00674.x.

Fraser, Nancy. *Cannibal Capitalism: How Our System Is Devouring Democracy, Care, and the Planet and What We Can Do about It*. London: Verso, 2022.

Fried, Marlene Gerber. *From Abortion to Reproductive Freedom: Transforming a Movement*. Boston: South End Press, 1999.

Gago, Veronica. *Feminist International: How to Change Everything*. London: Verso, 2020.

Gerstein, Josh, and Alexander Ward. "Supreme Court Has Voted to Overturn Abortion Rights, Draft Opinion Shows." *Politico*, May 2, 2022. https://www.politico.com/news/2022/05/02/supreme-court-abortion-draft-opinion-00029473.

Global Survivors Fund. *Global Reparation Study: Executive Summary Report of Preliminary Findings*. Geneva: Global Survivors Fund, 2021. https://www.globalsurvivorsfund.org/fileadmin/uploads/gsf/Documents/Resources/Global_Reparation_Studies/GSFReportColombia_ENG.pdf.

Goffman, Erving. *Stigma: Notes on the Management of Spoiled Identity*. Reissue ed. New York: Touchstone, 1986.

Goldstein, Daniel. *Qualitative Research in Dangerous Places: Becoming an "Ethnographer" of Violence and Personal Safety*. New York: Social Science Research Council, 2014. http://webarchive.ssrc.org/working-papers/DSD_ResearchSecurity_01_Goldstein.pdf.

Gómez, Diana, and Diana Ojeda. "Feminismo y antropología en Colombia: Aportes epistemológicos, diálogos difíciles y tareas pendientes." In Caicedo, *Feminismo y antropología*, 101–133.

Gonzáles Villamizar, Juliana, and Pascha Bueno-Hansen. "Promise and Perils of Mainstreaming Intersectionality in the Colombian Peace Process." *International Journal of Transitional Justice* 15, no. 3 (2021): 553–575.

Gonzalez Velez, Ana Cristina, and Carolina Melo Arevalo, eds. *Causa justa: Argumentos para el debate sobre la despenalización total del aborto en Colombia*. La Mesa por la Vida y la Salud de las Mujeres, 2019. https://causajustaporelaborto.org/wp-content/uploads/2020/09/Argumentos_CausaJusta-virtual-final.pdf.

Goodhart, Michael. "Children Born of War and Human Rights: Philosophical Reflections." In Carpenter, *Born of War*, 188–209.

Grey, Rosemary. "The ICC's First 'Forced Pregnancy' Case in Historical Perspective." *Journal of International Criminal Justice* 15, no. 5 (December 1, 2017): 905–930. https://doi.org/10.1093/jicj/mqx051.

Grieg, Kai. *The War Children of the World*. Bergen: War and Children Project, 2001. http://www.academia.edu/2189623/The_war_children_of_the_world.

Gutiérrez, Raquel, and Huáscar Salazar. "Reproducción comunitaria de la vida: Pensando la transformación social en el presente." *El Apantle: Revista de Estudios Comunitarios* 1 (2015): 21–44.

Guzmán, Álvaro, and Alba Nubia Rodríguez. "Social Order Reconfiguration in the Middle of an Armed Conflict Situation: Case Studies of Three Municipalities in the Cauca State North Region (1990–2010)." *Sociedad y Economía*, no. 26 (June 2014): 155–184.

Halbwachs, Maurice. *On Collective Memory*. Chicago: University of Chicago Press, 1992.

Humanas-CIASE. *Vivencias, aportes y reconocimiento: Las mujeres en el proceso de paz en La Habana*. Bogotá: Corporación Humanas, 2007. https://humanas.org.co/pazconmujeres/las-mujeres-en-el-proceso-de-paz-en-la-habana/.

Instituto de Estudios para el Desarrollo y la Paz (Indepaz). "Lideres sociales, defensores de DDHH y firmantes de acuerdo asesinados en 2022." December 31, 2022. https://indepaz.org.co/lideres-sociales-defensores-de-dd-hh-y-firmantes-de-acuerdo-asesinados-en-2022/.

———. "Masacres en Colombia durante el 2020, 2021, 2022 y 2023." September 13, 2023. https://indepaz.org.co/informe-de-masacres-en-colombia-durante-el-2020-2021/.

Jackson, Cecile. "Speech, Gender and Power: Beyond Testimony." *Development and Change* 43, no. 5 (2012): 999–1023.

Jaramillo Gomez, Olga Elena, Angelica Ocampo Talero, and Flor Edilma Osorio Perez. "¿Qué jóvenes rurales deja el conflicto armado colombiano? Retos en tiempos de posacuerdo?" In *Juventudes e infancias en el escenario lationamericano y caribeño actual*, edited by Maria Camila Melina Vazquez and Maria Isabel Ospina Alvarado, 199–220. Buenos Aires: CLACSO, 2018.

Jaramillo-Sierra, Isabel Cristina, and Lina Fernanda Buchely-Ibarra, eds. *Etnografías burocráticas: Una nueva mirada a la construcción del estado en Colombia*. Bogotá: Universidad de los Andes, 2019.

———. "La etnografía burocrática como herramienta critica en el derecho administrativo" In Jaramillo-Sierra and Buchely-Ibarra, *Etnografías burocráticas*, 9–36.

Jelin, Elizabeth. *Los trabajos de la memoria*. Madrid: Siglo XXI, 2002.

Jimeno, Myriam, Ángela Castillo, and Daniel Varela. "A los siete años de la masacre del Naya: La perspectiva de las víctimas." *Anuário Antropológico* 2 (2010): 183–205.

Justicia Transicional. *Una radiografía sobre la violencia reproductiva contra mujeres y niñas durante el conflicto armado colombiano*. Bogotá: Centro de Derechos Reproductivos, 2020. https://reproductiverights.org/wp-content/uploads/2020/12/Violencia-Reproductiva-en-el-conflicto-armado-colombiano.pdf.

Kirby, Paul. "Ending Sexual Violence in Conflict: The Preventing Sexual Violence Initiative and Its Critics." *International Affairs* 91, no. 3 (May 1, 2015): 457–472. https://doi.org/10.1111/1468-2346.12283.

Krystalli, Roxani C. "Narrating Victimhood: Dilemmas and (In)Dignities." *International Feminist Journal of Politics* 23, no. 1 (January 1, 2021): 125–146. https://doi.org/10.1080/14616742.2020.1861961.

Langer, Lawrence L. *Holocaust Testimonies: The Ruins of Memory*. New Haven, Conn.: Yale University Press, 1993.

Laverty, Ciara, and Dieneke de Vos. "Reproductive Violence as a Category of Analysis: Disentangling the Relationship between 'the Sexual' and 'the Reproductive' in Transitional Justice." *International Journal of Transitional Justice* 15, no. 3 (November 1, 2021): 616–635. https://doi.org/10.1093/ijtj/ijab022.

Lee, Sabine. *Children Born of War in the Twentieth Century*. Manchester: Manchester University Press, 2017. https://www.manchesterhive.com/view/9781526104601/9781526104601.xml.

———. "Unintended Consequences or Desired Outcome? Children Born of War and Their Role in National Rebirth." In Theidon, Mazurana, and Anumol, *Challenging Conceptions*, 56–86.

Lemaitre Ripoll, Julieta. *El estado siempre llega tarde: Una reconstrucción de la vida cotidiana después de la guerra*. Bogotá: Siglo XXI Editores and Universidad de los Andes, 2019.

———. "Transitional Justice and the Challenges of a Feminist Peace." *International Journal of Constitutional Law* 18, no. 2 (August 4, 2020): 455–460. https://doi.org/10.1093/icon/moaa050.

Levi, Primo. *The Drowned and the Saved*. New York: Simon & Schuster, 1988.

Link, Bruce G., and Jo C. Phelan. "Conceptualizing Stigma." *Annual Review of Sociology* 27 (January 1, 2001): 363–385.

Lock, Margaret. "The Tempering of Medical Anthropology: Troubling Natural Categories." *Medical Anthropology Quarterly* 15, no. 4 (2001): 478–492. https://doi.org/10.1525/maq.2001.15.4.478.

Lozano, Tatiana, and Margarita Restrepo. "Libres en la clandestinidad." Produced by Tatiana Lozano and Margarita Restrepo. *Un periódico de ayer*, April 2022. Podcast. https://www.lanoficcion.com/podcast/un-periodico-de-ayer/episode/libres-en-la-clandestinidad.

Lozano Lerma, Betty Ruth. "El feminismo no puede ser uno porque las mujeres somos diversas: Aportes a un feminismo negro decolonial desde la experiencia de las mujeres negras del pacífico colombiano." *La manzana de la discordia* 5, no. 2 (2012): 7–24.

———. "Mujeres negras (sirvientas, putas, matronas): Una aproximación a la mujer negra de Colombia." *Temas de nuestra América revista de estudios latinoaméricanos* 26, no. 49 (2010): 135–158.

MADRE. "Charo Mina-Rojas Speaks at UN Security Council on Children Born of Rape." Accessed October 14, 2022. https://www.madre.org/press-publications/blog-post/charo-mina-rojas-speaks-un-security-council-children-born-rape. Page no longer extant.

Markovic, Milan. "Vessels of Reproduction: Forced Pregnancy and the ICC." *Michigan State Journal of International Law* 16 (2007): 439–458.

Mazurana, Dyan, and Susan McKay. "Child Soldiers: What about the Girls?" *Bulletin of the Atomic Scientists* 57, no. 5 (September 1, 2001): 30–35. https://doi.org/10.2968/057005010.

Médicos sin Fronteras. "Acceder a la salud es acceder a la vida." March 2011. https://www.colectivodeabogados.org/acceder-a-la-salud-es-acceder-a-la-vida-977-voces/.

Meertens, Donny, and Margarita Zambrano. "Citizenship Deferred: The Politics of Victimhood, Land Restitution and Gender Justice in the Colombian (Post?) Conflict." *International Journal of Transitional Justice* 4, no. 2 (July 1, 2010): 189–206. https://doi.org/10.1093/ijtj/ijq009.

Merry, Sally Engle. *The Seductions of Quantification*. Chicago: University of Chicago Press, 2021.

Mertus, Julie. "Key Ethical Inquires for Future Research." In Carpenter, *Born of War*, 180–187.

176   Bibliography

Mina-Rojas, Charo. *Derrotar la invisibilidad: Un reto para als mujeres afrodescendientes en Colombia; El panorama de la violencia y la violación de los derechos humanos contra las mujeres afrodescendientes en Colombia en el marco de los derechos colectivos.* Proyecto de Mujeres Afrodescendientes Defensoras de Derechos Humanos, Proceso de Comunidades Negras, 2012.

Mochmann, Ingvill C., and Stein Ugelvik Larsen. "'Children Born of War': The Life Course of Children Fathered by German Soldiers in Norway and Denmark during WWII—Some Empirical Results." *Historical Social Research / Historische Sozialforschung* 33, no. 1 (January 1, 2008): 347–363.

Mochmann, Ingvill C., and Sabine Lee. "The Human Rights of Children Born of War: Case Analyses of Past and Present Conflicts / Menschenrechte Der Kinder Des Krieges: Fallstudien Vergangener Und Gegenwärtiger Konflikte." *Historical Social Research / Historische Sozialforschung* 35, no. 3 (January 1, 2010): 268–298.

Mookherjee, Nayanika. *The Spectral Wound: Sexual Violence, Public Memories, and the Bangladesh War of 1971.* Durham, N.C.: Duke University Press, 2015.

Mukangendo, Marie Consolee. "Caring for Children Born of Rape in Rwanda." In Carpenter, *Born of War,* 40–52.

Municipio de Buenos Aires. "Nuestro municipio: Indicadores." Accessed October 1, 2016. http://buenosaires-cauca.gov.co/indicadores.shtml. Page no longer extant.

Muñoz, Federico. "Procesos de desterritorialización en Buenos Aires (Cauca): Una historia de victimización." In *Identidades, enfoque diferencial y construcción de paz,* coordinated by Blanca Inés Arteaga Morales, Diego Andrés Walteros Rangel, and Oscar David Andrade Becerra, 99–126. Documentos para la paz 3. Bogotá: Universidad de Bogotá Jorge Tadeo Lozano, 2012. https://www.utadeo.edu.co/sites/tadeo/files/node/wysiwyg/pdf _identidades_enfoque_diferencial_y_construccion_de_paz_.pdf.

Neenan, Joanne. *Closing the Protection Gap for Children Born of War: Addressing Stigmatisation and the Intergenerational Impact of Sexual Violence in Conflict.* London: London School of Economics, 2018. https://www.lse.ac.uk/women-peace-security/assets/documents/ 2018/LSE-WPS-Children-Born-of-War.pdf.

Ng'Weno, Bettina. *Turf Wars: Territory and Citizenship in the Contemporary State.* Redwood City, Calif.: Stanford University Press, 2007.

Obradović-Wochnik, Jelena. "The 'Silent Dilemma' of Transitional Justice: Silencing and Coming to Terms with the Past in Serbia." *International Journal of Transitional Justice* 7, no. 2 (July 1, 2013): 328–347. https://doi.org/10.1093/ijtj/ijt011.

Ojeda, Diana, Jade S. Sasser, and Elizabeth Lunstrum. "Malthus's Specter and the Anthropocene." *Gender, Place & Culture* 27, no. 3 (March 3, 2020): 316–332. https://doi.org/10.1080/ 0966369X.2018.1553858.

Oliveira, Camile, and Erin Baines. "'It's like Giving Birth to This Girl Again': Social Repair and Motherhood after Conflict-Related Sexual Violence." *Social Politics: International Studies in Gender, State & Society* 29, no. 2 (June 1, 2022): 750–770. https://doi.org/10.1093/sp/ jxab033.

Olufemi, Lola. *Feminism, Interrupted: Disrupting Power.* London: Pluto Press, 2020.

Osborn, Catherine. "What the United States Can Learn from Latin American Abortion Rights Activists." *Foreign Policy,* May 6, 2022. https://foreignpolicy.com/2022/05/06/ mexico-argentina-brazil-abortion-united-states-roe-wade-green-tide/.

Paarlberg-Kvam, Kate. "What's to Come Is More Complicated: Feminist Visions of Peace in Colombia." *International Feminist Journal of Politics* 21, no. 2 (March 15, 2019): 194–223. https://doi.org/10.1080/14616742.2018.1487266.

Pastor, Lejandrina, and Angela Santamaría. "Experiences of Spiritual Advocacy for Land and Territorial Itineraries for the Defense of Wiwa Women's Rights in Postconflict Colombia." *International Journal of Transitional Justice* 15, no. 1 (March 1, 2021): 86–107. https://doi.org/10.1093/ijtj/ijaa033.

Pellegrino, Valentina. "Cifras de papel: La rendición de cuentas del gobierno colombiano ante la justicia como una manera de incumplir cumpliendo." *Antipoda: Revista de Antropología y Arqueología*, no. 42 (2021): 3–27.

———. "El papel de la respuesta y la respuesta como papel: Etnografía al papeleo de una orden judicial." In Jaramillo-Sierra and Buchely-Ibarra, *Etnografías burocráticas*, 217–254.

Prada, Elena, Susheela Singh, Lisa Remez, and Cristina Villarreal. "Unintended Pregnancy and Induced Abortion in Colombia: Causes and Consequences." Guttmacher Institute, September 1, 2011. https://www.guttmacher.org/report/unintended-pregnancy-and-induced-abortion-colombia-causes-and-consequences.

Price, Kimala. "What Is Reproductive Justice?" *Meridians* 19, no. S1 (2010): 340–362.

Recalde Castañeda, Gabriela. "'En lo que esté a mi alcance les ayudo': Los funcionarios de base y las víctimas en el proceso de declaración para la inscripción en el Registro Único de Víctimas del conflicto armado." In Jaramillo-Sierra and Buchely-Ibarra, *Etnografías burocráticas*, 141–176.

Recalde Castañeda, Gabriela, and Gloria Marcela Abadía Cubillos. "Un día en la casa de justicia: Atención en violencia doméstica y la banalización del estado a través de la justicia." In Jaramillo-Sierra and Buchely-Ibarra, *Etnografías burocráticas*, 149–172.

Rivera Cusicanqui, Silvia. *Violencia (re)encubiertas en Bolivia*. Santander: Otramérica, 2012.

Roberts, Dorothy. "Reproductive Justice, Not Just Rights." *Dissent* 62, no. 4 (2015): 79–82.

Romero, Mario Diego. "Familia afrocolombiana y construcción territorial en el pacífico sur, siglo XVIII." In *Los afrocolombianos*, edited by Adriana Maya, 6:84–94. Geografía Humana de Colombia. Bogotá: Instituto Colombiano de Cultura Hispánica, 1998.

Ross, Fiona. "Speech and Silence: Women's Testimony in the First Five Weeks of Public Hearings of the South African Truth and Reconciliation Commission." In *Remaking a World: Violence, Social Suffering, and Recovery*, edited by Veena Das, Arthur Kleinman, Margaret Lock, Mamphela Ramphele, and Pamela Reynolds, 250–279. Berkeley: University of California Press, 2001.

Ross, Loretta J. "Reproductive Justice as Intersectional Feminist Activism." *Souls* 19, no. 3 (July 3, 2017): 286–314. https://doi.org/10.1080/10999949.2017.1389634.

Ross, Loretta, and Rickie Solinger. *Reproductive Justice: An Introduction*. Berkeley: University of California Press, 2017.

Rubio-Marín, Ruth, and Pablo de Greiff. "Women and Reparations." *International Journal of Transitional Justice* 1, no. 3 (2007): 318–337.

Sánchez Gómez, Olga Amparo. "Cuarta tertulia: Entrelazando feminismos en Colombia; Parte de 40 tertulias sobre feminismos, Casa de La Mujer Colombia." Facebook webinar. March 25, 2021. https://www.facebook.com/302384689824328/videos/486927452342406.

Sánchez León, Nelson Camilo, and Clara Sandoval Villalba. "Go Big or Go Home? Lessons Learned from the Colombian Victims' Reparation System." In *Reparations for Victims of Genocide, War Crimes and Crimes against Humanity*, edited by Carla Ferstman and Mariana Goetz, 547–570. Leiden: Koninklijke Brill, 2020.

Sanchez Parra, Tatiana. "What's Killing Them: Violence beyond COVID-19 in Colombia." *Crime, Media, Culture* 17, no.1 (July 27, 2020). https://journals.sagepub.com/doi/10.1177/1741659020946379.

Sanchez Parra, Tatiana, and Sergio Lo Iacono. "(Re)Productive Discourses: Media Coverage of Children Born of War in Colombia." *Bulletin of Latin American Research* 39, no. 1 (2019): 22–36. https://doi.org/10.1111/blar.12976.

Sanchez-Rivera, R. "From Preventive Eugenics to Slippery Eugenics: Population Control and Contemporary Sterilisations Targeted to Indigenous Peoples in Mexico." *Sociology of Health & Illness* 45, no. 1 (2023): 128–144. https://doi.org/10.1111/1467-9566.13556.

Sandoval Villalba, Clara, Tatiana Sanchez Parra, Juliana Laguna, and Tatiana Olarte. *Study on the Situation and Opportunities of the Right to Reparation for Victims and Survivors of Conflict-Related Sexual and Reproductive Violence in Colombia: Victims at the Centre of Reparation.* Geneva: Global Survivors Fund, 2022.

Sandvik, Kristin Bergtora, and Julieta Lemaitre. "Beyond Sexual Violence in Transitional Justice: Political Insecurity as a Gendered Harm." *Feminist Legal Studies* 22, no. 3 (2014): 243–261. https://doi.org/10.1007/s10691-014-9274-0.

Santamaría, Angela, Dunen Muelas, Paula Caceres, Wendi Kuetguaje, and Julian Villegas. "Decolonial Sketches and Intercultural Approaches to Truth: Corporeal Experiences and Testimonies of Indigenous Women in Colombia." *International Journal of Transitional Justice* 14, no. 1 (March 1, 2020): 56–79. https://doi.org/10.1093/ijtj/ijz034.

Schaap, Andrew. "Forgiveness, Reconciliation, and Transitional Justice." In *Hannah Arendt and International Relations: Readings across the Lines,* edited by Anthony F. Lang and John Williams, 67–93. New York: Palgrave Macmillan, 2005. https://doi.org/10.1057/9781403981509_4.

Schulz, Philipp. *Male Survivors of Wartime Sexual Violence: Perspectives from Northern Uganda.* Berkeley: University of California Press, 2020. https://doi.org/10.1525/luminos.95.

———. "Towards Inclusive Gender in Transitional Justice: Gaps, Blind-Spots and Opportunities." *Journal of Intervention and Statebuilding* 14, no. 5 (October 19, 2020): 691–710. https://doi.org/10.1080/17502977.2019.1663984.

Schulz, Philipp, and Heleen Touquet. "Queering Explanatory Frameworks for Wartime Sexual Violence against Men." *International Affairs* 96, no. 5 (September 1, 2020): 1169–1187. https://doi.org/10.1093/ia/iiaa062.

Semana. "'Los paraquitos.'" August 20, 2010. http://www.semana.com//nacion/articulo/los-paraquitos/120819-3.

Skjelsbaek, Inger. "Sexual Violence and War: Mapping Out a Complex Relationship." *European Journal of International Relations* 7, no. 2 (June 1, 2001): 211–237. https://doi.org/10.1177/1354066101007002003.

Stepan, Nancy. *"The Hour of Eugenics": Race, Gender, and Nation in Latin America.* Ithaca, N.Y.: Cornell University Press, 1991.

Sylvester, Christine. *War as Experience: Contributions from International Relations and Feminist Analysis.* London: Routledge, 2012. https://doi.org/10.4324/9780203100943.

Taussig, Michael T. *Defacement: Public Secrecy and the Labor of the Negative.* Redwood City, Calif.: Stanford University Press, 1999.

Theidon, Kimberly. "Gender in Transition: Common Sense, Women, and War." *Journal of Human Rights* 6, no. 4 (December 11, 2007): 453–478. https://doi.org/10.1080/14754830701693011.

———. "Hidden in Plain Sight." *Current Anthropology* 56 (December 2, 2015): S191–S200. https://doi.org/10.1086/683301.

————. *Legacies of War: Violence, Ecologies, and Kin.* Durham, N.C.: Duke University Press, 2022.

————. "Reconstructing Masculinities: The Disarmament, Demobilization, and Reintegration of Former Combatants in Colombia." *Human Rights Quarterly* 31, no. 1 (2009): 1–34.

Theidon, Kimberly, Dyan Mazurana, and Dipali Anumol, eds. *Challenging Conceptions: Children Born of Wartime Rape and Sexual Exploitation.* Oxford: Oxford University Press, 2023.

Toogood, Kimairis. "Bad Blood: Perceptions of Children Born of Conflict-Related Sexual Violence and Women and Girls Associated with Boko Haram in Northeast Nigeria." International Alert, February 13, 2016. https://www.international-alert.org/publications/bad-blood/.

Unidad para las Víctimas. "El estado expresó voluntad para mejorar atención a hijos de la violencia sexual." September 9, 2019. https://www.unidadvictimas.gov.co/es/atencion-victimas/el-estado-expreso-voluntad-para-mejorar-atencion-hijos-de-la-violencia-sexual.

————. "Indemnización." Accessed April 19, 2022. https://www.unidadvictimas.gov.co/es/indemnizacion/8920.

————. "Ocultos a plena luz: Niños y niñas nacidos de violencia sexual en el marco del conflicto armado." November 8, 2019. https://www.unidadvictimas.gov.co/es/enfoques-diferenciales/ocultos-plena-luz-hijos-e-hijas-nacidos-raiz-de-violencia-sexual-en-el-marco.

————. "Registro Único de Víctimas." January 1, 2017. https://datospaz.unidadvictimas.gov.co/registro-unico-de-victimas/.

————. "Registro Único de Víctimas (RUV)." August 31, 2022. https://www.unidadvictimas.gov.co/es/registro-unico-de-victimas-ruv/37394.

————. "Reparación colectiva." August 5, 2015. https://www.unidadvictimas.gov.co/es/atencion-asistencia-y-reparacion-integral/reparacion-colectiva/119.

————. "Resolución 00171: Por la cual se define el confinamiento como hecho victimizante en el marco de la Ley 1448 de 2011." February 24, 2016. https://www.unidadvictimas.gov.co/sites/default/files/documentosbiblioteca/resolucion00171de24febrero2016.pdf.

————. "Resolución 1049: Por lo cual se adopta el procedimiento para reconocer y otorgar la indemnización por vía administrativa, se crea el método técnico de priorización, se derogan las Resoluciones 090 de 2015 y 01958 de 2018 y se dictan otras disposiciones." March 15, 2019. https://www.unidadvictimas.gov.co/wp-content/uploads/2019/03/010 49de15marzodel2019.pdf.

————. "Ruta de atención y reparación integral para sujetos colectivos." July 2022. https://www.unidadvictimas.gov.co/es/folleto-ruta-de-atencion-colectivos/73564.

————. "Sistema Nacional de Atención y Reparación Integral a las Víctimas (SNARIV)." Accessed October 1, 2022. https://www.unidadvictimas.gov.co/es/gestion-interinstitucional/que-es-el-sistema-nacional-de-atencion-y-reparacion-integral-las-victimas. Page no longer extant.

UN News. "Eradicating Sexual Violence in Colombia Requires Investment in Communities—UN Envoy." March 4, 2015. http://www.un.org/apps/news/story.asp?NewsID=50246#.VIcdur9SoYs.

Uprimny-Yepes, Rodrigo, and Diana Esther Guzmán-Rodríguez. "En búsqueda de un concepto transformador y participativo para las reparaciones en contextos transicionales." *International Law, Revista Colombiana de Derecho Internacional*, no. 17 (2010): 231–286.

Uribe, Maria Victoria. "Dismembering and Expelling: Semantics of Political Terror in Colombia." *Public Culture* 16, no. 1 (2004): 79–95.

Bibliography

Vallejo, Catalina. "Pricing Suffering: Compensation for Human Rights Violations in Colombia and Peru." PhD diss., University of Virginia, 2019. https://libraetd.lib.virginia.edu/public_view/jq085k41q.

Van Dijk, Jan. "Free the Victim: A Critique of the Western Conception of Victimhood." *International Review of Victimology* 16 (2009): 1–33.

Vera Lugo, Juan Pablo. "The Humanitarian State: Bureaucracy and Social Policy in Colombia." RUcore: Rutgers University Community Repository, 2017. https://rucore.libraries.rutgers.edu/rutgers-lib/54032/.

Verdad Abierta. "El recorrido sangriento del Bloque Calima por Cauca." April 25, 2012. http://www.verdadabierta.com/component/content/article/35-bloques/3987-el-recorrido-sangriento-del-bloque-calima-por-cauca.

———. "La larga y cruel lucha por la tierra en el Cauca." January 15, 2014. http://www.verdadabierta.com/lucha-por-la-tierra/5087-la-larga-y-cruel-lucha-por-la-tierra-en-el-cauca#l3.

Viveros Vigoya, Mara. "Dionisios negros: Sexualidad, corporalidad y orden racial en Colombia." Institutional Repository of the Universidad Nacional de Colombia. Accessed September 1, 2022. https://repositorio.unal.edu.co/handle/unal/57932.

———. "La interseccionalidad: Una aproximación situada a la dominación." *Debate Feminista* 52 (October 1, 2016): 1–17. https://doi.org/10.1016/j.df.2016.09.005.

Viveros Vigoya, Mara, and Carmen Gregorio Gil. "Sexualidades e interseccionalidad en América Latina, el Caribe y su diaspora." *Revista de Estudios Sociales*, no. 49 (2014). https://doi.org/10.7440/res49.2014.01.

Weber, Sanne. "From Gender-Blind to Gender-Transformative Reintegration: Women's Experiences with Social Reintegration in Guatemala." *International Feminist Journal of Politics* 23, no. 3 (May 27, 2021): 396–417. https://doi.org/10.1080/14616742.2020.1768879.

Weitsman, Patricia. "Children Born of War and the Politics of Identity." In Carpenter, *Born of War*, 110–127.

Wills, María Emma. *Inclusión sin representación: La irrupción política de las mujeres en Colombia (1970–2000)*. Bogotá: Editorial Norma, 2007.

Woolner, Leah, Myriam Denov, and Sarilee Kahn. "'I Asked Myself If I Would Ever Love My Baby': Mothering Children Born of Genocidal Rape in Rwanda." *Violence against Women* 25, no. 6 (2018): 703–720.

Zulver, Julia. *High-Risk Feminism in Colombia: Women's Mobilization in Violent Contexts*. New Brunswick, N.J.: Rutgers University Press, 2022.

INDEX

Abadía Cubillos, Gloria Marcela, 165n14
abortion: decriminalization of, 45–47, 147;
  forced, 33; individual choice rhetoric, 41, 45,
  46; and intersectionality, 45; and legalization
  of, 42–44, 51; and Malthusian agenda, 41, 43
absent father. *See* paramilitaries
accountability, 6, 14, 25, 83, 126, 147, 151.
  See also transitional justice system
Agamben, Giorgio, 137
Akello, Grace, 167n25 (chap. 3)
Alejandra, 69–72, 75–81
Anumol, Dipali, 132, 163n74
Apio, Eunice, 162n32, 166n3
Arach, Janet, 167n26 (chap. 3)
Arocha, Jaime, 166n23
Arthur, Paige, 161n4, 166n35
Association of Afro-Colombian Women of
  the North of Cauca (ASOM), 78
Astrid, 86, 110, 117; on San Miguel's collec-
  tive reparation, 120–125
attendance sheet, 78, 122. *See also* bureaucra-
  cies of reparations

Baaz, Maria Eriksson, 39, 161nn14–15, 161n17
Baines, Erin, 161n8, 163n23, 166n40, 167n27
  (chap. 3), 167n11 (chap. 4)
Bangura, Zainab Hawa, former U.N. SRSG
  on Sexual Violence in Conflict, 30
bastards, 97
Bell, Christine, 161n8
Bergallo, Paola, 165n81
Berman-Arévalo, Eloísa, 168n4
Bosnia and Herzegovina, 7, 37
Brown, Kris, 161n8, 161n11
Bueno-Hansen, Pascha, 4, 161nn6–8,
  161n16, 161n18, 164n50, 168n1
Buenos Aires, 1, 14–17, 48, 56, 77, 81, 115,
  138, 145
bureaucracies of reparations, 24, 57, 74, 76,
  79, 80, 83
Butler, Judith, 19

Caceres, Paula, 161nn7–8
Caicedo, Alhena, 163n69
Cali, 21, 42, 78
Camacho Segura, Juana, 166n20
care: and abortion, 47; and children born of
  conflict-related sexual violence, 48; and
  labor of motherhood, 54, 86, 105, 147;
  psychosocial, 64, 69, 72, 79, 81, 83, 117;
  and reproductive justice, 41; and social
  reproduction, 3, 7
Carmen (Victims' Unit head of the
  collective reparation process in
  San Miguel), 120, 122, 134–135,
  142–143
Carmen (woman from San Miguel), 128
Carpenter, Charli, 162n28, 162nn30–31,
  162nn33–35, 163n3, 163nn5–6, 35, 37,
  166n5
Casas Isaza, Ximena, 165n79, 165n82
Castillejo Cuéllar, Alejandro, 138, 162n62,
  163n72, 167n13, 167n20
Castillo, Ángela, 167n5
Cauca River, 1, 111, 116
Causa Justa, 45–46. *See also* abortion
Cecilia, 80–81
Centro Nacional de Memoria Histórica,
  162nn55–56, 164n42
Cerosetenta, 164n52
Céspedes-Báez, Lina M., 164n48, 164n70
Chaparro-Buitrago, Julieta, 161n23, 161n25,
  164n66
Chaparro González, Nina, 165n78
child recruitment, 32, 33, 149
children born of conflict-related sexual violence: on concealment, 18, 28, 139–140,
  155; and knowledge gap, 8–9, 49, 51, 149,
  150; as secondary characters, 29, 38; on
  unintelligibility, 22, 29, 54, 74, 149; and
  unwanted lives, 23, 54, 109, 149. *See also*
  impossible witnesses
children born of war, 22, 34

182   Index

Children Born of War H2020 Marie Curie Innovative Training Network, 32
Chile, 98
citizenship: and children born of conflict-related sexual violence, 8, 90; and reproductive rights, 40; and transitional justice mechanisms, 13–14
Clemencia, 58–59; and absence of the father, 95–96; and bureaucracies of reparation, 65–66, 78; on disclosure, 131–133; and family, 105–108; on knowing who the father is, 99; and presence of the father, 87–89, 94; on reparations, 100, 135, 147
Cockburn, Cynthia, 162n39
Coll, Alejandra, 163n30
Collective Reparations Support Group, 122, 134–135
Colombia: armed conflict, 10–11; transitional justice system, 11–17
Colombian Commission for the Clarification of the Truth, Coexistence, and Non-recurrence, 11, 33, 48, 52; on children born of conflict-related sexual violence, 34; and reproductive violence, 48; on war-affected children, 33–34
Colombian Constitutional Court, 28, 33, 40, 44, 61
Colombian Family Welfare Institute (ICBF), 50, 63
Comisión de Seguimiento y Monitoreo a la Implementación de la Ley 1448 de 2011, 165n9, 165n28
community action board, 117–120, 122, 134, 136, 142
community council, 118; Community Council of the Cauca River Basin and Micro-basin of the Teta and Mazamorrero Rivers, 118–122, 128, 134
compensation, 60–63, 69, 75, 80. See also reparations
complex political perpetrators, 32
complying incompliantly. See incumplir cumpliendo
confinement: and children born of conflict-related sexual violence as impossible witnesses, 108, 112; and collective reparations, 116–117, 119, 121–124, 154; and label paraquitos, 102; and poultry farm, 142, 144;

and San Miguel, 16, 24, 57, 86, 91; within victims' registry, 70. See also occupation
conflict-affected children, 28, 49–50, 67, 82, 149. See also war-affected children
COVID-19, 34, 56, 62, 81, 145
Cruzat, Daniela, 164nn71–72

Dalen, Annika, 165n78
Das, Veena, 129, 162n61, 162n63, 166n8
database, 71–72, 74, 75. See also bureaucracies of reparations
Dávila Sáenz, Juana, 163n16
Davis, Angela, 41
De Greiff, Pablo, 161n5, 161n8, 166nn36–37
DeLaet, Debra, 162n32, 163n19
Denmark, 97
Denov, Myriam, 106, 162n28, 163n3, 164n35, 167nn25–26 (chap. 3), 167n28 (chap. 3)
de Vos, Dieneke, 161n10, 161n22, 168n2
disclosure, 131–134
Doña Libia, 85
Doña Miriam, 125
Doña Rosa, 126
Doña Teresa, 125, 126
Don Efraín, 125–127
Don Gabriel, 126
Don German, 101
Drumond, Paula, 161n20

economies of war, 58, 81
Ecuador, 98
Eichert, David, 161n16
Enloe, Cynthia, 18–19, 162n39, 163n21
Esguerra Muelle, Camila, 162n26, 167n29 (chap. 3)
Esquivel, Gloria Susana, 164n63
ethnography, 18–19
Excel, 71, 74, 135. See also registry
experts: on expertise inertia, 67; and knowledge, 57, 75, 82

Federici, Silvia, 105, 162n27
feminism: and abortion, 40–44; and conflict-related reproductive violence, 6, 9, 53, 113; and conflict-related sexual violence, 38–39, 103; on consciousness, 19; ethnography, 10, 19; on high-risk, 120; and Latin American social movement, 11, 43, 46–47, 150;

peace building, 9, 146–147; and political struggles, 23, 42, 50; and transitional justice, 4, 48, 139

Fleischer, Friederike, 162n26, 167n29 (chap. 3)

Flórez Flórez, Juliana, 162n40, 165n83

Fobear, Katherine, 161n8

forced contraception, 6, 33, 47, 104. *See also* reproductive violence

forced sterilization, 6, 43, 104. *See also* reproductive violence

Forcey, Linda Rennie, 168n6

form, 72, 76. *See also* bureaucracies of reparations

Fraser, Nancy, 162n26, 167n29 (chap. 3)

Fried, Marlene Gerber, 164n53

Gabriel (one of the heads of the Victims' Unit Assessment and Registry Subdirectorate), 69–72, 74–76

Gabriel (San Miguel's president of the community action board), 120

Gago, Veronica, 47, 162n40, 168n3

gendered victimhood: and children born of conflict-related sexual violence, 51, 108, 153; and conflict-related reproductive violence, 6, 47, 54, 104, 150; and conflict-related sexual violence, 3, 6, 35, 39, 154; and transitional justice, 1, 5

gender justice, 113, 120–121, 154

Gerstein, Josh, 165n79

Global Survivors Fund (GSF), 26

Gloria, 59, 65–66, 89; and bureaucracies of reparations, 77; on disclosure, 131–132; on fathers, 100; and recruitment, 81–82, 145; on reparations, 135, 147

Goffman, Erving, 166n1

Goldstein, Daniel, 162n61

Gómez, Diana, 163n69

Gonzalez Velez, Ana Cristina, 40, 165n77

González Villamizar, Juliana, 161n8, 168n1

Goodhart, Michael, 162n32

Green, Amber, 167n26 (chap. 3)

Gregorio Gil, Carmen, 162n68, 163n70

Grey, Rosemary, 161n24

Grieg, Kai, 162n30, 163n3, 163n20

Gutiérrez, Raquel, 162n26, 167n29 (chap. 3)

Guzmán, Alvaro, 162n53

Guzmán-Rodríguez, Diana Esther, 165n78 (chap. 1), 165n1 (chap. 2)

Halbwachs, Maurice, 123

harm, 48, 137, 147; and children born of conflict-related sexual violence, 133–134, 147, 149, 156; on harm-centered model of transitional justice, 3, 5, 85, 151, 155; and reparations, 50, 72, 75, 83, 128; and sexual violence, 129, 152

Humanas: Corporación Humanas, 167nn32–33; Humanas-CIASE, 162n46

identity, 37, 54, 86, 90, 92–93, 97, 102

impossible witnesses, 138, 140

incumplir cumpliendo, 79

institutional violence, 25, 51, 84, 133, 136, 140, 155. *See also* bureaucracies of reparations

Instituto de Estudios para el Desarrollo y la Paz (Indepaz), 162n54, 163n73

International Network for Interdisciplinary Research on Children Born of War (INIRC), 32

intraparty sexual violence, 33. *See also* reproductive violence

Jackson, Cecile, 167n11

Jaramillo Gomez, Olga Elena, 163n27

Jaramillo-Sierra, Isabel Cristina, 165n81 (chap. 1), 165n12 (chap. 2)

Jelin, Elizabeth, 123, 137

Jimeno, Myriam, 167n5

Jorge, 126–127

Justice and Peace Law, 12–13, 44, 58, 128. *See also* transitional justice system

Kahn, Sarilee, 167n25 (chap. 3)

Kirby, Paul, 161nn11–12

Krystalli, Roxani, 163n78 (intro.), 163n15 (chap. 1)

Kuetguaje, Wendi, 161nn7–8

labor of motherhood, 86, 104–107, 109, 112, 140

Laguna, Juliana, 161n9, 162n41, 162nn48–49, 165n11, 165n13, 166n33

184   Index

Lakor, Atim Angela, 106, 162n28, 164n35, 167n26 (chap. 3)

Langer, Lawrence, 129

Larsen, Stein Ugelvik, 162n30, 163n4, 166n14

Latin American feminist movement. *See* feminism

Laverty, Ciara, 161n10, 161n22, 168n2

Law 70 of 1993, 118. *See also* community council

Lee, Sabine, 162n30, 163n4, 163n18, 166n5, 166n15

Lemaitre Ripoll, Julieta, 161n8, 164n50, 166n39

Levi, Primo, 137

Liliana, 115–119, 120, 134

Link, Bruce G., 166n2

local biologies, 92–93

Lock, Margaret, 92

Lo Iacono, Sergio, 38–39

Lozano, Tatiana, 164n62

Lozano Lerma, Betty Ruth, 166n22

Lucia, 80–81

Lunstrum, Elizabeth, 164n65

MADRE, 163n10

Mantilla, Julissa, 31, 35, 48, 49, 50

Markovic, Milan, 162n29

Márquez, Francia, 52, 145

Martinez, Catalina, 165n79, 165n82

masculinities, 5, 39

Mazurana, Dyan, 162n31, 163n22

McKay, Susan, 163n22

media coverage, 37–38

Médicos sin Fronteras, 164n76

Meertens, Donny, 164n69

Melo Arévalo, Carolina, 164nn74–75, 165n77

memories, 87, 96; of absence, 110; and collective memories, 111–113, 122–124, 139; and collective reparations, 24, 142, 153; on gendered, 125–126; and naming practices, 94; as object of labor, 123–124, 129–130, 136; and people born of conflict-related sexual violence, 140

Merry, Sally Engle, 67

Mertus, Julie, 162n36, 163n75, 164n33, 164n35

Mesok, Elisabeth, 161n20

military service, 59, 81

Mina-Rojas, Charo, 30

Ministry of Education, 63

Ministry of Health, 12, 61, 63

Mochmann, Ingvill C., 162n30, 163n4, 166n5, 166nn14–15

Mojica, Rocío, 31

Mookherjee, Nayanika, 161n3, 162n64

Morales, María Eugenia, 31, 70

motherhood: forced, 29, 48, 103–106; as labor, 104

Muelas, Dunen, 161nn7–8

Mukangendo, Marie Consolee, 166n3

Munderere, Samuel, 132, 163n74

Municipio de Buenos Aires, 162n50

Muñoz, Federico, 162n52, 162n57

National Commission of Reparation and Reconciliation (CNRR), 115

National Committee for Victims' Participation, 63, 64, 71

National Congress, 42, 44, 49, 51, 63, 64, 71

National System for Comprehensive Victim Support and Reparation (SNARIV), 12. *See also* reparations

Naya, 115–116

Neenan, Joanne, 162n66, 165n19

Ng'Weno, Bettina, 162n51

Ní Aoláin, Fionnuala, 161n8, 161n11

Nigeria, 92–93

Norway, 97

novedad, 77, 80. *See also* bureaucracies of reparations

Obradović-Wochnik, Jelena, 167n25 (chap. 4)

Ocampo Talero, Angelica, 163n27

occupation, 1; and collective memories, 88, 123–125, 127; and collective reparations, 112, 120–121, 141–143, 154; and forced and strategic partnership, 106–107; and motherhood, 101–103, 108, 110; and paramilitaries as absent fathers, 91, 95; and poultry farm, 144–145; and sexual violence, 152. *See also* confinement

offspring, 92, 105
Ojeda, Diana, 162n26, 163n69, 164n65, 167n29 (chap. 3), 168n4
Olarte, Tatiana, 161n9, 162n41, 162nn48–49, 165n11, 165n13, 166n33
Oliveira, Camile, 166n40, 167n27, 168n7
Olufemi, Lola, 164n56
ombudsman, 48, 63, 72, 114, 117, 148, 158
O'Rourke, Catherine, 161n8
Osborn, Catherine, 165n80
Osorio Perez, Flor Edilma, 163n27

Paarlberg-Kvam, Kate, 168nn1–2
paramilitaries: as absent fathers, 38, 95, 108; biological fathers as, 2, 85–86, 89–93; and demobilization, 96, 115–116, 124, 152; as perpetrators of sexual violence, 8, 38–39, 92, 101–102, 105, 128, 152; United Self-Defense Forces of Colombia (AUC), 15–16, 110
paraquitos (little paramilitaries): and identity transmission, 24, 86, 91; and mark of victimhood, 25, 89, 112; and naming practices, 2, 91; and whispers, 1, 124, 153
Pastor, Lejandrina, 161n8
Patten, Camila, former U.N. SRSG on Sexual Violence in Conflict, 26
Pellegrino, Valentina, 79, 166n38
people born of conflict-related sexual violence, 22. See also children born of conflict-related sexual violence
Perea, Yolanda, 63
perpetrator: biological fathers as, 8, 85–94, 102; of conflict-related sexual violence, 38–39, 93, 122, 152; victim-perpetrator binary, 32, 33
Peruvian Truth and Reconciliation Commission, 32, 129
Petro, Gustavo, 52, 145
Phelan, Jo C., 166n2
photo-voice, 21
Piolanti, Antonio, 167n28 (chap. 3)
Popayán, 48
population control, 6, 40, 43
poultry farm, 146
Prada, Elena, 164n73
Price, Kimala, 164n58

prioritization method, 61. See also compensation
Proceso de Comunidades Negras, 30

Recalde Castañeda, Gabriela, 165nn14–15, 166n30
registry, 60, 67–76. See also bureaucracies of reparations
Remez, Lisa, 164n73
reparations: and children born of conflict-related sexual violence, 27, 49, 57, 63–67, 77; collective, 24, 110, 113–122; and conflict-related reproductive violence, 6, 65; and conflict-related sexual violence, 26, 64–65, 80; and domestic reparations program, 4, 12–14; individual, 24, 58–63; measures of, 60, 68. See also transitional justice system
reproductive freedom, 40, 42, 51
reproductive justice, 9, 41–42, 46, 146, 148; and reproductive injustice, 39
reproductive rights, 23, 40, 44, 46, 50–51
reproductive violence, 5, 35, 113, 130, 146; and decriminalization of abortion, 45; and domestic reparations program, 65; and gendered justice, 47; and gendered victimhood, 54, 150
Restrepo, Margarita, 164n62
Rivera Cusicanqui, Silvia, 165n12
Roberts, Dorothy, 164n58
Rodríguez, Alba Nubia, 162n53
Roe v. Wade, 46
Romero, Mario Diego, 97
Rome Statute, 6
Rosa, 94–97, 99, 103, 121
Ross, Fiona, 129, 162n65, 167n11, 167nn16–17,
Ross, Loretta J., 162nn37–38, 164nn59–61
Roux, Father Francisco, 52–53
Rubio-Marín, Ruth, 161n8, 166n36
Ruiz, Esther, 31
Rwanda, 104, 132

Salazar, Huáscar, 162n26, 167n29 (chap. 3)
Sánchez Gómez, Olga Amparo, 43
Sánchez León, Nelson Camilo, 165n10
Sanchez Parra, Tatiana, 161n9, 162n41, 162nn48–49, 164nn43–45, 165n11, 165n13, 166n33, 166n34

Sanchez-Rivera, Rachell, 164n66
Sandoval Villalba, Clara, 161n9, 162n41, 162nn48–49, 165nn10–11, 165n13, 166n33
Sandvik, Kristin Bergtora, 164n50
San Miguel, 1, 14–17, 55, 85, 110
Santamaría, Angela, 161nn7–8
Santander de Quilichao, 56, 59
Sasser, Jade, 164n65
Schaap, Andrew, 161n7
Schulz, Philipp, 161n8, 161n16, 161nn18–19, 161n20, 164nn50–51
Semana, 161n1, 168n8
sexual slavery, 33
silence: and agency, 129; and children born of conflict-related sexual violence, 30, 36, 38, 112, 131; gendered, 18, 139; and unintelligibility, 25, 28; in war and transitional justice contexts, 17–18, 128–130, 151, 154
Singh, Susheela, 164n73
Skjelsbaek, Inger, 161n12
social cartography, 123–127, 130
Solinger, Rickie, 162n37, 164nn59–60
South African Truth and Reconciliation Commission, 129
Special Jurisdiction for Peace (JEP), 11, 33, 63, 76
Stepan, Nancy, 164n64
Stern, Maria, 39, 161nn14–15, 161n17
Stewart, Beth, 167n11
stigma, 90–91
storytelling, 21, 58
survivor-centered approach to transitional justice, 8, 27. *See also* victim-centered approach to transitional justice
Sylvester, Christine, 168n6

Tamayo, Diana, 70, 131
Taussig, Michael, 162n60
testimonies, 71, 137–139; gendered, 125–128; and sexual violence, 128–129; and silence, 128–130
Theidon, Kimberly, 22, 36, 90–92, 106, 129, 133
Toogood, Kimairis, 166nn12–13
Touquet, Heleen, 161n8, 161nn18–19

transitional justice system, 3–4, 12, 44, 82, 147; and children born of conflict-related sexual violence, 2, 12, 83, 108, 155; with a gendered approach, 4, 11–12; and gendered victimhood, 5–6, 23, 150; on mechanisms, 13, 58, 115; and silence, 128–130, 139, 154

Uganda, 7, 90, 104, 106
Unified Form for Testimonies (FUD), 72–75; for Collective Subjects, 114. *See also* form
Unified Registry of Victims, 67–76. *See also* registry
unintelligibility, 3, 29, 149. *See also* children born of conflict-related sexual violence
United Nations: UNICEF, 31; UN News, 163n11; U.N. Security Council, 30; U.N. SRSG on Children and Armed Conflict, 32; U.N. SRSG on Sexual Violence in Conflict, 30, 32; U.N. Women, 30–31
United States Supreme Court, 46
Unit for the Assistance and Integral Reparations of Victims, 12, 28, 55, 76, 83
Uprimny-Yepes, Rodrigo, 165n1
Uribe, Maria Victoria, 163n72

Vaggione, Juan Marco, 165n81
Vallejo, Catalina, 163n16
Van Dijk, Jan, 163n77
Varela, Daniel, 167n5
Vera Lugo, Juan Pablo, 163n79 (intro.), 163nn15–16 (chap. 1)
Verdad Abierta, 162nn58–59
victim-centered approach to transitional justice, 4, 11–12, 25, 85. *See also* survivor-centered approach to transitional justice
victimhood: bureaucracies of, 67, 79; and site of power, 23; and system, 59
victimizing event, 60–62, 64, 70–71, 75
Victims' and Land Restitution Law (Law 1448 of 2011), 12, 49, 59. *See also* reparations
Victims' Unit. *See* Unit for the Assistance and Integral Reparations of Victims
Villarreal, Cristina, 164n73
Villegas, Julian, 161nn7–8
Viveros Vigoya, Mara, 162n68, 163n70, 166n23

war-affected children, 32, 33. *See also* conflict-affected children
War and Children Identity Project (WCIP), 32
Ward, Alexander, 165n79
Weber, Sanne, 163n24, 164n50
Weitsman, Patricia, 37, 161n25, 162nn28–29, 163n19, 166n15, 166n19, 166n24
Wills, María Emma, 164n68
witness, 137–138

Women's Link Worldwide, 44
Woolner, Lea, 167n25 (chap. 3)
World War II, 97

Yugoslavia, 38

Zalewski, Elizabeth, 161n20
Zambrano, Margarita, 164n69
Zulver, Julia, 120, 164n50
Zúñiga, Mariana, 164nn71–72

ABOUT THE AUTHOR

TATIANA SANCHEZ PARRA is a Marie Skłodowska-Curie Actions fellow in the School of Social and Political Science, University of Edinburgh. Her background is in anthropology, human rights, and sociology. Working at the intersection of feminist, sociolegal, and Latin American studies, her research focuses on issues of feminist peace building, reproductive justice, and reproductive violence in contexts of war and political transitions. In 2025, Tatiana will join the Department of Anthropology at the University of Tennessee as an assistant professor.

Available titles in the Genocide, Political Violence, Human Rights series:

Nanci Adler, ed., *Understanding the Age of Transitional Justice: Crimes, Courts, Commissions, and Chronicling*

Bree Akesson and Andrew R. Basso, *From Bureaucracy to Bullets: Extreme Domicide and the Right to Home*

Jeffrey S. Bachman, *The Politics of Genocide: From the Genocide Convention to the Responsibility to Protect*

Andrew R. Basso, *Destroy Them Gradually: Displacement as Atrocity*

Alan W. Clarke, *Rendition to Torture*

Alison Crosby and M. Brinton Lykes, *Beyond Repair? Mayan Women's Protagonism in the Aftermath of Genocidal Harm*

Lawrence Davidson, *Cultural Genocide*

Myriam Denov, Claudia Mitchell, and Marjorie Rabiau, eds., *Global Child: Children and Families Affected by War, Displacement, and Migration*

Daniel Feierstein, *Genocide as Social Practice: Reorganizing Society under the Nazis and Argentina's Military Juntas*

Joseph P. Feldman, *Memories before the State: Postwar Peru and the Place of Memory, Tolerance, and Social Inclusion*

Alexander Laban Hinton, ed., *Transitional Justice: Global Mechanisms and Local Realities after Genocide and Mass Violence*

Alexander Laban Hinton, Thomas La Pointe, and Douglas Irvin-Erickson, eds., *Hidden Genocides: Power, Knowledge, Memory*

Douglas A. Kammen, *Three Centuries of Conflict in East Timor*

Eyal Mayroz, *Reluctant Interveners: America's Failed Responses to Genocide from Bosnia to Darfur*

Pyong Gap Min, *Korean "Comfort Women": Military Brothels, Brutality, and the Redress Movement*

Fazil Moradi, *Being Human: Political Modernity and Hospitality in Kurdistan-Iraq*

Walter Richmond, *The Circassian Genocide*

S. Garnett Russell, *Becoming Rwandan: Education, Reconciliation, and the Making of a Post-genocide Citizen*

Victoria Sanford, Katerina Stefatos, and Cecilia M. Salvi, eds., *Gender Violence in Peace and War: States of Complicity*

Irina Silber, *Everyday Revolutionaries: Gender, Violence, and Disillusionment in Postwar El Salvador*

Samuel Totten and Rafiki Ubaldo, eds., *We Cannot Forget: Interviews with Survivors of the 1994 Genocide in Rwanda*

Eva van Roekel, *Phenomenal Justice: Violence and Morality in Argentina*

Anton Weiss-Wendt, *A Rhetorical Crime: Genocide in the Geopolitical Discourse of the Cold War*

Kerry Whigham, *Resonant Violence: Affect, Memory, and Activism in Post-genocide Societies*

Timothy Williams, *The Complexity of Evil: Perpetration and Genocide*

Ronnie Yimsut, *Facing the Khmer Rouge: A Cambodian Journey*

Natasha Zaretsky, *Acts of Repair: Justice, Truth, and the Politics of Memory in Argentina*